Sam

Samuel Smith

The Hero of Baltimore
in the War of 1812

HANK H. COX

McFarland & Company, Inc., Publishers

Jefferson, North Carolina

LIBRARY OF CONGRESS CATALOGUING-IN-PUBLICATION DATA

Names: Cox, Hank H., 1945– author.
Title: Samuel Smith : the hero of Baltimore in the War of 1812 / Hank H. Cox.
Other titles: Hero of Baltimore in the War of 1812
Description: Jefferson, North Carolina : McFarland & Company, Inc., Publishers, 2024 |
    Includes bibliographical references and index.
Identifiers: LCCN 2024010692 | ISBN 9781476693132 (paperback : acid free paper) ∞
    ISBN 9781476650753 (ebook)
Subjects: LCSH: Smith, Samuel, 1752-1839—Leadership. | Baltimore (Md.)—
    Biography. | Baltimore, Battle of, Baltimore, Md., 1814. | Baltimore (Md.)—
    History—War of 1812. | United States—History—War of 1812. | Politicians—
    Maryland—Baltimore—Biography. | United States. Congress. Senate—
    Biography. | Legislators—United States—Biography. | BISAC: HISTORY /
    Wars & Conflicts / War of 1812 | BIOGRAPHY & AUTOBIOGRAPHY / Military
Classification: LCC E302.6.S575 C69 2024 | DDC 328.73/0924 [B]—dc23/eng/20240306
LC record available at https://lccn.loc.gov/2024010692

BRITISH LIBRARY CATALOGUING DATA ARE AVAILABLE

ISBN (print) 978-1-4766-9313-2
ISBN (ebook) 978-1-4766-5075-3

Front cover image: Major General Samuel Smith 1817-1818 painting
by Rembrandt Peale, Baltimore City Life Museum, courtesy
of the Maryland Center for History and Culture, BCLM-CA.681

Printed in the United States of America

*McFarland & Company, Inc., Publishers
    Box 611, Jefferson, North Carolina 28640
    www.mcfarlandpub.com*

Contents

Preface

Many years ago, I heard a veteran prosecutor say that anytime several witnesses told the same story about a crime, he knew the fix was in. "People never see the same thing," he said. "They just don't."

As an historian I always approach research for a possible book with that wisdom in the back of my mind. I know that whatever I am writing about, other people have been there before me. But it is unlikely they saw it through my eyes. I always aspire to bring a fresh perspective to whatever I'm writing about.

Back in the early '80s I read *Lincoln* by David Herbert Donald, a highly respected historian, and I thoroughly enjoyed the journey. Of course, there have been thousands of books about Abraham Lincoln and one would think they have pretty much covered the story from top to bottom. But there were two to three pages in that book that took me by surprise. I learned that there had been a major Sioux uprising in 1862 that Lincoln had to handle when the world was coming down around his shoulders. It was the bloodiest Indian uprising in our history and led to the largest public execution—38 men—in our history. I had read many Lincoln books but had never encountered that story. So I wrote a book about it—*Lincoln and the Sioux Uprising of 1862*—which got a good bit of ink. My angle was that the U.S. Army was about to execute 303 Indians based on flimsy evidence and Lincoln put a stop to it. In a time when almost no one championed the cause of Native Americans—the Sioux had murdered an estimated 800 settlers—Lincoln's innate decency overruled political expediency.

Lincoln's magnanimity to the Sioux was not appreciated by the Minnesota settlers who had seen the carnage close up and Minnesota barely went to Lincoln in the election of 1864. Later a senator told Lincoln, "If you had hanged more Indians you would have gotten more votes," to which Lincoln replied, "I could not hang men for votes." What a man!

More recently I took on another tough subject—the career of Lieutenant General John Clifford Hodges Lee who served as Eisenhower's senior supply officer in World War II. Just about every scholar writing about World War II has castigated Lee as a martinet. I thought there must be another side to that story. I could not find one so I wrote it: *The General Who Wore Six Stars*, published in 2018. It didn't exactly resuscitate Lee's reputation (that was a heavy lift) but there was a reason Eisenhower kept him on the job when everyone was calling for his head—he got the job done.

This time I am on safer ground—a genuine American hero who in my opinion has not received his due in the history books. Major General Samuel Smith organized Baltimore from top to bottom and they fought off the British when they tried to storm Baltimore in 1814 right after they burned Washington. I ran across Smith's story when I picked up one of the older books in my library, *The Dawn's Early Light* by Walter Lord, published a half century ago. He gave Smith three cheers and by the time I finished the second read I was wondering why I had not reacted more strongly when I first read it. Possibly because I was a different person half a century ago. Smith was a hero in the Revolution and served in Congress for 40 years. He practically owned Baltimore and his fellow citizens acted like he did when he called them out to pick up shovels and build fortifications. He was an awesome character.

Walter Lord seemed to agree though he did not, in my humble opinion, give Smith his due. Nor did Frank A. Cassell in *Merchant Congressman in the Young Republic*, published the year before Lord's work. A reader will notice that in Cassell's expansive title he doesn't even mention the terms soldier or general or inspired military leader and most of his book is about Smith's legislative career. To be sure, Smith's career in Congress—some of it in the House and some in the Senate—was remarkable. But I have spent a lifetime in Washington and my eyes glaze over when anyone writes or talks about legislation. But show me a man who took on the British military when it was the most awesome in the world (it had recently brought Napoleon Bonaparte to heel), and kicked their butts on land and sea at the same time, and I'll show you a man qualified to wear Superman's cape, even if Superman did not come along until many years later.

As for Alan Taylor in *The Civil War of 1812*, published in 2010, he goes on and on about the endless farce up north where our ancestors tried to conquer Canada and lumbered from one debacle to another for years and doesn't even mention Sam Smith in passing. He does mention Andrew Jackson's "great victory" in New Orleans, a strategically meaningless battle fought after the war was over. But then as that prosecutor said so many years ago, witnesses never see the same thing, even when they're offering their accounts many years after the fact.

The reader is forewarned that despite their flaws (in my view), I rely heavily on Lord and Cassel, and less on other historians, as I relate this account of one of our history's greatest moments. I regret that I cannot offer accounts from eyewitnesses who have all long since passed on. If it seems that in some places I have abandoned skepticism in favor of awe, I plead guilty. As one of my sources, John Pancake, wrote, "These were not small men." Others who saw this drama play out close up were likewise astounded and honored to play their parts in this great drama—whether great or small. It was a time when tens of thousands of ordinary people responded to an inspired leader and did whatever they could—whether firing a musket or cannon or digging for hours on end to create earthen barriers to discourage the invaders.

I should mention another work, *Sam Smith, Star-Spangled Hero*, by Marc De Simone and Robert Dudley, published in 2014. This is an interesting work but it is more of a college or business school primer on leadership than a history of the War of 1812. (Oddly, in their book on leadership the authors do not even mention how Smith was obliged to usurp command from the general who outranked him before he could lead Baltimore into battle.)

In this day and time, it is wonderful to have such a story to tell—of a time when our ancestors stood together, swallowed their fears and fought for that great flag flying over Fort McHenry. That flag is to this day on display at the Smithsonian. It is ripped and torn in places, raggedy and faded.

It is still as beautiful as the day it was sewn.

Introduction

The War of 1812 is mostly treated as a sidebar of American history, when it even rates a passing mention. Even those of us who fancy ourselves historians take scant notice of it. By and large it was a messy affair in which American successes were few and far between. When and if that conflict is remembered today it is usually in the context of the Battle of New Orleans in which brave Americans under the command of future president Andrew Jackson gave the British a thorough thumping—though we now know that due to the delays of early 19th-century communication, that battle was actually fought after the war was over.

Those who dive a bit deeper into the War of 1812 learn of a flailing attempt to add Canada to the United States and an embarrassing rout at the Battle of Bladensburg in Maryland after which the victorious British troops invaded Washington itself and burned and looted much of it—including the White House, the Capitol building and the Library of Congress. A sad business, that, at least from the American point of view.

If you dive really deep into the War of 1812 you will learn that the people of Baltimore rallied to the flag and sent the British packing, but somehow that heroic event seldom gets its due in our popular culture. The story of war needs heroes even if, like Jackson, they came along after the fact and their heroism was of little consequence. It would seem the Battle of Baltimore lacked a certifiable hero.

In fact, the Battle of Baltimore itself has curiously excited minimal attention, except here and there a reference to Francis Scott Key and "The Star-Spangled Banner." In *The Civil War of 1812, American Citizens, British Subjects, Irish Rebels & Indian Allies*, published in 2020, historian Alan Taylor does not mention the Battle of Baltimore or Francis Scott Key or "The Star-Spangled Banner" even in passing, and certainly not the hero of this work, Samuel Smith.

Stand by, dear reader. If you have not heard about Samuel Smith—wealthy merchant, congressman, senator, major general in the Maryland militia—you are in for a treat. This guy was there at the beginning, fighting

5

closely with George Washington in the Revolution and playing a key role in getting this country up and going in its formative years. He organized his hometown of Baltimore like no one ever has before or since and sent the British packing.

For the record, Samuel Smith—just called Sam by his friends—had no middle name. President Harry S. Truman had no middle name either, but at least he has an initial. (Recently added, by the way. In his own time Truman used no middle initial.) There was no middle initial for Sam Smith, not even an initial. Just Sam, thank you very much.

1

Declaring War

I have already given two cousins to the war, and stand ready to sacrifice my wife's brother.—Artemis Ward

On June 17, 1812, the Senate, at the behest of President James Madison, approved a House resolution declaring war on Great Britain. The vote was 79–49 in the House and 19–13 in the Senate. It was the first time the U.S. government had declared war since its inception and appropriately enough it was against the same world power the United States had won its independence from in 1783. On June 18, Madison like Caesar crossed his own Rubicon, formally declaring war on the greatest world military power when we didn't have a battleship worthy of the name.

But Madison was no Caesar. His was, to put it mildly, a bold and intemperate act—at least partly due to the fact that almost a third of the members of the 1811 Congress were newly elected and really had no idea what they were getting into. At the time, the total strength of the U.S. Army was 11,744 troops, most of them green recruits. The navy had only 15 ships that were seaworthy, none of them comparable to British battleships of the line. In contrast, the British army consisted of a quarter million seasoned troops, almost all of them highly trained, experienced veterans who had been under fire. The British navy had nearly 1,000 combat ships including 137 ships of the line deployed worldwide—the 74-gun behemoths that had blown the combined French and Spanish navies out of the water at the Battle of Trafalgar in 1805. They carried crews of 620 men, give or take, and weighed 1,700 tons. Britain's navy was the world's greatest navy up until that time. "Britannia Rules the Waves" was first sung in 1745, and it reflected the reality of sea power. Generations of Americans—most all of whom were born residents of British colonies—knew the song well and could sing it. (Well, maybe Francis Scott Key couldn't sing it. Friends said he was tone deaf and could not sing anything.)

The idea of going to war on the strength of a divided vote seems preposterous today but it must be remembered that this was early in the nation's brief history. The United States itself was the first serious attempt to create a working democracy since the days of ancient Greece more than 2,000 years before. The U.S. government was feeling its way along. The war vote was largely along party lines which in itself was a departure from what had come before. The first president of the country, George Washington, was haunted by the prospect of political parties taking root in this country. He warned against them in his farewell address. As of 1810, there was no real party structure in the national government, only shifting patterns of coalitions. But two years later, at the time of Madison's war crisis, a sharp distinction between Federalists and Republicans was beginning to appear.

There had been serious efforts during the Washington Administration by France to recruit the United States into joining its ongoing war with Great Britain. Thousands of French had fled to the United States from the Caribbean island of St. Dominque (Haiti) after they were uprooted by a slave rebellion. In July 1793, more than 1,500 French refugees from St. Dominque had landed in Baltimore. Thousands more poured into Philadelphia and New York. There was a strong sentiment among those and other French immigrants that the United States owed France for all the aid provided during the American Revolution. But President George Washington would have none of it. He was conciliatory enough to express gratitude but not enough to join France's war against England. He knew this fledgling nation was ill-prepared for another conflict and in any event he had had enough war for one lifetime. He had seen what war does early on as a young officer in the French and Indian War (the Seven Years War in Europe). He got a lot more as commander of the American side in the Revolution. He appreciated France's support in the American Revolution, but in international politics, gratitude will only get you so far. Washington had looked askance at France's bloody revolution, which Jefferson admired, and saw no compelling reason to join forces with France in its struggle with Great Britain which, despite everything, was still this nation's major trading partner.

To be sure, the Americans of the post–Revolutionary War era were not averse to fighting. The government had squelched domestic rebellions such as Bacon's Rebellion in New England and the Whiskey Rebellion in western Pennsylvania and of course the combat with Native American tribes was more or less constant. Then as now, most everybody in the country had at least one gun in the house and knew how to use it. The standard weapon of the time featured the flintlock firing mechanism which was a primitive technology that required diligent attention. An Indian could fire several arrows in the time it took to load a musket—so the seemingly endless war against the Native Americans was by no means a one-sided affair.

The United States was an evolving nation state struggling to be born. It was touch and go for a long time. It had little money and less prestige. There was a continuing debate about what the proper role of government in American life should be. Generally speaking the Federalists wanted a strong central government and the Republicans preferred a weak one. Presidents John Adams and Thomas Jefferson who followed Washington had heeded our first president's parting admonition in his farewell address to avoid foreign entanglements. They had not yet noticed the evolution of parties, but war was on the table front and center. They knew, or at least many of the more thoughtful people knew, that they had enough trouble on their hands and most certainly did not need another open war with the world's greatest superpower.

But apparently Madison didn't get the memo. He was thoroughly ticked off by the conduct of the British and had exhausted diplomatic efforts to get them to change their ways peaceably. On November 5, 1811, Madison had called on Congress to prepare the nation for war against Great Britain, which he accused of "trampling on rights which no independent Nation can relinquish." Everyone saw the war declaration coming and for many it could not come soon enough. But Madison did not impress anyone as a credible wartime leader. He stood only five foot six and always dressed in black with knee britches that made him look even smaller and younger. The writer Washington Irving, author of "The Legend of Sleepy Hollow" and "Rip Van Winkle," was quoted as saying Madison was a withered little applejohn. An applejohn is a withered apple that has lost its moisture and shriveled up.

Still the narrow votes in Congress represented a sharp split among the nation's political class regarding the need for and justification of another war against Great Britain, which was conspicuous along party lines. The Republicans, the party of Thomas Jefferson and President Madison, supported the war and pushed through the declaration. The Federalists were in opposition. The Republicans largely represented rural and small town America and resented Great Britain's highhanded contempt for the United States. The Federalists were centered largely in New England and spoke for commerce and trade. They did not want to interrupt trade with Great Britain even though the Brits were pushing the United States around on the high seas, stopping our ships, kidnapping our seamen to man their own ships, and often confiscating our trade goods if they suspected we were trading with their enemy France, which we often were. There was money to be made and the New Englanders did not want to kill the goose that laid the golden eggs, all because of a little international larceny.

At the outset of this war the U.S. government was hopelessly riven by factionalism. The president's wife Dolley Todd Madison was an energetic hostess who deliberately brought diverse legislators together at social events in an effort to foster bipartisanship. By common agreement, she had a more forceful personality than her husband. Then as now, bipartisanship was an uphill process.

The Revolution Continued

Any understanding of the War of 1812 must begin with recognition that the American Revolution had not been resolved by the climactic 1781 battle at Yorktown, Virginia, in which the American army caught the British army under Cornwallis on the coast with the French fleet at their back. That battle was a fluke. Britain had a bigger, more formidable navy than France, but the English couldn't be everywhere at once. The English ground soldiers under Lord Cornwallis were trapped in that time and place and had to surrender. General George Washington deserved great credit for recognizing this opportunity and seizing it, but up until then, his battlefield record had been spotty at best, as had the records of other American commanders. The Americans were never a match for the British on the battlefield in those days. With the exception of our daring exploit at Trenton when we captured a bunch of Hessians, professional soldiers hired by the British, we lost almost every encounter. The fellows in red uniforms were well trained and ably led. They marched in lockstep and did not panic when some of them were smashed to smithereens by cannonballs. Also, the Americans had learned the hard way that when the British soldiers locked their bayonets in place on their muskets, it was going to be a long day. When the Americans heard that telltale click their hearts sank and more than a few of them fled the battlefield.

But having to supply an army in America across 3,000 miles of ocean with sailing ships was wearing the British out and draining their bank account, especially when they were locked in a life or death struggle with France led by Napoleon Bonaparte, arguably the most brilliant military leader of history. Likewise the British public had grown weary of the American adventure and, while they did not enjoy direct political participation, the English people conveyed their displeasure with their government in various ways. There were many outspoken critics of the American war in Parliament. The voices of dissent were coming through loud and clear, at least in part because most of the Americans were of British descent and shared a common culture. So King George III, on the advice of his senior advisors, decided to give it up.

To the surprise of many, the American patriots negotiated a favorable peace treaty. The Americans won their independence along with a remarkably generous northern boundary with Canada and a vast country stretching all the way south to Florida, west to the Mississippi and north to the Great Lakes. The British ostensibly gave up their main forts at Oswego, Niagara and Detroit. It was a big win for the Americans, at least on paper.

But the British military establishment did not embrace the peace treaty with anything resembling enthusiasm. They were a proud group at the height of their power—they ruled the seas and would soon humble the great legions of Napoleon on land (with a little help from the Prussians)—and they did not consider the Americans to be worthy foes, much less victors. Thus the British surreptitiously continued to maintain their forts along the great lakes and worse yet to encourage the Indian tribes to make life miserable for settlers along the American side of the border. The Native Americans did not have the technology to make their own guns, but they had bows and arrows and tomahawks, and they continued to receive firearms and gunpowder from the British. The Indians regarded the Americans as interlopers upon their ancient lands and were determined to drive them out of Indian country, which in their view encompassed everything west of the Atlantic Ocean (which few of them had ever seen). The British encouraged them in this attitude with warm words and modern weapons.

The struggle with Native Americans was a continuing process that had been going on since the earliest days of the European invasion of North America and would continue for another century. The Indians could not long withstand direct conflict with the white man's organized armies, but they could and did terrify farm families scattered among the caliginous hills and forests that the white man was steadily chopping down to make way for farms and towns. It wasn't so much the total death toll attributable to Indians that caused consternation among the whites, which is an abstract concept in any case, but rather the Indian brutality that the tribes had honed over the ages in endless conflicts with each other and which inspired terror among settlers who imagined bloodthirsty Indians behind every tree. Horror stories of Indian atrocities, many of them based on real events, abounded.

The Native Americans had earned their reputation. They ran around half naked (in the winter—in Canada) painted in bright colors and were at home in the primeval forest. They were masters of sudden raids and savage screams in the middle of the night, which intimidated their adversaries. They chopped the tops off heads of their victims, taking scalps. They raped women and butchered children. Some tribes employed sophisticated torture techniques that would have been appreciated in the dungeons of Medieval Europe. For example, they would slowly cut away their victims' outer layers of skin or roast them over an open fire. The reputation of savage Indians was in and of itself a major propaganda weapon. The British were harshly criticized for arming and arousing the Indians, but insisted they tried to restrain the red men. In some instances they actually did try to restrain their Indian allies. Or so they claimed.

Alan Taylor captured the impact of fear generated by Indian atrocities—and rumors of atrocities—in *The Civil War of 1812*: "The fear of warriors generated loathing, a categorical hatred of all Indians as murderous savages who deserved extermination. Dread and hatred were alternating emotional currents affecting the same people depending on circumstances. When endowed with superior numbers over vulnerable natives, Americans would butcher natives of all ages and both genders, which the vindictive called a just revenge. But fear trumped hatred when Americans ventured into a densely forested country possessed by Indians who had British help. In forest combat, American troops confronted their own nightmares, something far more terrible than real Indians. An American soldier's greatest foe lurked in his own imagination."[1]

Out west in Indiana (which was the Wild West in those days) Governor William Henry Harrison launched an aggressive offensive against an Indian federation led by the great Shawnee warrior Tecumseh and his brother who was called the Prophet. The Prophet foresaw a great victory. If he were around today he would have his own show on Fox. That particular expedition ended in the Battle of Tippecanoe which was really indecisive but would later figure prominently in Harrison's successful presidential campaign. Be that as it may, the whole campaign against the Indians raised tension along the frontier and provoked support for a stronger stand against the Native Americans who were seen, appropriately enough, as British allies. Some in Congress dubbed the "War Hawks," including such luminaries as Henry Clay of Kentucky and John C. Calhoun of South Carolina, urged Congress to roust the British from Canada and stifle their campaign to stir up the Indians. Many people were urging Congress to declare war and there was no restraining voice of Washington, Adams or Jefferson to tamp down the war fever.

An even more provocative activity of the British was the impressment of American seamen into the British navy. As the war against Napoleon waxed hotter, the British were rapidly expanding their navy to meet the threat. The Americans were presumptuous in declaring war on Great Britain, but Great Britain was itself even more presumptuous—a small island nation attempting to be a world power. "The Royal navy grew to a mammoth and unprecedented scale during the long hard war against the French Revolution and later Napoleon's empire," Taylor wrote. "In 1793, when the war began, the Royal Navy had 16,600 sailors. The number soared to 119,000 by 1797, a strength sustained into the next decade. Desertion, illness, injuries, and combat deaths combined to produce a

10 percent annual attrition, which meant that the swollen navy annually needed 12,000 new sailors to replace the losses."[2] "When Captain Thomas Masterman Hardy sailed HMS *Victory* through the French line at Trafalgar and into *Redoubtable*'s port, twenty-two impressed American sailors were serving on Nelson's flagship."[3]

The royal navy needed sailors and so did the American merchant marine which was expanding by leaps and bounds. Like the royal navy, it also faced a labor shortage and responded in the time-honored American way by raising wages. Scores of British sailors deserted the royal navy to earn up to double their pay on American ships. Thus began an ongoing personnel heist as thousands of British sailors claimed American citizenship to work on American ships. Under British law, however, no such transfer of nationality was legal. If you were born an Englishman, you died an Englishman. In a constant search for more sailors, British warships would stop American merchant ships on the high seas, take a hard look at the sailors and arbitrarily decide certain ones were actually British deserters. There were no photographs in those days and in any case the British would not accept the plea that a British sailor had switched nationality. It simply wasn't legal to do that, in the British view. The process of capturing sailors of suspect nationality was called "impressment." Roaming "press gangs," comprised of some of history's most frightening characters, prowled ocean ports all over the world looking for likely candidates for the British navy who were then mugged, bound and delivered to the nearest British warships, which were never hard to find.

The tendency of the British sailors to shift their allegiance to the Americans also was evident among the British land-based troops who deserted in droves during the American Revolution and were doing the same again in the War of 1812. Of course, the fact that they all spoke the same language made this transition fairly simple.

What was a minor irritant became a major issue after 1803 when the British war against Napoleon got serious. Over the next eight years leading up to the War of 1812, the British impressed an estimated 10,000 men from American ships who either claimed American citizenship by birth or naturalization.

Matters came to a head on June 22, 1807, when the British frigate *Leopard* confronted the American frigate *Chesapeake* a few miles off the coast of Virginia. The American commodore James Barron was expecting no trouble and left his cannon stowed on his deck which was littered with cargo. The *Chesapeake* was headed for the Mediterranean. When the British captain Calusbury P. Humphreys ordered the *Chesapeake* to yield to a search, Barron refused. Then the *Leopard* opened up with 26 cannon at close range. After a third broadside, the American ship surrendered. Three

Americans were killed and 18 wounded. Humphreys sent a search party to board the *Chesapeake,* and it returned with four sailors who were allegedly deserters from the royal navy.

The unprovoked attack on the *Chesapeake* occasioned much outrage in the United States and led to spirited protests that got exactly nowhere. There was a casual contempt in the British attitude that rankled American sensibilities. It highlighted a continuing conflict between the United States and Great Britain in a time when there was no United Nations to broker a settlement. The British continued to impress American sailors from both American merchant and navy ships. It was one of the irritants, perhaps the main one that drove the American government ever closer to adopting a war resolution.

By 1811, a series of events had seemed to be laying the groundwork for war. The British were routinely interfering with American shipping. In May, the American frigate *President* commanded by Captain John Rodgers, having been ordered to protect American commerce in the Atlantic, engaged the smaller British sloop *Little Belt* and emerged victorious. Though it was an uneven contest, many took it as revenge for the Chesapeake affair. The *Little Belt* business seemed to open a Pandora's box of American hostility toward Great Britain.

But probably the most aggravating item among the new nation's grievances against Great Britain was the so-called Orders in Council through which the British forbade the United States from trading with Continental Europe and seized U.S. ships on the high seas suspected of trading with France, wherever they were found. The gripes among Americans were building: the agricultural south saw its crop values drop in the wake of British trade restrictions, western settlers were in constant fear of the Indians stirred up by Britain, and a growing number of land-hungry "war hawks" were openly calling for an invasion of Canada.

The U.S. declaration of war could not have evoked great concern in London. Economically, the United States appeared almost hopelessly weak. The new nation was committed to low taxes, and when the Madison Administration tried to borrow funds for the war, money proved hard to get. Foreign banks were understandably reluctant to loan money to the United States and New England—the wealthiest corner of the nation— opposed the war. Here was a lesson for future leaders of any fledgling democracy—do not declare war unless you have a consensus of support and a lot of money to spend.

But it seemed like the nation was boxed into a corner and only war could defend the nation's sovereignty being challenged on the Canadian frontier and on the high seas. Despite the prospect of conflict, Madison seemed unperturbed. There is an old saying in Washington that if you can keep your head when all about you are losing theirs, you probably don't understand the seriousness of the situation. Madison may have been the original source of that saying.

On to Canada

The opening salvos of the War of 1812 came along the Canadian border. There had always been a few obstinate troublemakers in the United States who thought Canada should have been part of the United States, yet it remained a British outpost loyal to the same old King George III who the patriots had reviled in 1776. (George was still on the throne but by this time was quite insane, surrounded by incompetent relatives who manipulated him for their selfish purposes.) But Canada was sparsely populated claiming only about 500,000 residents compared to 7.5 million in the States. Canada is a vast country larger than the United States, but much of it is too cold for comfortable human habitation. It is a nation of extremes. The Great Bear Lake, a huge reservoir of fresh water in northern Canada, is comparable in size to some of the Great Lakes, bigger than a couple of them, but it is frozen over most of the year. Getting in and out of key Canadian cities back then was especially dicey in winter when most rivers froze over.

Therefore, then and now, most Canadians lived in shouting distance (or thereabouts) to the U.S. border. The vast hinterland was left mostly to hunters, trappers and—of course—Native Americans who somehow lived off the land and water and ran around half naked when combat broke out.

Many Americans assumed Canada would gladly join the United States if given a little push. Despite a sizable French minority, most Canadians spoke English and shared the same heritage of their southern neighbors. The War Hawks in Congress exhorted Madison to launch a major invasion of Canada which would serve the double purpose of taking revenge on Great Britain and augmenting the geographical and demographic reach of the United States. It seemed like a simple proposition. The general perception was that the New York militia could take Canada in a flatbed wagon in a week or two.

It didn't turn out that way. Tens of thousands of those Canadians were expatriates of the colonies who fled the revolution to preserve their attachment to the mother country and their king. They generally exhibited a certain bitterness toward their southern neighbors for the mistreatment they had experienced during the American Revolution which induced them to give up their farms and businesses at fire sale prices to shift their families and loyalty to Canada. They flocked to the British banner when asked to take up arms to defend their snow-covered homeland, and by and large they proved at least as tough and resilient as the invaders.

Which in reality was a pretty low bar. Many if not most of the Americans called to the fight were untrained, unfed and poorly led. There simply was no training system for military officers at that time. West Point was a small outpost used to train military engineers. Interestingly, an act of Congress on April 29, 1812, expanded the West Point population to 250 and authorized a four-year curriculum. The man generally recognized as the father of West Point, Colonel Sylvanus Thayer, led the organization from 1817 to 1833, by which time it was producing graduates with some semblance of military training. But that evolution came too late to benefit the U.S. Army in the War of 1812 which was essentially a ragtag assembly of state militias with no uniforms or winter clothing, inconsistent weapons and scant military training. Thus, the U.S. "invasion" of Canada was a fiasco.

It was and remains a popular myth that anytime a battle broke out the British soldiers stood stolidly in line during a battle enabling clever Americans to conceal themselves and pick off the British at will. That myth bore scant relation to the reality of the war in Canada. For example, on May 25, 1813, the United States had won the Battle of Fort George, capturing the fort. The British fell back to a position at Burlington Heights near the western end of Lake Ontario, briefly abandoning the entire Niagara Peninsula to the invading force. The United States attempted to pursue the British, but their advance was checked at the Battle of Stoney Creek by a British counterattack. At the same time, the U.S. flotilla of warships which had been supporting their army on the Niagara Peninsula was hastily withdrawn to face a threat to their own base, and a British flotilla threatened the U.S. line of communications. The Americans fell back to Fort George. The British followed up and established an outpost at DeCou's house in the present-day city of Thorold, Ontario, from which natives and militia harassed U.S. outposts.

The U.S. commander at Fort George, Brigadier General John Parker Boyd, decided to clear the threat posed by enemy raiders and to restore his men's morale by making a surprise attack on the outpost at DeCou's stone house near present-day Brock University.

Which led to the Battle of Beaver Dams on June 24, 1813. A U.S. column marched from Fort George and attempted to surprise a British outpost at Beaver Dams, billeting themselves overnight in the village of Queenston, Ontario. Laura Secord, a resident of Queenston, had earlier learned of the U.S. plans and had struck out on a long and difficult trek to warn the British at DeCou's stone house. When U.S. warriors resumed their march, they were ambushed by Indians and eventually surrendered to a small British detachment led by Lieutenant James FitzGibbon. About 500 U.S. troops, including their wounded commander, were ambushed in a thickly wooded area 1.5 miles (2.4 km) east of Beaver Dams. They were taken prisoner by the British army and its Indian allies. The main contingent of natives were 300 Kahnawake, also referred to as *Caughnawaga* in contemporary accounts, who were Mohawk people who had earlier converted to Christianity via Jesuit missionaries. They were nominally commanded by Captain Dominique Ducharme of the Indian Department, with lieutenants Isaac LeClair and J.B. de Lorimier. There were also 100 Mohawks under Captain William Johnson Kerr.

This story was repeated about 100 times all over southern Canada for the better part of two years. All along the northern borderlands between the United States and Canada, the scattershot American offensive was stymied by a powerful combination of British soldiers working with Native Americans that repeatedly defeated the invaders. The Indians were consummate guerrilla fighters. They controlled the flanks as the regular British soldiers held the center, repeatedly terrorizing the Americans with bayonet attacks that terrified Americans as much as the Indians did. Whenever the Americans broke and fled, which happened often, the Indians tracked them down and made short work of those who were wounded or slow. The few American victories such as happened at York and Fort George invariably occurred near a lake in warm weather—Canada is replete with lakes—where superior American numbers along with supporting fire from warships deterred the Indians, leaving the few British regulars vulnerable. But when the lakes froze over, early in autumn, the warships could not sail.

Madison grew frustrated with repeated reports of reverses in the field. He blamed his lack of success on "the forests to be penetrated, the savages to be encountered, and the Lakes and other waters to be passed in order to reach a distant theater, where the adversary was at home in the midst of all his resources for defence."[4] The British leaders back in London no doubt heard a hollow echo of their own anxiety in Madison's words left over from the American Revolution. Welcome to our world, Jimmy.

Ever fearful of Indian ambushes, the American commanders in the north preferred the security and ease of movement on the Great Lakes. But even there the American advantage proved fleeting because their commanders on the scene eschewed fighting in favor of building more warships at Kingston and Sackett's Harbor. Every military reverse, and there were plenty, sent them scurrying back to the harbors to build more ships. This erratic give and take anticipated the challenge that the U.S. government would encounter in the Civil War half a century later when General George McClellan spent most of his time organizing and very little fighting. This was a disadvantage for the Union because it had to win while its opponent needed only to survive. What little Canadian support for the American invaders that existed when the war began to erode rather quickly in light of continued American ineptitude.

When Napoleon was finally run to ground the first time, after his abortive invasion of Russia, Britain was free to turn its undivided attention to the pests in America. Madison and his generals knew this would happen. Soon fresh fleets of British warships and troop ships would be rounding the capes headed into the Chesapeake Bay with orders to teach the upstart American patriots a lesson or two. For many of the British commanders who had never forgotten that hard day at Yorktown in 1781, it was a consummation devoutly to be wished—to employ a phrase coined by one of their playwrights a couple of centuries before. It was payback time.

2

Something Wicked
This Way Comes

The Redcoats are coming!
The Redcoats are coming!—Paul Revere

"That a republic boasting of its freedom should have stooped to become the tool of the Monster's ambition, that it should have attempted to plunge the parricidal weapon into the heart of that country from whence its own origin was derived, that it should have chosen the precise moment when it fancied that Russia was overwhelmed, to attempt to consummate the ruin of Britain—all this is conduct so black, so loathsome, so hateful, that it naturally stirs up the indignation that we have described."[1]

So said the *London Times* on April 15, 1814. The "Monster" it referred to was Napoleon Bonaparte. But now that the Monster was slain—or at least put away on the island of Elba—it was time to settle up with the upstart nation that dared declare war on Britain when it was fighting for its survival. Up until now Great Britain had conducted operations in North America with its gloves off. But now that vast navy and army for so long preoccupied with Napoleon could turn its full attention to the west.

Actually the people in Washington knew nothing of Napoleon's defeat and exile—it took a long time for news to cross the ocean in those days—but they found out eventually and knew full well what it meant. When the British newspapers weren't castigating President Madison they were ridiculing the American military. Its officers were a "strange, uncouth set."[2] The objectives of the British were stated clearly in the news media and on the floor of Parliament: the Canadian border should be at least 100 miles below the Great Lakes, there should be an expanded region set aside for the Native Americans, the United States should be excluded from Canadian fisheries and from trading with the British West Indies, the United States also should be forbidden to take over Florida and by the way it should also cede New Orleans to the mother country, too.

Great Britain was essentially bankrupted by its prolonged war with France and now had an opportunity to downsize that huge military which it could never afford in the first place and return to normalcy, if anyone in the realm could remember normalcy, but the war fever still burnt as hot as ever—only now the enemy was no longer Napoleon, it was America.

The American envoy Albert Gallatin was in London at the time trying to negotiate a peace treaty with Great Britain when that nation was aflame more than ever in war fever. "To use their own language," he wrote to Secretary of State James Monroe, "they mean to inflict on America a chastisement that will teach her that war is not to be declared against Great Britain with impunity."[6]

Of course, simple rage or the urge for vengeance was not worthy of a great power. The ostensible purpose of the coming onslaught was to reduce pressure on the British forces in Canada which along with Canadians and Indians were at least holding their own against the invaders. Other than that, the British naval forces under Vice Admiral Sir Alexander Cochrane based in Bermuda, Rear Admiral George Cockburn already running amok in the Chesapeake Bay, and army units under Major General Robert Ross were to employ their forces "in such operation as may be found best calculated for the advantage of H.M. service, and the annoyance of the enemy."[7] So within a few weeks, ships filled with thousands of sailors and soldiers were on their way to the United States to annoy the Americans.

The British made no effort to conceal their plans and soon reports of their large-scale preparations were leaking into Washington and other cities, especially those with active ports like Boston, New York, Philadelphia and Baltimore. Commodore Joshua Barney of the U.S. Navy was one of the few who recognized what was coming and the need for a creative response. Barney had distinguished himself in the Revolution and again in 1812, as commander of a privateer out of Baltimore named *Rosie*, with which he captured 15 vessels worth more than a million dollars in the aggregate over a three-month period. Any suggestions from an officer of his standing commanded attention.

Barney knew the United States had nothing to compete with the British ships of the line which were like the U.S. aircraft carriers of a later era. They owned the seas. But they did not necessarily own the bays and estuaries because their deep draft keels could not operate in shallow water. Barney envisioned a flotilla of well-armed, shallow draft vessels manned by Baltimore sailors who were unemployed because of the British blockade and were looking for gainful employment. They would attack and harass the large British ships in a form of waterborne guerrilla warfare. "Barney submitted designs of the craft he had in mind along with the costs," Joseph A. Whitehorne wrote in *The Battle for Baltimore.* "His proposal was approved by the Navy Department and scheduled to begin on August 20, 2013. The flotilla would be distinct from the rest of the Navy with Barney reporting directly to Navy Secretary William Jones. The cutter Scorpion and the schooner Asp soon joined Barney's forces."[5]

Contracts to build the flotilla were given to Spencer's Shipyard in St. Michaels on the Maryland Eastern Shore and Thomas Kemp at Fells Point near Baltimore. Construction continued through the winter of 1813–14 in the absence of large-scale British navy activity in the bay. Barney recruited crews and clarified his discreet operational links with Secretary of the Navy Jones. His special status and most positions were filled by March.

By April 17, 1814, the flotilla consisted of 26 different vessels and 900 men, mostly in Baltimore, and was ready for a shakedown cruise. They put to sea (or bay) and learned a few things that led to corrections. They were opposed by British rear admiral Cockburn who had a small armada running amok around the bay, was terrorizing local inhabitants, and was setting up shop on Tangier Island lower down in the bay closer to the capes. Barney learned of

Commander Joshua Barney had a well-earned reputation as a captain of a privateer who harassed British shipping. He knew the fledgling American navy could not stand up to British warships so he petitioned the Navy Department to permit him to build a flotilla of smaller boats that harassed British ships in the Chesapeake Bay and retreated into inlets where the big ships could not pursue them. Before the Battle of Bladensburg the British finally caught up with Barney's little ships but before they could capture them Barney had them blown up. His flotilla men, all tough fighters, then joined the American army as soldiers and gave a good account of themselves (c. 1817 painting by Rembrandt Peale, Baltimore City Life Museum collection, image ID BCLM-CA, courtesy Maryland Historical Society).

this and set out on May 24 with *Scorpion*, two gunboats, 13 barges and a lookout boat to harass enemy traffic. His force engaged in some sporadic firefights with British ships. They holed up in one of the estuaries which are plentiful throughout the Chesapeake Bay and fought it out with smaller British boats which were trying to lure the flotilla out into deeper water where their larger ships could pounce. Barney's crews were wise to the scheme. They all engaged in a fencing match with much shooting but without much effect.

But the anticipated arrival of the main British fleet brought a new sense of urgency to the patriots who simply could not compete with the big 74-gun ships of the line, and Cockburn started getting a bit cocky. He conducted a raid on the small town of Havre de Grace on the upper bay near where the Susquehanna empties into the bay. Some local militia in the town fired a small cannon which was all the provocation Cockburn needed. His Marines looted and torched the town, burning 40 of 60 houses and other buildings. One American was killed. Another was wounded and taken prisoner and released soon after. But the real fight was on.

Cockburn had roamed freely about the bay for most of 1813 and into 1814, all the while waiting for major reinforcements from the home country. He routinely socialized with country squires in Virginia and Maryland who presumably hoped to dissuade him from allowing his troops to loot their plantations and manhandle their women. Joshua Barney penned a note to Navy Secretary Jones informing him that the British fleet was already in the Patuxent River, the main conduit to Baltimore. He reported also that Cockburn had boasted to one of the locals that he planned to destroy Barney's flotilla and dine in Washington on Sunday.

Soon everyone in Washington knew about that vow. Jones ordered Barney to take his flotilla as far upstream as he could get and to burn it if the British approached. Barney was to fall back with his men into Washington to assist in its defense. The flotilla men, largely Baltimore seamen who were unemployed because of the British blockade, were to prove effective fighters on land as well as on the water.

Major General Ross was a formidable character—one of those inspired military leaders who dot the history books with tales of triumph over adversity. Historian Walter Lord described him as a "47-year-old Irish country gentleman with bright blue eyes and a ready smile. But behind that pleasant front, he was also the toughest of disciplinarians. Despite this, the men respected him, for like most soldiers they would put up with almost any qualities in a commander as long as his system paid off."[3]

Because of his harsh discipline, his commands routinely suffered fewer casualties than others wearing the red coats. And whatever the danger, he was always right there with his men, not safe and secure somewhere behind the lines. He had been wounded twice and had two horses shot out from under him. So he enjoyed the confidence of his men (if not his horses). Admiral Cochrane was to pick the targets, but Ross was entitled to "freely express" his views. He had veto power over the use of his troops and once ashore had complete control of their operations. He was also specifically charged "not to engage in any extended operations at a distance from the coast." In other words, he was to stay close to the big ships with the big guns, not wander off into firefights in the countryside.

When word came that the French had formally surrendered, the navy swung into action. Led by the 74-gun HMS *Royal Oak*, 13 other warships and three troop transports were soon under way headed toward the western horizon. The trip from Britain to America under sail took seven weeks plus a day or two, depending on the weather. All that time thousands of troops and naval personnel were crowded below decks, hot and damp. No fans or air conditioning relieved the atmosphere. The odors emitted by thousands of dirty men using primitive toilets soon became unsupportable. They survived on salted beef, hard cheese and biscuits full of maggots. The officers drank a lot of wine, though their food was not much better than that of the common soldiers. On the other hand they were hardy soldiers accustomed to hardship and they knew the sea voyage would not last forever.

Somewhere along the long voyage a ship from the Chesapeake appeared bearing a missive from Cockburn who was thinking big. "Within forty-eight hours after the arrival in the Patuxent of such a force as you expect, the City of Washington might be possessed without difficulty or opposition of any kind," he said. Thus, the seeds of conquest were planted.[4]

Already, Cockburn had gone up the Patuxent near Baltimore taking soundings of the water depth and putting local guides on the payroll. But after a quick foray he told his commander he was leaving the river lest the enemy get suspicious. It was too late for that—the Baltimoreans had seen him and recognized his ensign on his frigate. They knew what he was up to. Meanwhile, another 24 British ships were leaving Bermuda to join in the fun. The first ships swept through the capes on August 11. Cockburn had been on station for more than two years leading raiding parties up and down the bay, Maryland on one side and Virginia on the other. If the people didn't resist, they might escape with the loss of their livestock and food. If any musket was fired, Cockburn brought out the torches.

Some of the British soldiers were apparently descended from the Viking raiders who once pillaged the countryside of their own country. They stripped beds, stole libraries and in one instance chopped down trees that lined a lane simply because they were English walnuts. One thing they did not burn was tobacco which could be easily transformed into cash.

It was loaded onto captured schooners and ultimately sent off to a prize agent in Bermuda. A month before the British convoy landed, Cockburn sent 84 hogsheads of tobacco off to be sold. Some of the money would go to senior officers and some to the ordinary seamen who captured it, but a major part of it was retained by Cockburn himself. To him it was war for fun and profit.

As he roamed to and fro, Cockburn became increasingly contemptuous of his American opponents. "The country is in general in a horrible state," he said in a letter. "It only requires a little firm and steady conduct to have it completely at our mercy." He added later, "It is impossible for any country to be in a more unfit state for war than this now is."[5] Which was probably true.

In early August, Cockburn led 500 British marines in a raid on Kinsale, Virginia, a small town a few miles from the bay. He routed the local militia, burned houses, and captured five schooners loaded with tobacco— at a cost of only three killed. He meant only three British killed. He took no note of the militia casualties. But obviously someone was shooting back.

When he learned that the size of the British force coming to join him was smaller than anticipated, he was not concerned. His only concern was that his senior commander Cochrane would

Rear Admiral George Cockburn was the primary instigator of British military action. When senior command balked at an invasion of Washington, he browbeat General Ross into going ahead, leading to the Battle of Bladensburg and the burning of Washington. He was goading Ross into attacking Baltimore when Ross was cut down by American sharpshooters (Image no. BHC2619, National Maritime Museum, Greenwich, England).

not be inclined to storm Washington. He was not acquainted with Ross except by reputation but he knew plenty about Cochrane who to his total lack of surprise did not believe they had enough force to take Washington. He assumed Cochrane simply did not realize how weak and disorganized the Americans were. He pointed out that he had been roaming to and fro anywhere he wanted with a battalion of marines meeting only scattered opposition. When the big force arrived in the bay, he took Ross on a foray into the Maryland countryside. They moved several miles inland on the St. Mary's River, burned a building or two and returned to the fleet without firing a shot. Ross was convinced.

While the Redcoats were gathering strength and pondering their next move, the powers that be in Washington were basically running around like chickens with their heads cut off. What little military strength President Madison had at his disposal was on the northern border thrashing about in a disconcerted, unfocused campaign in which no coherent strategy was discernible. There were militias in the District of Columbia, Virginia, and Maryland, but they were a mixed lot and lacked cohesion. In desperation, Madison appointed Brigadier General William Winder as commander of the 10th District which included D.C. and the two states—Virginia and Maryland.

Winder was a young lawyer from Baltimore who served as a captain in one of the city's militia companies. When the war broke out, he volunteered for active duty and was commissioned lieutenant colonel in the 20th U.S. Infantry. He had no formal military training, but then neither did anyone else. He led the 20th to the northern border. He was promoted to brigadier general in the spring of 1813 and seemed to perform competently but he was captured at the Battle of Stoney Creek where he was interned as a prisoner. During his year as a prisoner, he moved on parole between Montreal and Washington as he negotiated a settlement of a hostage crisis between the rival governments. In this role his work brought him into contact with President Madison and Secretary of State James Monroe who became a lifelong friend. Winder was also the nephew of Maryland governor Levin Winder. He was formally exchanged in June 1814 which made him available, if not necessarily qualified, for a new command.

Thus command of the 10th District was his first independent command, but all he got from Madison was a piece of paper confirming his appointment. He got no staff or active subordinates. He had to go find some. Meanwhile, it was just him running around thinking about the British and what he should do about them. He reasonably undertook a tour of the landscape but apparently lent little thought to developing a strategy. He requested 4,000 militia be assembled for the defense of Washington. In a letter to War Secretary John Armstrong, he pointed out that

Norfolk, Annapolis and Baltimore were already reasonably well defended and fortified, leaving Washington as default easy target for the British. So he needed some soldiers.

History records numerous instances of ordinary men rising to daunting military challenges, but in Winder and Armstrong history presents two people conspicuously miscast in roles for which they both were in over their heads. Winder wanted to do the right thing but could glean no support from anyone and really had no experience to fall back on. His titular head, Armstrong, simply did not believe—or perhaps did not want to believe—there was a crisis and he refused to do anything. He fended off Winder's requests by expressing his long held view that militia were more effective when called upon in an imminent crisis—which in his view did not exist. Armstrong continued to downplay the threat to Washington even when he learned from Norfolk of the arrival of the 3rd Battalion of royal marines. By that time newspapers were circulating the names of ships coming into the bay and regiments either on the ground or on their way.

"Armstrong showed no sense of urgency, even sending Winder crucial orders and authorizations through the ordinary mails," Joseph A. Whitehorne wrote in *The Battle for Baltimore*. "One of these took three weeks to reach the general though he was never more than three or four hours away by mounted courier. Armstrong ignored reports from units in contact such as Steuart's Fifth Maryland Brigade, even rejecting their pleas for supplies, and forcing the President to intervene on their behalf. His opinion that the defense of Washington was a local problem to be dealt with by Winder persisted until the situation was irretrievable."[6]

In later years, Henry Adams wrote of Armstrong: "In spite of Armstrong's services, abilities, and experience, something in his character always created distrust. He had every advantage of education, social and political connection, ability and self-confidence; he was only fifty-four years old, which was also the age of Monroe; but he suffered from the reputation of indolence and intrigue. So strong was the prejudice against him that he obtained only eighteen votes against fifteen in the Senate on his confirmation; and while the two senators from Virginia did not vote at all, the two from Kentucky voted in the negative. Under such circumstances, nothing but military success of the first order could secure a fair field for Monroe's rival."[7]

Predictably, when the British landed in Maryland and began moving north, Armstrong was spending his time with matters in New York. His mind was elsewhere. He had a warlike reputation based on his service in the Revolution, but in reality he had served as a staff officer for the brass. There is no evidence he ever heard a shot fired in anger.

The authorities in Maryland, on the other hand, did act quickly. The 11th Maryland Brigade consisting of two regiments left Baltimore on August 19 and reached Bladensburg on the 22nd where they began working on earthworks. Bladensburg, then and now, was a small village east of Washington. On August 23, they were joined by Lieutenant Colonel Joseph Sterett's Fifth Maryland Infantry. The latter had left Baltimore on August 21 to a glamorous send-off full of music, flags and cheering crowds. (Among the gathering throng was Major General Samuel Smith who will be heard from later in this account.) Thus, there were a few people here and there cognizant of the challenge and eager to meet it.

Meanwhile, on August 19 Secretary of the Navy Jones responded to Barney's news of the British landings by ordering him to move his flotilla upriver to Pig Point near Upper Marlboro and to bring most of his men to Washington. Barney took as many of his guns and equipment as he could and 400 men and set out for Bladensburg which had become the default assembly area.

The one thing Winder did have, and he had it in abundance, was a surplus of gratuitous advice and interference from well-meaning but inept officials. Despite these handicaps, he worked against growing odds but sensed an impending disaster. He confided in Major John H. Briscoe, one of his newly found aides, "I am but a nominal commander. The President and the Secretary have interfered with my intended operations and I fear for the success of the day."[8]

When others besides Winder sought to persuade Armstrong of the gravity of the crisis, and one in particular said he expected a serious blow, Armstrong pushed them aside. "Oh yes. By God they would not come with such a fleet without meaning to strike somewhere, but they certainly will not come here—what the devil will they do here?" When someone offered other thoughts, such as Washington was the symbolic capitol of the nation, Armstrong gave him another brush-off. "No, no," he said. "Baltimore is the place, sir, that is of so much more consequence. They are foraging, I suppose. If an attack is meditated by them upon any place, it is Annapolis."[9]

The District of Columbia's militia was called out for the third time that summer and were apparently growing weary of it. Some had no shoes, others lacked weapons. One company of riflemen had not one rifle among them. Winder looked them over in despair. He needed soldiers but preferably with shoes and guns. They were dismissed and ordered to report back fully equipped in the morning.

Meanwhile, Admiral Cochrane was vigorously promoting the notion of recruiting American slaves to aid in the British war effort and ordered Cockburn to make it happen. However, after months of serious effort,

Cockburn had been able to raise only 120 black recruits. "If you attach importance to forming a corps of these Blacks to act against their former masters," he wrote to Cochrane, "I think, my dear sir, your proclamation should not so distinctly hold out to them the option of being sent as free settlers to British settlements, which they will most certainly all prefer to the danger and fatigue of joining us in arms. I shall therefore only mention generally our willingness and readiness to receive and protect them."[10] Nothing much would come of these efforts. The slaves weren't particular which side cracked the whip over them, preferring neither the one nor the other.

There was continuing discourse among the British leaders about where to strike when the full complement of soldiers and ships was on hand. Cockburn thought the Chesapeake Bay port town of Benedict— small then, still small today—would be the ideal jumping off point. "Within forty eight hours after the arrival in the Patuxent of such a force as you expect, the City of Washington might be possessed without difficulty or opposition of any kind," he wrote to Cochrane, and he offered good reasons: the ease and speed of such an operation, the éclat of taking the enemy's capital, "always so great a blow to the government of a country," and the relative difficulty of taking Baltimore or Annapolis.

Cockburn added judiciously: "If Washington (as I strongly recommend) be deemed worthy of our first efforts, although our main force should be landed in the Patuxent, yet a tolerably good division should at the same time be sent up the Potowmac [sic] with bomb ships etc. which will tend to distract and divide the enemy, amuse Fort Washington, if it does not reduce it, and will most probably offer other advantages."[11]

On August 17, the captains of all the British ships rowed over to Admiral Cochrane's flagship the *Tonnant* to get their final briefing. Several ships led by the frigate *Seahorse* followed by smaller vessels headed up the Potomac. The remainder of the fleet was also underway going north on the Chesapeake. As the waterway became narrower and shallower the further north they went, the ships of the line began making contact with the bottom so they dropped anchors and began transferring troops to the smaller vessels. Word passed along that the next day they would land at dawn. The troops were loaded up with arms, ammunition, blanket, knapsack, canteen, three pounds of pork and two and one half pounds of biscuits crawling with bugs.

The most amazing thing to the recent arrivals was the complete lack of organized opposition. Of course, Cockburn's troops had fought several small engagements with local militias, but for the majority of the British force, all of this was new. They spent most of the day setting up camp near Benedict, all the while looking about for possible ambush. The British had neglected to bring horses along on their trip—seven weeks is a long time to keep a horse bouncing around in a sailing vessel—and though they had confiscated a few farm animals, they had nothing resembling a cavalry to scout the countryside. Like Robert E. Lee at Gettysburg, whose cavalry under Jeb Stewart had gone astray, they were basically groping around in the dark.

The Americans learned of the British landing and began to move, albeit uncertainly. The District of Columbia militia was up and moving east of the city in the general direction of Bladensburg, uncertain where the British might be. They marched down Pennsylvania Avenue to the eastern branch of the Potomac River. Here they crossed the lower of two bridges to the Maryland countryside. Taking the road to the Wood Yard, a well-known lumber yard, they continued another four miles and then stopped for the night. There was no sign of tents or cooking equipment. Most of them were clerks and tradesmen in their normal work clothes. They had to sleep in their clothes out in the open. Fortunately for them it did not rain that night. Back in the White House, Madison huddled with colleagues trying to guess where the British were going. Armstrong continued to insist they had no designs on Washington, but his credibility was waning rapidly.

Next morning the British rose early, raided local farms for breakfast and prepared to move out. In the absence of horses, Ross deployed skirmishers all around to be alert to any organized resistance. The soldiers struggled forward through thick underbrush, sweating in the heat and dust. It was slow going. After moving about six miles, Ross declared a camp for the night. Great dark clouds dominated the sky lit by lightning bolts and a major thunderstorm engulfed the soldiers who had few tents. There were thunderstorms in Great Britain, but when they happened, most people, even those in the military, had access to shelter. These fellows were out in the downpour with no brollies.

Next morning the British soldiers continued their trek sloshing through the mud. By five o'clock in the afternoon they reached another small Maryland town, Nottingham, whose name must have sounded familiar to them. Ross was looking for Barney and his flotilla, but Barney had seen them coming and moved on up the river. The British obsession with Barney's little boats seems curious but they lacked cover from their big ships and the small gunboats could have done some damage, given their shortage of their own artillery.

Meanwhile, Winder's force was gradually growing—240 Maryland militia already camped at Bladensburg, 300 regulars from Piscataway, New Jersey, 125 dragoons from Carlisle, Pennsylvania, and 120 Marines and five heavy guns from the District. By afternoon he had some 1,800 men, some cavalry, 20 pieces of artillery—others trickling in. But no one knew how many British there were or their intentions. Some believed— or at least wanted to believe Armstrong—that they were not heading to Washington.

Ross could not have told him even had he been inclined to. He had strict orders not to engage in any extended operations far from the coast. But he was already 40 miles from the bay. In addition, he had been instructed to avoid any engagement that would expose his troops to loss disproportionate to the advantage which it may be the object of the attack to attain. This must have seemed like doubletalk to Ross. Any military engagement poses the possibility of loss. Ross had no cavalry, little intelligence and minimal artillery. He was a gutsy officer but he was getting more anxious with every passing hour.

Cockburn learned of Ross' concerns. He found a horse and early on the 22nd quickly caught up with him. Cockburn said they had Barney on the run and could not leave off the chase at this delicate hour. He quickly got Ross back on board for a big adventure.

Ross was now on the road to Upper Marlboro seeking Barney's flotilla. He kept moving up the Patuxent until he reached Pig Point where the river narrowed into a small stream. Beyond the point he and his officers could see the masts of Barney's flotilla. They had them at last. But suddenly they saw smoke rising followed by a huge explosion and a mushroom cloud of smoke. The small boats had been scuttled on Jones' order.

The British beat the bushes looking for the flotilla crewmen but most of them were long gone on their way to join Winder's army at the Wood Yard where they arrived about noon. It seemed obvious to Winder at this juncture that the British were headed toward Washington. He ordered his troops to fall back toward the city and sent a note to Madison that the British were coming.

There was no need for that admonition. Word had spread all over town and Washington was in an uproar. Meanwhile, at Upper Marlboro a few miles east of Washington, General Ross was spending a quiet and comfortable night at the home of Dr. William Beanes, the only local resident still home when the British entered about mid-afternoon. Beanes was a prominent man. He was the community's leading physician. That wasn't much to celebrate given the primitive state of medical science at the time, but Beanes was also a major landowner, proprietor of the local grist mill, and owner of the finest house in town. He had offered it to Ross as a headquarters which was likely a devious ploy to save it from looting and possible arson. Ross was happy to accept. It was a pleasant house and Beanes was an obliging host. The good doctor also gave Ross the impression he was a Federalist opposed to the war, which may have been true. But this seemingly benign interaction between Beanes and Ross would have far-reaching implications reflected in the opening ceremonies of millions of sports games into the present time. About which more anon.

For his part, Ross was again having doubts about the whole operation. Barney's vaunted flotilla was no more. So what was the incentive to attack Washington, especially given his overall instructions to avoid complicated engagements far from the fleet which was now 40 miles away? He was at least getting some limited intelligence having stolen 40 horses, but given the confused state of the American forces, he wasn't learning much.

Admiral Cochrane had given specific orders to Cockburn to develop a clandestine network of agents, but stealing tobacco and burning farms was much more fun and Cockburn never got around to it. As for Ross, he had young officers on his staff who shared Cockburn's opinion that Washington was easy prey. They found Cockburn resting on one of his boats and warned him that Ross was beginning to waver. Early in the morning of August 23, Cockburn rode to Upper Marlboro to steel Ross' resolve. It didn't take long. Ross was soon sending for his senior officers to join him in Upper Marlboro.

Madison was up early to greet Winder and Armstrong. Winder told him Ross was in Upper Marlboro but it was clear he had designs on Washington. Armstrong repeated his conviction that whatever the British did, there would be no attack on Washington. At most there might be a quick hit and run foray, and for that exigency, Armstrong suggested also that Winder put his troops in the Capitol building the minute the Redcoats showed up, if they showed up. "On the success of this plan," Armstrong said, "I would pledge both life and reputation."[12]

By that time, Armstrong's reputation was not much of a wager. Armstrong comes across not so much as an inept functionary but as an early example of what would become a standard Washington type—a blowhard who adamantly insists he is right amid mounting evidence that he is a fool. Only Armstrong was not taking a stand in blind obedience to some arcane political philosophy or egotistical charlatan as is common in modern times. He was just making a complete fool of himself which was rapidly becoming evident to all but him.

For his part, Winder suddenly saw a golden opportunity for military victory. He had troops trickling in from all over. According to his calculations, altogether, he would soon have upwards of 6,000 men within 20 miles of each other. The only trick was to get them all together. His plan was to bring them together and attack Ross' regulars in Upper Marlboro the next day. That would have been difficult enough with modern communications technology. Winder was sending couriers on horseback trying to find widely separated military units without being caught by the British.

James Monroe had been riding around here and there for two days trying to get a fix on where the British were and what they were doing and how many of them there were. He rode back to Bladensburg, the small town east of Washington. When he got there he sat on his horse a while watching the motley crowd of would-be soldiers wandering around aimlessly in search of leadership. He had no idea where Winder was, but he knew the British were nearby and coming his way. Monroe somehow got the idea that he should provide leadership, though he had scant military experience to fall back upon.

3

The Battle of Bladensburg

War is hell.—General William Tecumseh Sherman

In his own way, Secretary of State James Monroe was as disoriented as Armstrong and his activities just as inexplicable. But Winder remained his own worst enemy. It occurred to him that moving his entire army to Bladensburg would leave the road open to Washington. Of course the enemy would have to cross the Eastern Branch of the river to get there, and Winder had given orders that the bridge be destroyed. But he suddenly had an anxiety attack about that and rode off to make sure the demolition was on schedule. Apparently, it did not occur to him that any junior officer could conduct that mission just as well as he could at a time when senior leadership was desperately needed to mold his gathering horde into an army and prepare for the coming onslaught.

Early in the afternoon First Lady Dolley Madison had received a note from her husband that the crisis seemed to be abating and that the British had no designs on Washington. Still the city around her was on edge. She got a note from Eleanor Jones, wife of the navy secretary who was scheduled to have dinner at the White House. "In the present state of alarm and bustle of preparation for the worst that may happen, I imagine it will be more convenient to dispense with the enjoyment of your hospitality today," Jones wrote.[1] Dolley was pleased to oblige. Toward evening she got another note from her husband who advised her to be ready "at a moment's warning" to get her carriage and leave the city. He said the British were stronger than expected and might very well move into Washington.

That very thought was being discussed by General Ross and Admiral Cockburn who had spent the night in a small shed that served as their headquarters. Historian Lord caught the moment: "Outside the last of the seamen and marines, ordered from their boats to join the army, bedded down for the night. Nearby, Lieutenant Gleig put in some anxious hours on picket duty, half-convinced that the Americans would attack him. At Upper Marlboro, Captain Robyns of the Royal Marines relaxed after a long day spent loading prize (stolen) tobacco for transport down the river. At Benedict, Admiral Cochrane's fleet lay silently at anchor in the black, quiet waters of the Patuxent."[2]

It was August 23. A Lieutenant Scott had been sent to Admiral Cochrane from Cockburn reporting destruction of Barney's flotilla and that he and Ross were next planning to assault Washington. Now Scott was on his way back with orders to Cockburn, but clearly also intended for Ross, to stand down. Cochrane said they had already accomplished a lot with a small force and should go no further. (Cochrane was clearly unaware of a pending clash at Bladensburg.) Cochrane was adamant that Cockburn should return to Benedict and re-embark on the ships. He said Cockburn would be jeopardizing his success by attacking Washington with insufficient means. Cochrane was the senior commander. Thus the assault on Bladensburg—and Washington—never should have happened if the senior British officers obeyed their orders.

But Cockburn was determined. This was the third time—or was it the fourth?—that his grand project had been on the chopping block. He wasn't going to give up now. He assured Ross that the goal was within their grasp. If they went ahead, he pledged "everything that is dear to me as an officer" that they would succeed. If they turned back without striking a blow, he said, it would be worse than a defeat, it would be dishonor ... "a stain upon our arms."[3]

Cockburn insisted he knew the enemy. "The militia, however great their numbers, will not—cannot—stand against your disciplined troops," he said to his colleague. (Not many miles away Armstrong was telling President Madison the same thing—that if the coming battle was between militia and regulars, the militia would be beaten.) "It is too late—we ought not to have advanced," Cockburn the navy guy a long way from his ships told the army guy whose troops would bear the brunt of the battle. "There is now no choice left us. We must go on."[4]

Cockburn and Ross got their army moving toward Bladensburg. At 5:00 a.m. on August 24, the troops swung out into the road—or at least what passed for a road—and began marching toward the capital of the United States.

Even with a highly organized force like the British army it took time to get things moving. The landscape was rugged and laced only with a few dirt tracks that did not merit the name roads. They were only generally clear of what direction to go, other than toward the west. The soldiers were burdened with their muskets and personal gear trudging through rough underbrush or forest land. By the time the sun was up, they were hot and exhausted. They were strung out over several miles, so advance units had to stop from time to time to enable following units to close the gap. Still, there was no dismay or undue concern, though the men in red coats surely knew many of them would die that day. They took a break whenever they could to wait for their comrades to trickle in.

As for the American side, reviewing the records of that time suggests something akin to a Keystone Cops movie being filmed, with hundreds of people moving back and forth in aimless confusion. Winder was running around frantically trying to cover every possible exigency ordering people to do things only to come back later and change the instructions. He lacked the experience of a senior officer to realize that this created confusion. There were two bridges over the stream that would separate the Americans from the British when the British got there, and Winder had given orders for the upper bridge, Stoddards bridge, to be blown up. The bridge was old and rickety but still usable. No one was guarding it.

He found the captain of the navy yard, who he had directed to blow the bridge, at one a.m. The captain assured him he had several casks of powder ready to go. Winder protested that the British could arrive at any moment and that it was necessary to blow that bridge up immediately. The captain did as told, getting dressed as he spoke to the frantic army officer who actually had no direct authority over him.

The lower bridge also remained. Winder had sent Commodore Barney with his 400 flotilla men along with Captain Samuel Miller's 120 Marines with five splendid guns to the bridge where they milled around increasingly anxious about the specter of men in red coats appearing at any moment. There they remained with little to do.

War Secretary Armstrong's inactivity was beginning to generate criticism. President Madison called him on the carpet and told him to get busy. Armstrong took that as an order to assume command of the army, and had an implied promise that Madison would back him up. But before he went off to do that, he joined Madison and other cabinet members for an inspection of the lower bridge. There Commodore Barney took the opportunity to give the president a tongue lashing, insisting it was folly to leave him there with 500 tough fighting men waiting to do a job—blow up the bridge—which any "damned corporal can do better with five."[5] Madison ordered him to go directly to Bladensburg and a "corporal's guard" would remain to blow the bridge.

It was becoming clear to everyone—with the possible exception of Winder—that the fight would be at Bladensburg. It was a small, insignificant place but there was a bridge there. There was a tangle of woods and brush to the north and west, and with the river widening to the south, it had over the years become a focal point for traffic headed toward Washington. Brigadier General Tobias Stansbury had his 2,200 troops from Maryland there, disobeying an order from Winder to send them into

Washington. He saw no benefit of taking his men into Washington. His troops were raw militia and Stansbury believed—rightly, as it turned out—that the British army was coming straight at him.

On his own volition, Stansbury was setting up a battle zone. His strongest spot was some earthworks thrown up by civilian volunteers. It was facing the river and about 350 yards from the bridge into Bladensburg. It was a large work designed for heavy cannon, too high for Stansbury's six pounders, but his men were busy clawing away the dirt making the setting right for their cannon.

To the left of the earthwork Stansbury put two companies of militia and to the right a battalion of riflemen. The earthwork stopped well short of these groups but they were still somewhat protected on the left by a tobacco barn and on the right by a rail fence. Taken together, the guns and supporting troops formed a line that covered both the bridge and the roads fanning out from the bridge. About 50 yards behind this line Stansbury put his remaining troops in an apple orchard. These guys were almost all from Baltimore—friends who drank together and sometimes drilled together. They seemed to be on a lark as young men often are before they find themselves in a battle situation.

Now begins a series of events that contributed mightily to the result of the battle. Secretary of State Monroe had been riding around for a couple of days looking for creative ways to help—ways that did not involve him handling a firearm. He saw what Stansbury had done and was quite sure he could do better. Without mentioning it to Stansbury, who wasn't there at the time, he ordered the troops in the apple orchard to move back to a hill farther in the rear. Monroe had not served in the army since the Revolution and was out of his element. These troops were now well beyond where they needed to be to support the line and were now themselves exposed, leaving a large gap on the left of the line with no support for the earthwork or the men stationed there.

He wasn't done. By and by a group of 800 militia from Annapolis showed up. Stansbury had been expecting them all morning, planning to put them to the left of his line, covering his flank. Monroe put them on the right of his line up another hill—this one more than a mile from the first line. They could barely see the main line, much less offer any support.

Winder came to the field about noon where he encountered the attorney Francis Scott Key who, like everyone else, had lots of suggestions where the troops should be placed. While fending off Key's suggestions, Winder received a visit from Monroe and Stansbury. Monroe noted proudly that he had been rearranging the battle lines and asked Winder to look them over to see if he approved. But time had run out. Here came the guys in red coats with glittering bayonets. Troops from Washington were beginning to appear in their rear. Stansbury positioned them as best he could.

Well off to the right, about 250 yards away, the 800 Annapolis militia men moved onto their isolated hill where Monroe had sent them. They watched in confusion, just standing there without orders, wondering what they should do.

Just then the cavalry appeared. Their commander went to Monroe of all people looking for orders. Monroe was up to the job. He pointed to a ravine far to the left of Stansbury's people. Obeying Monroe's orders, the riders found themselves in a gully they couldn't even see out of. They were soon joined by other horsemen. They eventually comprised almost 400 horsemen without orders or any sense of where they were in terms of the overall military alignment or what they should be doing.

Armstrong rode up and looked around. He was under the impression that Madison had put him in charge of the battle but like Winder he seemed confused and disoriented. Madison came riding up but his horse began bucking around and a man on a bucking horse has no thought beyond regaining control of his mount. The little army quivered in anticipation of dire things as the British hove into view. Winder figured that if Barney's men showed up in time they would be 6,000 in number but that number was deceiving. All of Winder's numbers were mostly guesswork.

As for the men in red, they had been on the road since 5 a.m., at first in the shade but then later in the broiling August sun—a time when most Washingtonians even in those primitive pre-air conditioning days sought refuge in the mountains or on the shore. Sometime around 10:00 in the morning they paused for half an hour and then got up and went on again. They were still innervated by their seven weeks on the ships. They wore heavy woolen uniforms in the blistering August sun. Dozens fell by the wayside. One fellow, a devoted aide to Ross, went delirious with sunstroke. They finally reached Bladensburg about noon after a 15-mile march.

The town itself was abandoned as locals saw what was coming and got out. Ross moved stealthily at first. There were many heavy buildings that would offer excellent cover for an ambush. The sturdy structures were perfect for sharpshooters. While Ross and his men waited for scouts to check the situation out, the men who arrived first collapsed on the ground while most of their comrades were trickling in behind them. Meanwhile, Ross went up a nearby hill and got an eyeful—of thousands of Americans with muskets moving around. He began to think that Admiral Cochrane's concerns were well founded. And then Colonel Thornton, leader of the 1st Brigade, insisted they attack right away. Thornton insisted his 1,100 regulars could march through the crowd of American militia with minimal difficulty. So they organized behind a hill and began to move to the sound of bugles and drums. And then they were in plain sight marching down the main street of Bladensburg toward the American lines. The sound of gunfire from undisciplined militia rent the air. The fight was on.

The first shots fell short or missed, but as the British neared the bridge, they began to hit home. Then the Americans could see little clumps of British soldiers setting up unfamiliar devices near a warehouse adjacent to the bridge. Then they heard whooshes and saw streaks of lightning across the sky. The militia men, many of whom had never heard cannon fire, were stunned by the sound and fury of the rockets. Winder rode along the lines trying to reassure them that the rockets were harmless. He took a moment to ride over to where President Madison sat on his horse among his entourage. Winder suggested the official party withdraw from the field which was likely to get hot within a few moments. Madison turned in his saddle and spoke to his colleagues. "Let us go and leave it to the commanding general," he said.[6]

They rode to the rear. Armstrong was unhappy. He had thought the president had given him command. But all of that had gone up in a puff of smoke. He went into a prolonged pout and declined any further participation in the proceedings, not that he had actually participated in the proceedings. "I now became, of course, a mere spectator of the combat," he said later.[7]

The Americans kept up a steady drumbeat of artillery fire. Then suddenly the Redcoats halted and scattered behind the nearby houses and trees for shelter. The American gunners let out a surprised whoop of triumph. It was premature. For a while, the British just fired the rockets which were ineffective but light and easy to carry, and their artillery, what little they had, was still a long way back. Given that their British artillery was far behind, the rockets were the best they could do at the time.

But then the men in red got serious. Colonel Thornton, who had earned his spurs on the battlefields of Europe fighting against Napoleon, decided it was time to charge the bridge. He emerged from cover on a big horse, drew his sword and called to his brigade to follow. He and his horse clattered onto the wooden span. The American artillery responded, knocking down several of Thornton's men as they attempted to follow their leader. But others came on to the sound of the buglers and Thornton seemed to shrug it off, the hot lead whizzing around him. Faster than the Americans could reload their cannon, the British were fanning out on the other side into the bushes and thickets, firing as they came.

What ensued was the classic encounter of militia with regulars. To the Americans, many of whom had never seen a battlefield or even participated in basic training, there was something eerie and discomfiting about the British regulars. Oblivious to the noise and smoke and the cries of their comrades taking hits, they came on in a steady pace, their deadly bayonets glittering in the midday sun. It was the same cold indifference to death their descendants would display a century later at the Marne and the Somme. A company of skirmishers broke first, then the artillery people. Without orders from above—just mere focus on self-preservation—all up and down the line men threw down their muskets and made a beeline to the rear. For those scattered further back by Monroe, including many who could not see what was going on, the process took a bit longer. But panic when it sets in is highly contagious.

Winder struggled to maintain some semblance of order, but soon a new pack of rockets—the British had adjusted their aim—came roaring in at head level. Winder's best regiments simply dissolved. There was no stopping them. If there was any latent respect for Winder among the troops it disappeared in a flash. Here and there a few men rallied but soon joined their comrades in pursuit of better environs. The rout was on. Winder gave an order to fall back and then almost immediately rescinded it. Here and there a man stopped to help a wounded comrade, but then they both kept moving.

The various infantry and artillery units were soon jumbled together in a single tidal wave of retreat. Anything it touched, it carried along. There was no Thermopylae in the making. The frenzied runners sought the quickest exit and for most it was the road to Georgetown which took them straight through Washington.

Among the hustling throng was President Madison and his retinue which was well to the rear when the rout began. It was only 2 o'clock when a note from Winder set the president in motion, heading back into the capital city. In the meantime, Winder's scattered troop formation was slow getting the word of what was happening. Barney's flotilla men were still in formation on the left of the reserve line which remained intact. They had five cannon and were perfectly willing to assume the role of infantrymen. The flotilla men—all sailors—were tough and aggressive. One of them, Charles Ball by name, was an escaped slave who did not choose to accept the British invitation to join them. He posed as a freedman and joined the flotilla as a cook. They and a few other groups still had fight left in them. As the British hove in sight, they opened up with their cannon and the flotilla men launched a charge.

The British reeled from the counter attack. Most of them scrambled for cover in the thickets near the Eastern Branch which was now behind them. Lieutenant Gleig was proud of the way his men handled the setback, retiring slowly and indignantly, halting from time to time, firing with effect. He was also relieved that the flotilla men did not press their advantage. Seeing no one rallying to their side, they retreated back up the hill to their big guns. The British lost several officers killed or wounded in this exchange.

Ross and Cockburn, watching the fight from a house porch, had not taken seriously the second American line running along a ridge more than a mile from the river which is where Monroe apparently sent them, well out of the fight until the main force collapsed. Ross called up fresh regiments just now reaching the battlefield, got on his horse and led them into the fray. His horse was shot out from under him so he got on another one and went on. Admiral Cockburn was also very much in evidence riding a white charger with his gold-laced hat and epaulets flashing in the sun, trying to get his rocket men close to the American line. One of his lieutenants suggested he move back from the fighting, but he kept going. The British reinforcements began to turn the tide.

Joshua Barney true to form was in the midst of the struggle. He saw a British soldier carefully pile up some stones and then lie down behind them, taking aim with his musket. "Oh," said Barney to himself, "you are a crack shot, I suppose but I'll bank you." Personally aiming one of his big guns, he fired into the stone pile. When the smoke cleared, both the pile of stones and the marksman were missing. Barney hoped the guy got away, which was the kind of thought process that distinguished him when the bullets were flying.

Barney and his crew kept fighting. A few others whose units had disintegrated made their way into Barney's group. Winder had ordered the regulars and militia to pull back but sent no word to Barney because Barney was a navy officer and presumably not subject to Winder's command. All of which meant more British fire at the flotilla men.

The British now had the upper hand on the top of the hill and began serious pounding of Barney's men. Barney's horse was killed and then he took a round in his leg. In a tight spot he deemed it best not to tell anyone and kept on fighting. Sailing masters Warner and Martin went down and then several more good men. But the worst thing was loss of their ammunition wagons which were being driven by civilians under contract who had not bargained for that situation. They fled the field. With his ammunition gone and his troops reeling, Barney had the guns spiked and ordered a retreat. His wound began to take its toll. His men tried to help him along, but it was useless. He ordered them to leave and stayed there with one lieutenant by his side awaiting the British. Soon he was chatting with Cockburn and Ross like old school mates—a typical kind of socializing of the old school of warfare, long since gone.

"Well, Admiral, you have got hold of me at last," Barney said to Cockburn.

"Do not let us speak of that subject, Commodore," Cockburn said. "I regret to see you in this state."[8] Cockburn and Ross chatted a bit and then told Barney he was paroled, asking where he wished to be taken. Barney picked a tavern near Bladensburg. Ross gave the necessary orders, summoned a surgeon to treat Barney's wounds, and got a group of his men to serve as stretcher bearers. Cockburn assigned a junior officer to see to Barney's needs. With all that out of the way, Cockburn and Ross went back to their battle.

It was a great victory for the British and an unmitigated disaster for the Americans. With only two-thirds of his force, some 2,600 men, Ross and Cockburn had beaten an American army of 6,000, taken 10 big guns, 220 muskets and 120 prisoners. They had also inflicted 150 casualties. The victory would sound impressive back home, but Ross' force had lost 250 killed and wounded, including 18 of his best junior officers. He had made major mistakes, sending his men into battle piecemeal and indulging a costly frontal assault when minimal reconnaissance would have shown him a shallow ford of the river just a short distance upstream.

The Americans lost the battle because of gross incompetence: putting Winder in charge without adequate instruction and cooperation; failure to defend the sturdy houses in Bladensburg; failure to make use of the cavalry; failure to bring other available units into the fight; but mainly letting a neophyte like Monroe put key portions of the army in places where they could not even see the battle, much less cooperate with other units.

Dispirited groups of militia and soldiers made their way through Washington wondering what they were supposed to do. There was no one to tell them. The residents looked around in wonderment at the chaos around them. Madison's freedman servant Jim Smith galloped up to the front door of the White House, waving his hat and yelling, "Clear out, clear out, General Armstrong has ordered a retreat."

First Lady Dolley Madison never lost her composure. She had a note from her husband telling her all was lost and to gather their things and go. Someone found a wagon and they quickly loaded it with silver, some papers, a few books, a small clock, and the red velvet curtains from the drawing room. It took a while to get the full-length portrait of George Washington by famed artist Gilbert Stuart off the wall. "Save that picture if possible," she said to the staff. "If not possible, destroy it. Under no circumstances allow it to fall into the hands of the British."[9] They finally got it out of the frame but had been forbidden by Mrs. Madison to roll it up. They somehow got it on the wagon and off it went.

Madison came away impressed by the performance of the British soldiers. Like most American leaders of his era, he believed that democratic freemen could outfight the stooges of royal governments. "I never could have believed that so great a difference existed between regular

First Lady Dolley Madison quickly organized a hasty exit from the White House as the British army approached, taking special care to save the portrait of the nation's first president, George Washington (drawing by Gerry Embleton, in *In Full Glory Reflected: Discovering the War of 1812 in the Chesapeake* by Ralph E. Eshelman and Burton K. Kummerow, published by the Maryland Center for History and Culture, July 15, 2012).

The two conquering British officers—Major General Robert Ross and Rear Admiral George Cockburn—toast their victory in the White House before setting it aflame (drawing by Gerry Embleton, in *In Full Glory Reflected: Discovering the War of 1812 in the Chesapeake* by Ralph E. Eshelman and Burton K. Kummerow, published by the Maryland Center for History and Culture, July 15, 2012).

troops and a militia force, if I had not witnessed the scenes of this day," he said.[10] Meanwhile, the patriotic soldiers of just a few hours before were getting drunk and ransacking government offices for anything valuable they might find. They did not find very much.

Leaving Bladensburg at twilight, General Ross, Admiral Cockburn and others rode into the city. The enemy's capital lay helpless at their feet. Some 1,460 men who had been late to the battlefield were with them. Ross and Cockburn went ahead moving toward the Capitol looming in the darkness. Suddenly a volley out of nowhere hit the group. Four men were wounded, one killed. Another shot took Ross' horse to equine heaven. (The man lost a lot of horses in battle.) No one knew who fired the shots, but it was probably some of Barney's flotilla men who were gathered near the Capitol for no particular reason. Everyone has to be somewhere.

The evening dark was suddenly riven by explosions and smoke from the navy yard which was a major enterprise built 14 years before. Winder had given orders that it be blown up rather than fall into the enemy's hands. The fire raced along among the many buildings there and the ships moored there—including the new frigate *Columbia* almost ready for launch and the sloop of war *Argus* completely finished. British troops lined up in front of the Capitol building and fired a volley into it, ostensibly to discourage any snipers that might be hiding there. Then they broke down the main door and went sightseeing, scooping up papers and souvenirs. Then the torches came out. Before long both chambers—the Senate and the House—were ablaze.

Then on to the White House. Ross thoughtfully sent a message ahead to Mrs. Madison assuring her of her safety but she was long gone. In the dining room they found a table set for 40 people who had been expected for dinner that night. Also there was wine in the coolers packed with ice. The unexpected guests raised the crystal goblets in a joyous toast to "the health of the Prince Regent and success to His Majesty's arms by sea and land." They savored the food found in the galley and had an all-around good time.[11]

Ross was in the Oval Room—today the Oval Office—piling together all the furniture he could find which was soon ablaze. As the flames rose in the night air, they turned their attention to the Treasury Building nearby. Because of the name the soldiers hoped to find some money there but no luck. Still they found lots of records that were soon on fire.

The British soldiers carefully set fire to all three of the ropewalks near the navy yard which contributed a major addition to the ongoing flames and smoke. The sailing ships of the early 19th century used vast amounts of rope, and the creation of rope in the pre-mechanical age was a complex undertaking. A typical ropewalk was a structure probably 300 meters

The White House was consumed by the fire the British set, leaving nothing but this lonely shell behind. It looks forlorn, but repairs were already underway (1814 ink and watercolor by George Munger, reproduction no. LC-DIG-ppms-ca-23076,LC-PPD, Library of Congress).

long filled with barrels of hemp, tar and other chemicals and fibers used in the process. Ropewalks involved substantial investment and labor, not to mention space, and could not be easily or quickly replaced.

Both Cockburn and Ross loudly condemned looting and actively sought to suppress it at convenient times. At least seven men were publicly flogged, some of them for what seems to be trivial offenses. One such floggee was heard to complain that it was "damned hard, after being in the service 18 years that I should be flogged for taking a damn Yankee goose." Such are the vicissitudes of warfare. As for the looting of farm goods to feed the British soldiers or the vast amounts of tobacco to be sold to agents in the Bahamas, well, that was normal military activity, not looting per se.

One of the bloodiest events of the Bladensburg battle did not involve shooting. The Americans had burned the navy yard but not the magazine that contained 150 barrels of explosive powder. One would think that the British navy could put powder to good use but for some reason that did not happen. Rather the soldiers were ordered to dispose of the powder. A deep well at the location seemed ideal for that purpose, so the troops began rolling the kegs to the well and dropping them in. But the well was not deep enough to accommodate all those barrels so they soon began to float to the top. No one knows how it happened but something—a stray cigar or spark from metal hitting metal—set the powder off. The result was a huge explosion that sent countless pieces of wood and human flesh soaring into the air. No one knows how many men were killed—possibly as many as 30. The 44 British soldiers who were badly injured were carried back to the Capitol where Ross had established a makeshift hospital in a big hotel on Carroll Row.

Then there was a violent thunderstorm—crashing thunder, lightning bolts across the sky, blinding raid, howling wind. It went on a while, obfuscating the relatively minor fracas of the day before. Cockburn was visiting a Doctor James Ewell in his house chatting about this and that when the front door flew open and in came four soaked men bearing a white flag. They had come from Alexandria, a few miles down the Potomac from Washington, braving the storm, to request surrender terms for their town. Cockburn was unaccustomed to people surrendering who were not under duress or even threat of duress, but he seized the opportunity.

It was an invitation not to be casually dismissed. Soon a few British ships were on the waterfront at Alexandria taking anything that wasn't nailed down and more than a few things that were. They made off with nearly 16,000 barrels of flour, 1,000 hogsheads of tobacco (which was like barrels of cash), and 150 bales of cotton, as well as a goodly amount of wine and sugar. Plenty more remained but there was no more room on the 21 prize vessels they had also captured during their visit.

Through it all the British had been terribly polite. After emptying one merchant's cellar, they invited the man aboard their lead ship for a glass of wine. "They dismissed him with many smooth words and good-natured recommendations to think no more about the flour," a witness recalled. Alexandria mayor Charles Simms was delighted at the good manners. "It is impossible that men could behave better than the British," Simms wrote approvingly to his wife.[12]

By late afternoon, Ross was ready to skip town. He and his team had had a good run and accumulated a goodly amount of booty. He heard rumors that the Americans had rallied 12,000 men just outside of town to regain their honor. It was time to leave. Quietly he passed word to his officers to get ready to move, without a word of warning to anyone. His commissary people conducted a raid into the countryside where they rounded up about 60 cattle to help feed the legions in red. But it was all very hush-hush and soon they were on their way.

Ross had rounded up a diverse collection of vehicles—farm wagons mostly—to cart off his wounded soldiers. He did not have enough to carry them all and several men, including those blown up at the well, had to be left behind. Ross fretted about that. Dr. Ewell assured him the men would be taken care of. And they were.

Ross and Cockburn now set their sights on Baltimore which was a much more attractive target than Washington. Baltimore was a major port with dozens of huge warehouses loaded with trade goods. It was also a place that loomed large in the British imagination, where dozens of privateers had preyed on British shipping for years. It was payback time. Ross and Cockburn reckoned if they could take Washington so easily, Baltimore would be another cakewalk. They reckoned their regulars could handle Baltimore's militia.

They reckoned without Sam Smith.

4

A Man for All Seasons

And there's a nice youngster of excellent pith—Fate tried
to conceal him by naming him Smith—Oliver Wendell
Holmes, Sr.

Cockburn and Ross were undoubtedly familiar with the name of
Major General Samuel Smith of the Maryland militia. For years, the British had attempted to enforce an embargo on American shipping in a key
part of their campaign against Napoleon—to prevent goods from getting to France. The United States had responded with a major privateering campaign against British shipping, taking hundreds of British ships
and their cargoes. Much if not most of that privateering operated out of
Baltimore and the biggest shipping company in Baltimore was Smith and
Buchannan—Sam Smith's operation. In fact, privateering—a fancy term
for piracy—had made many American fortunes, including Sam Smith's.

Privateering was carried out all along the Atlantic coast. The Maryland privateers differed from those of other states in that taking prizes—
ships—was more or less incidental to their trading activities. The British
restrictions on American trade before the war had already forced Baltimore merchants to seek more favorable trade to the south—in particular the West Indies. With the outbreak of war, they redoubled their efforts
down there.

The Baltimore schooners and brigs usually sailed with cargo which
could yield good value in regular trade, while the ships coming out of Boston and New York were going out without cargo, focusing entirely on taking prizes. The armament of a Baltimore ship was as much for defense as
offense, although the superior sailing qualities of the Baltimore-built ships
made them especially dangerous in a fight. They could out-sail anything
Great Britain had on the briny deep. A few of the Baltimore captains, such
as John Rodgers and Joshua Barney, were the exception rather than the
rule, and even they usually carried cargo to the West Indies before cruising for prizes.

Smith had fought hard and well for Washington's army in the Revolution, but he resigned in 1779 to go to Baltimore to revive his family's sagging fortunes. Most of their wealth was in shipping and the British were strangling that effort. On Smith's initial privateering cruise in the summer of that year he turned a profit of £5000, a magnificent sum in a time and place where there were no income taxes, and certainly none on British money. He wrote to his friend Otto H. Williams that it was enough "to help me set up house-keeping."[1]

Smith was without doubt the most prominent citizen of Baltimore and likely Maryland as well. He was a successful businessman—probably the richest man in Baltimore—and also a U.S. senator. He was almost six feet tall in a time when most men were five foot six or so, and built like a modern day linebacker; his very physique commanded attention. He had the air of a man born to lead, and lead he did. Where petty bureaucrats or government rules seemed likely to impede him, he simply ignored them and where necessary walked over them. Over time, most people in Baltimore learned not to get in his way, and as prudent to follow him.

At Washington before the Bladensburg battle, there had been seemingly endless debates about where the British would go—to Annapolis, Baltimore, anywhere but Washington. No one expected a battle at Bladensburg, followed by a destructive raid on the nation's capital. At Baltimore, there was not a shred of doubt that the British were coming their way next. The Baltimoreans were the ones who had chased British ships all over the ocean and hijacked hundreds of them. They were the ones with warehouses bursting with valuable trade goods, much of it lifted from British ships. And what is perhaps more important, the people of Baltimore knew the British were coming because Sam Smith said they were.

At Washington there had been continuing debates about who was in charge. Everybody was free and easy with advice about what should be done and who should do it and where they should do it. General Winder could barely cut through all the gratuitous advice coming his way instead of the practical assistance he really needed. In Baltimore there was no debate about who was in charge—Sam Smith.

At Washington there were many officers with dubious credentials. There were no West Point graduates with high fancy titles because West Point wasn't spitting them out yet. Some of the senior leaders at Bladensburg had never seen a battle up close. But Smith had been a junior officer in George Washington's army during the Revolution earning Washington's praise for his field leadership in combat—including tight situations where he was wounded but kept fighting. In a letter to his wife Abigail dated 25 October 1777, John Adams wrote: "We have accounts that are pleasing. Commodore Hazelwood, with his Gallies, and Lt. Col. Smith in the Garrison of Fort Mifflin, have behaved in a manner the most gallant and glorious. They have defended the River, and the Fort with a Firmness and Perseverance which does honor to human nature."[2] Sam Smith was a proven warrior—and leader.

Samuel Smith walked like a leader and acted like a leader and talked like a leader and it was abundantly clear to everyone in Charm City that he was their leader. When word came that Napoleon was defeated and the British army was suddenly free to attend to other matters, Smith saw the future lying before him and his city with consummate clarity. And he knew what he and Baltimore had to do about it.

One of his first tasks was to verify his leadership position. On paper, General Winder was senior because he was in the regular army and therefore outranked Smith who was in the militia. Also General Winder's uncle Levin Winder was governor of Maryland. But General Winder's performance at Bladensburg did not inspire confidence. For whatever reasons he clearly did not have control of the situation. That is ever and always a conspicuous character defect in a military leader.

When his army was defeated and scattered, Winder—undeterred by the debacle—gathered what remaining forces he could find and struck out for Baltimore to assume control. He was on paper at least the commander of the 10th District of which Baltimore was a part. Thus he assumed his job was to take over what appeared to be the next British target. On the way he received a letter from Smith telling him what to do—a letter he found presumptuous in the extreme. He hurried ahead to Baltimore to confront this challenge to his authority.

Somehow Smith had anticipated this turn of events the year before. As a businessman and politician and also as a warrior he had a knack for knowing what enemies, competitors and rivals would do, and he was almost always right. Certainly, Governor Winder saw him as the natural leader of Baltimore. As early as May 16, 1813, Governor Winder had written to Smith, apparently in response to a query:

> My general order of the thirteenth of March last directing you to take the earliest opportunity of making the necessary arrangements of the militia for the protection of the Port of Baltimore did not confer on you any authority beyond that which you possessed under the militia law. The meaning of the order was that you would proceed to complete the organization of the militia under your command and place them in the best possible state for defense; of course your command as Major General commenced for that period.

> P.S. The British fleet are not to be seen from the top of the State House this morning.[3]

Everybody in Baltimore that mattered was aware of a possible—indeed certain—challenge to Smith's authority. On August 25, Brigadier

General John Stricker, Fort McHenry commander Major George Armistead, Commander Oliver Hazard Perry, hero of the Battle of Lake Erie, and Lieutenant Robert T. Spense, new chief of the Baltimore naval station, made a trip to Annapolis to meet with Governor Winder about Smith's status. They told the governor that the Committee of Public Vigilance and Safety, a citizens' group organized to oversee the defense of Baltimore, had resolved that in the present crisis Smith should take "command of the forces that may be called out for the defense of our city." It was clear Smith enjoyed broad public support in his hometown.

It is not clear whether Smith was in on this scheme but he undoubtedly knew about it. They would not have undertaken this mission without his foreknowledge. Those gentlemen were integral parts of a tight group around Smith. They were all knowledgeable about military affairs, had military experience and would play key roles in Baltimore's defense. One of Smith's most conspicuous assets was this cadre of experienced military leaders who knew what they were doing and were unquestionably loyal to him. It gave him a strong hand to play and he played it to the hilt.

To put the icing on the cake, one of the influential citizens backing Smith was a wealthy property owner, General John Eager Howard. Howard, a Revolutionary War hero of the Battle of Cowpens, one of the few patriot victories, had bitter political differences with Smith, but they were resolved to work together in this pending crisis.

Smith also wrote a letter to Governor Winder which may have been delivered by the delegation, requesting confirmation of his command. Here is an excellent example of Smith's ability to dance around presumably awesome hurdles. Governor Winder was the uncle of General Winder, but he was not one to put family ahead of expediency. After deliberating for more than 24 hours, the governor obligingly wrote a letter that went a bit further than the one he had written to Smith the previous year. The governor implied that Smith's assignment was also a federal appointment, declaring: "By the requisition of the President of the United States of the 4th of July last, one Major General is required of this state. In conformity to which you have been selected."[4]

That was a frail endorsement but Smith chose to see it as the formal last word confirming his authority. General Winder was slow to realize he was no longer in command. In the meantime, he organized survivors of Bladensburg and others who had joined after the defeat and started them for Baltimore. He sent orders ahead to Smith to hold all troops in the city as he expected it to be attacked next and directed rations and munitions be gathered. When Winder got to Baltimore, expecting to assume command, he was stunned to learn that although he was commander of the 10th District, of which Baltimore was a part, he had been preempted by the

Committee of Vigilance and Safety and that the governor (his uncle) had subordinated him to Smith.

He pointed out that Governor Winder had no authority to put Smith in command, and indeed the governor's letter is a model of political ambiguity, but it was clear Smith was asserting control anyway and had no intention of yielding it. The younger man was enraged. In the following days, General Winder wrote whining letters to President Madison and War Secretary Armstrong to no avail. Madison was fully engaged in trying to restore the nation's capital city and had little time or interest in Winder's complaint. And Armstrong had been muscled out of office and was gone—who knew where? The controversy was more or less resolved on September 11, the eve of the attack on Baltimore, by which time Armstrong had left the capital in disgrace. After Armstrong's ouster, James Monroe was acting secretary of war and though he had promoted Winder's career in the past, he let the young general down as gently as he could. "Gen'l Smith's command must extend to Annapolis & to other points along the bay, to which the enemy may direct their movements," he said in a letter to General Winder, "and the troops must be under his control. Monroe expressed full confidence that you will do everything in your power to promote the success of our arms in defense of our Country."

In an enclosed copy of that letter to Smith, Monroe shut the door on the fledgling controversy: "Gen. Winder, who as Commander of the District has made calls for militia from different quarters, is instructed to cooperate and give you all the aid in his power."[5]

Thus, Smith's position was unshakable basically because he had been getting Baltimore organized to resist the British invasion for several months. Governor Winder knew this very well, and with all deference to his nephew, he knew it would be disruptive to interfere with Smith's activities at this juncture, especially to promote a relative who was widely held responsible for the debacle in Bladensburg and the burning of Washington.

And Smith had been busy—very busy. By that time, he had the people of Baltimore in hand. Initially, there was great concern over the fate of local troops who had fought at Bladensburg, "but that was soon replaced by a sense of pride after news of their overall performance was received," Joseph A. Whitehorne wrote in *The Battle for Baltimore.* "Many persons evacuated their families and valuables but Samuel Smith's iron control mitigated panic and instilled a will to get the city ready for defense. Suspense turned to determination and each day without a British attack lessened people's fears and inspired greater efforts at preparedness. Smith's preemptory manner had not set well with some residents before the emergency. However, his past performance marked him as just the man for the moment. His Revolutionary War record, long prominence in state and local politics, and impressive performance during 1813 led to great public confidence in his leadership and assured him the widest connections to draw on for material support."[6]

A major support for Smith's efforts in Baltimore was the Committee of Vigilance and Safety, which succeeded the earlier Committee of Public Supply. It was even stronger than its predecessor and went about its business with zeal. Its records reveal that it had total responsibility not only for defending the city but also administering it during the crisis. Among other duties it raised money, built barracks for soldiers, arrested suspected spies, purchased supplies of all sorts, and made provisions for the city's sick and poor. It also undertook to represent the city's interests before the state and federal governments. It was the indispensable mechanism necessary to free the city's resources and effectively use them. A critical element of the committee's success is that its members were elected by the citizens, not appointed by the mayor, as was the case with its predecessor. Thus it had a broad popular constituency that insured its decisions would be respected. Though elected, its members were members of the merchant and other business classes and consequently had access to the upper crust in controlling the city's wealth. It gave Smith the imprimatur of democratic leadership that enabled him to avoid any potential accusations of arbitrary rule, and it backed him to the hilt.

The key to defense of the Port of Baltimore was Fort McHenry which had been allowed to deteriorate over the years. As late as April 1814, many of its guns had not been mounted because of a lack of gun platforms. Smith arranged to have local carpenters construct gun platforms or carriages. At some point it was reported to Smith that some bureaucrat at the War Department had insisted that the big guns belonged to the federal government and had to be transferred to Washington. "The guns belong to the U.S.," Smith wrote to the Committee of Vigilance and Safety, "but the carriages are the property of the city. I have therefore not conceived myself at liberty to deliver them without the consent of your Committee. I consider these guns as indispensable."[7] The committee took the cue and told the War Department that it could have the guns but not the carriages. That way they would be of little use to anyone and Washington quietly capitulated. That was the last Smith heard about that problem.

At Fort McHenry, Smith found a strange situation in which an elderly commander ruled an extended family of servicemen and their families. Smith was a senator and knew how to manipulate the bureaucracy. By early spring, that elderly fellow was gone and Colonel Decius Wadsworth, prodded by Smith, was working to rectify the situation by emplacing 36 big 42-pounders and some smaller guns from the broken French warship

L'Eole marooned in the harbor. Major George Armistead was now in command, a vigorous officer in the Smith mold.

Smith's quartermaster Paul Bentalou reported he had no money and could get none from the War Department in Washington, which was essentially broke. Then as now, Washington had trouble managing its fiscal affairs. Smith went straight to the Committee on Vigilance and Safety where his friends quickly engineered an immediate loan of $100,000 from Baltimore banks. He worked closely with Smith until he had a full complement of soldiers on hand who knew how to use the big guns. He had several cannon emplaced down at the water level and a full complement of soldiers to operate them. Fort McHenry was ready to earn its lasting fame.

To be sure, there was a brief period of uncertainty. Probably no other city had been as loud as Baltimore in fanning the war fever, but when the shattered remnants of Stansbury's and Sterett's militia trickled into town, a wave of defeatism swept the city. "You may be sure this is the most awful moment of my life," one of the city's stunned inhabitants, David Winchester, wrote to a relative in Tennessee. "Not because, if the place is defended, I shall put my life at hazard in common with my fellow citizens, but because I am positively sure we shall not succeed."[8]

Few had much confidence in defense of the city. "I think the only way to save the town and state will be to capitulate," wrote Private Henry Fulford in a letter to the folks back home after his harrowing day at Bladensburg. "We shall have to receive the British without opposition and make the best terms we can," echoed a local ship owner in a letter to a friend in New York. He said he had to close the letter because he had to go scuttle his own vessel in the harbor to block it against the largest British war vessels.[9]

The postmaster of Baltimore made plans to shift the mail out of town. The banks began moving their real money to New York. Some members of the Committee of Vigilance and Safety seemed more interested in arranging capitulation than arming for defense. But through it all were voices of defiance. John Eager Howard, for one, tried to buck his friends and neighbors up. Pointing out that he had four sons in the field and as much property as anyone, he said he would rather see his sons killed and his property in ashes than surrender and bring disgrace upon the country. It's hard to imagine any American talking like that today.

Meanwhile, Commodore Rodgers sought to pour oil on troubled waters. "General Winder has in a manner much to his honor I conceive, consented to waive his pretensions to rank for the present," he wrote to Navy Secretary Jones. Rodgers had been present during Winder's confrontation with Smith, and as a regular himself, he had to agree with Winder's position that he outranked Smith. But he had been in Baltimore since the night of August 25, had seen the panic firsthand and knew how desperately a strong leader was needed. Somehow he managed to give his sympathy to Winder and his support to Smith without alienating either of them.

Rodgers was a pillar of strength backing Smith. "As senior officer of the U.S. Navy, his presence alone gave new heart to Baltimore, while his 300 seamen from Philadelphia were the first tangible evidence that help was on the way," Lord wrote in *The Dawn's Early Light*. "By combining them with the 500 flotillamen in town—plus Commodore David Porter's force, soon down from New York—Rodgers put together a makeshift brigade which he made as conspicuous as possible."[10]

Meanwhile, Rodgers was here, there and everywhere supplying a calming voice to balance the somewhat driven language of Smith. He even extracted a personal pledge from the Committee on Vigilance and Safety that they would defend the city "to the last extremity." Calm gradually returned to the city streets. On the 27th, Porter wrote to Secretary Jones that, thanks to Rodgers, "the citizens of Baltimore have recovered from their panic, and I hope, Sir, the Navy may yet be enabled to render some service to their country."

There was a lot to be done and high on the list was the basic matter of rounding up the Baltimore troops who had scattered across the countryside after Bladensburg. When Smith issued a call to Stansbury's men to report, only 600 showed up. He ordered

Commodore John Rodgers of the U.S. Navy was a "tower of strength" in the defense of Baltimore. His 300 seamen from Philadelphia were the first tangible evidence that help was on the way. Adding Barney's 500 flotilla men plus Commodore David Porter's force soon down from New York, Rodgers put together a makeshift brigade that figured prominent in the fighting (c. 1814 oil painting by John Wesley Jarvis, National Gallery of Art).

Winder to bring Stansbury's tents and equipment, but it was lost somewhere in Virginia. As for Sterett's elite 5th regiment, it seemed to have vanished from the earth.

Of course, there was no Internet or iPhone service in those days, nor even a *Washington Post* or *Baltimore Sun*, or a CNN or Fox, so rounding up people scattered across the landscape was problematical at best. Smith put ads in the *Patriot and Evening Advertiser*, pleading with his riflemen and artillerists to report for duty in Baltimore, ready to fight again. An even more desperate plea summoned "elderly men who are able to carry a firelock, and willing to render a last service to their country."

This was a situation made to order for Sam Smith and everyone in Baltimore knew it. On August 27 the citizens of the city were ordered to collect all the wheelbarrows, pickaxes and shovels they could find. On the 28th they started digging. A line of fortifications gradually took shape along the eastern edge of the city—the side most exposed to a British landing and, perhaps more importantly, where Smith said the British would land. If Smith were wrong, if the British came from the west, it would be disastrous. But Smith did not have the forces he would need to cover all possibilities. He decreed the British would come from the east because that was what he would do were he the British commander—and that they did.

A man of action, Smith seemed to be everywhere at once riding around on his horse in his major general's cocked hat with a high white plume and his blue coat faced with buff in the Revolutionary tradition—blue ribbon and eagle of the Order of Cincinnati hanging from his left lapel to show he had fought in Washington's army, as if anyone didn't know. His message to them was clear and direct—buckle on your arms and prepare to defend your homes with all you have and all you are worth. His was the spirit of Winston Churchill long before Churchill was born.

Smith created the City Battery, also called Fort Babcock, about one and one quarter miles west of Fort McHenry. It was begun near Winan's Wharf in late April and was completed in the summer as a crescent-shaped earthwork with six of the 18-pounder cannon from the French ship *L'Eole* and a hotshot furnace needed to prepare the ammunition. (They heated the cannonballs so they would start fires and were especially effective against wooden ships of the era.) Located near where Hanover Street Bridge crossed the Patapsco, it was manned by Sailing Master John A. Webster and 52 flotilla men. It was sometimes called Fort Webster. Fort Covington, one quarter of a mile west of Fort Babcock, slightly below Spring Gardens, had been completed the previous December and may have had as many as 10 guns.

The 38th U.S. Infantry commanded by Lieutenant Colonel William Steuart, continued to work on Fort Covington until June when it was turned over to Addison's U.S. Fencibles (seamen drafted into combat duties) who occupied it until September. After that it was manned by 80 sailors from the French battleship *Guerriere* which had been sunk by the USS *Constitution*—sailors who apparently did not want to return to France. It was built to dominate the Ferry Branch approaches into the city and support Fort Babcock. A seven-gun circular battery commanded by Lieutenant George Budd of the U.S. Navy was built at the foot of Light Street (present-day Battery Square) to provide cover and support. A small earthwork right at Ferry Point manned by some Virginians completed the system of the Ferry Branch side of Whetstone Point where the Patapsco split into two branches—the Northwest Branch to the east and the Ferry Branch to the west.

As noted earlier, Cockburn had sailed up the Patapsco in 1813 to scout it ahead of future operations, a trip that was duly noted and reported to Smith, who began making plans to receive Cockburn the next time he paid a visit. One of Smith's "welcome wagon" concepts was construction of a boom across the harbor mouth as a supplement to Fort McHenry's cannon fire. State sea fencibles under Lieutenant Solomon Rutter began work in May and finished in August, making a barrier that extended to both shores as well as 450 feet in front of Fort McHenry's water batteries. (Water batteries were the cannon emplacements at water level where they could do harm to both ships and small craft as necessary.) The boom consisted of a chain fastened to masts laid end to end and bolted together, while the part in front of the shore was made of timber laid end to end and anchored on piles. Smith was working with people who knew what they were doing and were committed to doing it well.

Smith ordered hulks—old ships that had lost their usefulness—to be sunk behind the chain boom. These were anchored in readiness until the fall of 1813 when they were taken to a wharf for maintenance before being brought out and sunk when the enemy fleet should appear—which was September 1814. These barriers were sustained by eight-by-eight flotilla barges armed either with an 8- or 12-pounder cannon, with a crew of 34 men. Additional flotilla barges patrolled the mouth of the Patapsco for added security. The three-gun battery with 45 men at Lazaretto Point commanded by Lieutenant Solomon Frazier of the flotilla could fire down the line of hulks as well as in support of Fort McHenry. The battery was secure from landward attack by positions occupied by 114 more flotilla men. (Lazaretto Point, across the water from Fort McHenry, was so named for a hospital built there accommodate immigrants with infectious diseases—the term lazaretto is Italian for hospital.)

Smith delegated these naval preparations to Commodore Rodgers, one of the more aggressive and capable officers in his retinue, while he focused his energy on completion of landward defenses on Hampstead

Hill and Patapsco Neck and integrating the growing numbers of incoming manpower. Construction of more than a mile of earthworks and gun positions was supervised by J. Maximilian M. Godefroy, a French émigré and architect, assisted by militia officers with some engineering and construction experience. It was expedited by zealous support of nearly every able-bodied resident working in the daily dawn to dusk shifts mandated by the committee. A Baltimore newspaper quoted one of the workers saying: "They are throwing up trenches all around the city, white and black are all working together. You'll see a master and his slave digging side by side. There is no distinction made whatsoever."[11] This was considered newsworthy. Slaves and their masters did not often work side by side.

While the British dallied in the Patuxent, Baltimore's fortifications grew by leaps and bounds. At Smith's call, every able-bodied man enrolled in the 3rd Division, with the exception of the 3rd Brigade, was marched to Hampstead Hill and there joined the thousands of militia troops from Pennsylvania, Delaware, and Virginia. Rather than the 5,000 men Smith had originally predicted, he now found himself at the head of 15,000 men by early September.

At 62 years of age, in a time when few men lived past 50, Smith showed more stamina than most of his subordinates—who by and large were an energetic lot. He seemed to be everywhere, inspecting the harbor fortifications, supervising the work on Hampstead Hill, or meeting with the Committee of Vigilance and Safety. Each day he wrote scores of orders creating hospitals, setting up horse relays to key points, disciplining recalcitrant militia men, and distributing arms and ammunition. Through it all he carefully followed intelligence reports on British movements sent to him by Barney who had performed the same service the year before. If discipline, planning and hard work could save Baltimore, Smith and his fellow Baltimoreans were ahead of the game.

Sam Smith's authority rested primarily on a cadre of seasoned warriors who were unfailingly loyal to him. This was not always the case in American history—or human history, for that matter. Battles have been lost and won due to jealousy, by petty spats over rank, by bureaucracy wrangles over "proper channels." Whole campaigns had failed and whole campaigns would fail again because famous officers could not take orders from fellow officers at least equally distinguished. General Charles "Light-Horse Harry" Lee had sneered at Washington and disobeyed him and twice almost wrecked the army and lost the Revolution. The famous Confederate cavalry general Jeb Stuart disobeyed Lee's orders at Gettysburg, going off on a random venture to capture a Union supply train, instead of providing Lee with critical intelligence regarding Meade's army, leaving him blind in the face of the Union host.

For his part, Sam Smith's authority was built on a flimsy pretext—a humble petition voted by a scratch committee of civilians and ratified by a governor who had no authority to do it. Without question Smith's authority was one grand presumption that could not have withstood serious challenge. But no serious challenge was in the offing. "If there were jealousies and bickerings in Baltimore, if any of these officers disputed Sam Smith's highly disputable authority, no record of such discord has survived," Neil H. Swanson wrote in *The Perilous Fight*. "The outcome itself is evidence that there was none. So is the thoroughness of the preparations for defense, and so is the speed with which those preparations were completed."

Swanson, who passed in 1983, was a prolific historian who clearly was taken by Smith who comes across in his pages as a Churchillian figure. "These were not little men," he wrote. "They were proud men, but not petty. They had the good sense and the good will to see Sam Smith as his fellow townsmen saw him—the symbol of last-ditch resistance. They made themselves into a team, and a situation that might easily have developed into a fatal weakness developed instead into strength. It provided the hometown general with an informal staff of battle-experienced officers—men with the habit of command, men not to be rattled by danger or by sudden, unforeseen crises. And Sam Smith had the sense to use them, the tact to get along with them, the self-confidence and the stature to give orders to these much more distinguished officers with no embarrassment and with no sense of inferiority."[12]

Only Winder comes through as recalcitrant—plaintive, critical and at times sarcastic. He did not return to Baltimore until September 4, and he quickly began finding fault with Smith. Before the sun went down that day, he wrote to Monroe that Smith apparently intended to give him a "patched up" brigade put together from the troops of "other brigadiers who may go away" but that no orders had been issued. Actually, Smith issued orders the following day that put Winder in charge of the defense of the Ferry Branch and gave him two small regiments of regular infantry, Colonel Laval's regular cavalry and two brigades of Virginia militia.

But Winder was not satisfied, Swanson wrote. He informed Smith of his displeasure in a tart letter: "After the candor I have evinced toward you, I cannot for a moment suppose that in the assignment of my command and station, any other motive that a just regard for my rank and other circumstances influenced you—and yet I cannot but believe that in a review of the arrangements you have made, you will be satisfied that it is unjust as relates to my rank and situation and in derogation of the ordinary principles of military service."[13]

Two days later Winder's complaints continued to spew forth. The garrison of Fort McHenry had not been placed under his command; he wanted it. There were two redoubts on the Ferry Branch shore and their garrisons were not included in the list of troops assigned to him; he wanted them, too. There were actually four redoubts in the sector which he had been charged to defend; apparently he had not yet found the others. Perhaps he was too busy finding things to complain about. He was reaching out for command of the troops stationed at Annapolis 30 miles away. And of course he continued nibbling away at Smith's authority like this in a letter to Monroe: "Every moment evinces more and more the impracticability of the present arrangement.... The present state of the Country requires that the command should be arranged without delay," he wrote.[14]

Monroe tried to let Winder down gently. "It was thought improper," Monroe wrote, "to make any change in the command at Baltimore, lest it might cause some derangement there injurious to the public interest." He reminded Winder that he had been offered the command of two brigades of militia called out for the defense of the Potomac but that Winder had insisted on returning to Baltimore. He also reminded Winder that, as acting secretary of war, he had offered to relinquish the command of Washington to him but that Winder had declined. Now he renewed the offer. "There is now no obstacle," he said, "to your resuming command here and in every other part of the district" except, of course, Baltimore.[15] But Winder proved even more stubborn in controversy than he had proved in battle, Swanson wrote. "He retorted that he apparently had failed to make himself clear. What he wanted, he said, was some order from the War Department that might fix with precision the Command respectively to be performed by the Major General of Militia and my duties as Commander of the District."[16] And once again, in the same letter, he reached out for the command of Annapolis.

This time Monroe, in apparent exasperation, let Winder have it with both barrels. "There can be but one Commander in every quarter for which any particular force is intended," Monroe wrote. "The force at Baltimore being relied on for the protection of that place, Annapolis and all other places in the District on this side of the Bay, being under General Smith, the movement of troops must be under his command. I thought this idea was conveyed in my last."

Winder had at long last exhausted his paperwork battle to regain his dignity. He had devoted to it almost the entire three weeks that had been granted to Baltimore by the sluggish British commanders to prepare for its fight for existence. On the day Monroe finally put Winder in his place, the British army landed to attack the city.

5

A City in Transition

Wagner's music is better than it sounds.—Mark Twain

One might easily construe that Sam Smith had Baltimore in the palm of his hand, and that does appear to be the reality of September 1814. But one cannot prudently conclude that Baltimoreans constituted a docile population. They were a rowdy bunch prone to occasional outbursts of extreme violence under the best of circumstances and these were far from the best of circumstances. And yet Smith did have them in the palm of his hand, or at least he had most of them cooperating.

It must be noted that as bustling seaport of more than 40,000, Baltimore was a die-hard Republican town and it had no patience with Federalists who opposed the war. For example, only a fool or a brave man would publish a Federalist newspaper in Baltimore and Congressman Alexander Contee Hanson was such a man. He was an unapologetic Federalist incapable of keeping his opinions to himself. In 1808 he had launched the *Federal Republican and Commercial Gazette* in Baltimore and merged it with another publication in the following year. The *Federal Republican* was known as one of the nation's most extreme Federalist publications. It did not make Hanson, a wealthy and well-educated planter and attorney, popular in Baltimore. Hanson's paper defended the British as liberty's true defenders and castigated the Republicans as stooges for the French dictator—Napoleon. Hanson represented Maryland's Third District and was also a member of the Maryland House of Delegates.

On June 18, 1812, four days after Madison declared war on Great Britain, the *Federal Republican* promised to resist the war effort. "We detest and abhor the endeavors of a faction to create civil contest through the pretext of a foreign war it has rashly and premeditatedly commenced, and we shall be ready cheerfully to hazard everything most dear to frustrate anything leading to the prostration of civil rights, and the establishment of a system of terror and proscription announced in the Government paper at Washington as the inevitable consequence of the measure now proclaimed."[1] You just don't see sentences like that anymore.

Two days later an organized mob wrecked the printing office, destroyed the type, smashed the presses and razed the building in which the *Federal Republican* was printed. The mob's leader declared "that house is the Temple of Infamy, it is supported with English gold, and it must and shall come down to the ground." Hanson was undeterred. He had the paper re-published at a plant in Georgetown and returned to Baltimore to distribute it. This time he came with a few friends to support him, or at least defend freedom of the press. Among his friends was Brigadier General James M. Linghan and General Henry "Light-Horse Harry" Lee who had fought with Washington in the Revolution before letting himself get captured by the British. Also present was the mayor of Baltimore and Brigadier General John Stricker, who was a close friend of Smith and would be one of his colleagues in the war. The mob came back. It was a scary situation. There was a tense standoff.

The local authorities cut a deal with the mob and took Lee and Linghan, along with several others, to the Baltimore City jail where they would presumably be safe. But the mob, numbering several thousand now, came back with even more virulence and extricated the prisoners. About eight of the prisoners managed to mingle with the mob and slip away, but nine were taken outside where the mob stripped them of their clothing, beat them senseless, tortured them with hot wax dripping from candles, and committed other outrages that are fairly common where mobs are out of control. Stabbed in the chest, Brigadier General Linghan died. Eleven others suffered crippling injuries including General Lee who lost sight in one eye. He was so distraught he moved to Barbados and never recovered, dying there four years later.

Meanwhile, the mob dismantled several ships suspected of trading with the British as well as the homes of several free blacks. There was no hint of suspicion that the free blacks were sympathetic to the British, but it was always open season on free blacks. As for Hanson, he never fully recovered his health either but continued publishing his newspaper in Georgetown and continued his political career. He served as U.S. senator from Maryland from 1813 to 1816, back when senators were appointed by the state legislature. As for the riot, a few token prosecutions resulted in only one conviction and that fellow only paid a small fine. A juror later explained "that the affray originated with them Tories and that they all ought to have been killed, and that he would rather starve than find a guilty verdict against any of the rioters."[2]

Sam Smith was not around for this particular riot. He may have been in Washington with other members of the Senate arguing about public policy and pending legislation. But if he had been in Baltimore when the mob trashed the publishing office and bashed a few heads in the process, it seems doubtful he would have been offended or attempted to mollify the angry rioters. Only three years before, he had himself led a mob of Baltimoreans into the print shop of William Goddard, whose newspaper had printed an article Smith considered unpatriotic. Smith assisted in the vandalism of Goddard's property and also the terrorizing of Goddard himself. One of Goddard's associates, Eleazer Oswald, promptly charged Smith with infringing on freedom of the press and challenged him to a duel with pistols. Smith tried to persuade Oswald to withdraw his challenge and then refused to fight because, he said, the challenge was not justified. Oswald replied by calling him a coward. That slur was not taken seriously, at least not by Smith.

On another occasion, when Smith was challenged for office by a young Federalist named James Winchester, and the politics was waxing hot. Smith and some of his followers broke up a Federalist meeting and beat up a number of Winchester's followers. All of this violence was just politics as usual in Baltimore. The Bill of Rights, including the First Amendment which protects free speech, had been ratified in 1791 but apparently the good people of Baltimore did not get the memo. It was often said in the old days, as it is still said today, that politics ain't beanbag.

These are the people Smith was organizing and rallying to his side. He offered no high-sounding sentiments, no oratorical pleas for patriotism or the flag. He was giving them an assignment with no frills, without trying to make it sound cheerful. He didn't even dress it up as a "call to arms." He called for picks and shovels, and the town provided them. Everyone had shovels. Even today city people have shovels packed away somewhere. You just never know when you will need a shovel.

But we don't turn out today when some presumptuous government official calls on us to dig trenches. In 1814, Baltimoreans did—in droves. In a rather lengthy memorandum, Smith enumerated the places for residents of each ward to assemble at 6:00 a.m. "with provisions for the day." There were no McDonald's franchises in Baltimore in those days, so each man had to pack his own lunch. "The owners of slaves are requested to send them to work on the days assigned in the several districts," he wrote. "Such of our patriotic fellow citizens of the county and elsewhere, as are disposed to aid in the common defence, are invited to partake in the duties now required on such of the days as may be most convenient to them."[3]

"It was a businessman's memorandum," Swanson wrote in *The Perilous Fight*. "But if there was nothing in it to quicken the pulse, it had certain other merits. It contained not only a plan but also the where and the when and the who and how of putting the plan to work. Bladensburg might had

had a different outcome if the cabinet or the War Department had been equally unconcerned with the public pulse; but the politically minded gentlemen in Washington could hardly have been expected to tell their constituents to get up at five o'clock in the morning and trundle a wheelbarrow to Centre Market by six; they could hardly have been expected to upset the voters by waking them up so early for such an unpleasant purpose."[4]

But Smith could.

This message from Smith brought the war home to the residents of Baltimore. It was no longer an article in the paper or a rumor. It was on their front doorstep. War was something a man could hold in his hands. It was the wheelbarrow he had used to pick up manure from the stable to fertilize his plants. It was the spade he had used to dig up that extra plot to make room for more tomatoes. And it also made him wonder if he would be around next spring or maybe should grab the wife and kids and head north. But this was home and north was just a direction. There was no one up north to take him and his family in. Home was the Fells Point market house or the seventh ward riding school. Everybody knew the British had it in for Baltimore. If they took over, they would steal everything not nailed down and burn the rest. There would be no more houses or shipyards or ropewalks or harness shops or iron foundry or any wagon works. Someone had to stand up to the British and it was clear that Washington was not up to the job. It was put up or shut up time for everyone in Baltimore.

Only a few days before, as Washington burned, the people of Baltimore, only 40 miles away, stood in the streets or leaned out of their dormer windows or climbed to the rooftops to watch the glare that pulsed and wavered in the southern sky. They likely told one another that it looked like a "right good far" which in Bal-morese meant a right good fire, which of course would mean a right bad fire. (The locals still pronounce their town Balamur.)

Baltimore liked fires. It liked the noise and the commotion that came with fires, the running about, jostling, hollering excitement. It was a lusty, rambunctious upstart of a town and of course there were no movie theaters or rock concerts in those days. If you were organizing a mob to ransack a Federalist newspaper office, that would do. The people needed entertainment.

Baltimore was young and brawny. It took its liquor straight and excitement in simple, direct forms. It liked crowds and fires but also ship launchings and mass picnics and parades, and its swift private schooners with big guns setting out to raid the English Channel and Irish Sea, and coming home past Lazaretto Light with the flags of a dozen prizes hanging out like the week's wash in the rigging. It liked to hear the guns of the homecoming privateers saluting the great fort on Whetstone Point—Fort McHenry. It liked to see the Franklin Artillery and the Baltimore Yagers, the Blues and the Sharp Shooters and the Baltimore light infantry tramping through the streets to drill on Loudenslager's Hill, with a pack of town dogs and rambunctious little boys running alongside.

Everybody was in the streets doing something useful or cheering other people on. It was a tough, rowdy town doing serious business and having a damn good time doing it. "Not even political meetings brought out such a mingling of frock coats and checkered shirts, of roundabouts and coatees, smocks and ruffles of gentlemen's elegant truncated-conical hats and mechanics' work grubby caps, of stable hands, bankers and 'free people of color,' lawyers, clerks, roustabouts, judges, merchants and slaves," Swanson wrote. "It was a combination of picnic, fire, political rally, cornerstone laying and drill day. Militia companies marched up the hill to the rowf-rowf-rowf of their drums; they stacked arms to the rowf-rowf-rowf of ecstatic, hysterical dogs. Supply wagons rumbled behind them, tools were tossed out with a clatter. A band played. Flags fluttered. A well-known, worthy and estimable Frenchman trotted briskly about, measuring, pointing, nodding his head at stakes in the ground and cords stretched over the grass. His name was Maximilian Godefroy, he was an architect and engineer, and Sam Smith had assigned him to superintend digging of the entrenchments laid out on the hill."[5]

The crowd grew and grew some more. On foot with picks over their shoulders, in gigs, in grocers' carts, in surreys and carryalls bristling with long-handled shovels, the men of the eighth ward and the eastern precincts came straggling out of the city. With them came the more energetic from districts not summoned until Monday or Tuesday or Wednesday. They looked like refugees, but they were men determined not to be refugees. A sense of duty was a factor in their coming but only one factor. They were driven by other, simpler motivations. Apprehension was one—the thought that what had happened to Havre de Grace, that had happened to countless helpless hamlets along the Chesapeake, and also to the nation's capital city, could soon be happening here in their city. Anger too was part of the mix—anger that this trouble had been permitted to come upon them, anger that the national government was too weak to help them and too stupid to help itself, anger at the federal politicians blaming their troubles on the "cowardice of the militia" to cover their own shortcomings, anger about the rancid beef being fed to them and the lack of knapsacks and blankets. It is fair and accurate to say that these people were having fun but they were also totally pissed off.

Even with the militia companies and flags and martial music and anger, the first wholesale muster of Baltimore manpower was certainly not a military spectacle. There were too many civilians, there were too many militiamen still wearing civilian clothes. There was much standing around and waiting, lots of shouting and arm waving as the eight citizens charged with the "superintendence" did what they could to wrest order out of confusion. The enemy would not have been greatly impressed. But the sight was impressive enough to hearten the man who conceived it. Sam Smith had given Baltimore no high-sounding appropriate "sentiments" which was standard fare for leaders in that day and time. He had given them a tough job without trying to make it sound like something other than a tough job. He had not dressed it up as a "call to arms." He had issued a call for picks and shovels and asked the town to provide them. The town had responded. Smith had plenty of guns and swords. What he needed at that moment was picks and shovels.

The top-hatted gentlemen began to dig. The bankers and the stevedores, the well-to-do merchants and the hostlers, the lawyers and the slaves and the free blacks and the harness-makers and the coopers and the wheelwrights and the soft-handed shop clerks began to dig. It was no picnic. It was a hot, dirty, back-aching, blistering business. They stuck to it all day, grimly. The newspaper would be able to say with some justification that "the work done demonstrates their power and zeal, to the astonishment of all who behold it." They themselves were astonished. As they dug, two long, curving lines of entrenchment began to take shape. The meaningless holes in the ground became rifle pits. Formless heaps of red earth turned into barbettes and fleches, into demilunes and redans—terms that ordinary people were unfamiliar with at the time and even less so today. A hard confidence grew, a defiance. They could take a grim satisfaction in hands that were blistered raw. They could put thumbs to sun-scalded noses and waggle stiff fingers in the general direction of Ross, Cockburn and Cochrane and their arrogant host in red coats somewhere out there on the bay, coming their way.

Swanson describes it in his 1945 book as if he were there: "From the top of Hampstead Hill a man could see a four-mile panorama of preparation. It started a mile away to the northwest where the Bel Air Road made a slanting line across the far end of the trenches, and it came southward along the curved face of the hill until it touched the harbor. Then it jumped the wide mouth of Harris Creek and followed the north shore of the harbor eastward to the Lazaretto lighthouse, crossed the narrow channel there and took in Fort McHenry. The low brick fort on the tip of Whetstone looked like the red-painted nail on a woman's finger, pointing toward the Chesapeake and the 'big mouth' of the Patapsco River. On the far side of Whetstone at the base of the long slender finger the shore curved in toward the city and then curved out again. It made a broad, ample cove behind the fort; it made Whetstone Point and the low ground behind it look like the back of a right hand, the forefinger pointing and the other fingers and thumb doubled under and the first joint of the little finger poking out to make the first headland of another, smaller cove called Ridgely. Westward way off to the right and past the mouth of Ridgely's Cove and then southwestward across the wider entrance of the Ferry Branch was Cromwell's marsh."[6]

Looking from a distance, Hampstead Hill looked like an anthill amid many other hills not quite so big but looking just as busy all around. Tiny figures crawled around the lighthouse and the red-brick fort. Others swarmed over the fresh mounds of earth thrown up at intervals along the shore of the larger cove. Over toward Ridgely's the figures dwindled till they looked like midgets hovering above the redoubt that was being built there. Whole congregations of water bugs were clustered in the narrow passage between the lighthouse and McHenry, not darting and skittering about but clinging close around a few sticks that protruded from the water like the stakes of pound nets. There was another cluster of them in the mouth of Ridgely's Cove.

With a spyglass you could see toy soldiers playing with toy cannon on the very tip of Whetstone—that would be George Stiles' crack Marine Artillery drilling with the French 42- pound cannon in the new water battery on the shore in front of Fort McHenry. You might be able to make out that the water bugs were in reality small boats and barges and that the sticks were the masts of sunken ships. The masts made an uneven row part way across the channel, like the end of a pasture fence running down into the water, a fence with its posts set crooked, with some of the posts missing. Other ships were being towed out from the inner harbor. Brigs, bay schooners, ship-rigged packets, Jamaican sloops and bugeyes, all creeping toward the harbor entrance.

The people who owned those craft being sunk to block the waterway to British battleships were without doubt upset at their loss. Every boat represented a substantial investment for someone. But then you would see one of Sam Smith's schooners being warped into an open space in the line, inshore by the Lazaretto. In Baltimore in those days everyone knew who owned which ship. The seamen are seen anchoring her, both bow and stern. She's starting to fill with water, sinking down. You can't get mad at Smith for sinking your boat if you see he is sinking his own. Well, maybe you can, but you don't.

And then you see barges in the creek—the last of the little gunships built for Barney. They weren't finished in time to join him down toward Bladensburg. They still have their guns, a long gun in the bow and a carronade aft. They didn't have time to remove the guns. But wait, Smith has another plan. He's setting up a cannon row behind the line of sunken ships. They will be there waiting for the Redcoats like militia men in one of the new trenches. Smith is always thinking of something. And every thought in Smith's brain soon becomes reality on the ground.

Not all of the vessels moving down the harbor were stopping in the narrow entrance. Some were being towed out past the Water Battery and around the end of Whetstone into the broad reach that lay between the fort and Cromwell's marsh. They were being anchored in a long row like a line of battle—which is what they were. So there you have it. Baltimore is scuttling its own ships not to save them but to barricade the city. Afloat they were of no use. They could not fight the British mortar ships and frigates but lying on the bottom they could impair movement of the big battleships the British needed to take on Fort McHenry.

One by one they sank, making that awful glug-glug sound that sailors are conditioned to fear and hate. The crooked row of masts made a slovenly, forlorn-looking fence from the Lazaretto to the Whetstone shore below the main gate of the fort and from the other side of Whetstone to the marshy shore beyond the Ferry Branch. It was a spectacle like no one in Baltimore had ever seen before or would ever see again.

In the channel that led to the inner harbor, with its wharves and warehouses, working parties in clusters of small boats rigged a boom above the sunken hulks, the heaviest chains that could be found in town, spiked to logs and timbers from the shipways. A second boom was being built across the mouth of Ridgely's Cove where British landing barges might attempt amphibious assault almost two miles behind Fort McHenry and almost in the city streets. In the channel between the lighthouse and the fort, the gun barges were creeping up to the barricade of ships. They were being moored bows-on behind the boom to point their long guns down the harbor.

All things considered, Sam Smith was doing a remarkable job of getting his city ready to fight. It isn't easy getting soldiers ready to fight, damn near impossible getting rank and file citizens ready to fight. It wasn't a matter of waving a sword or shouting commands or maneuvering troops in neat blocks of regiments and brigades, though he knew how to do those things. Rather it was being able to surmount the steady onslaught of details about this and that. The details did not come in tidy bundles; they were more like a sea of hornets buzzing around your head constantly, day and night—from swarms of drafted men and worried townsfolk who were scared and confused about what they were supposed to do and what was being done to them. Sam Smith did not have a large staff to handle the small stuff, and in any event, in this crisis there was no small stuff.

For example, hungry men have to eat. A man named J. Winchell living at 59 South Street had an idea about that. He put an ad in the local paper addressed to "colonels of regiments and captains of companies, now on service in Baltimore." Calling himself "the subscriber," he "respectfully announces to officers of the above description, that he will bake and deliver for the men under their command, Bread of any description agreeably to order—and will receive flour in pay, pound for pound."[7] The ad did not express respect for the commanding general which would have been prudent.

Winchell probably meant well but he was a civilian and did not realize he had gone over the general's head which is something a prudent man does not do. He may or may not have intended to be a profiteer—actually the term did not yet exist—but flour for bread, pound for pound, looks like a high price. Of course, a commanding general cannot permit his men to go hungry. Frederick the Great liked to starve his men. He said "hungry dogs fight well," but he wasn't dealing with volunteers, and he wasn't dealing with Baltimore. So where was Smith to get the bread for his men? If the senior commanders of armies spend their time looking for flour to trade with Winchell, their companies will get precious little drill, a critical need for militias. There must be a better way and Sam Smith was accustomed to finding better ways to do things. By the third of September, he had a contract with someone named Francis W. Bolgiano to bake bread for the troops.

Men need bread and they also need a place to sleep. Smith seemed to keep going 24 hours a day but he could not expect that of the men in the trenches they were even then digging. He can't let them sleep in the streets or the trenches, but there aren't enough barracks and tents. So he calls on the Committee of Vigilance and Safety to build sheds. They don't have to be palaces, just a place to get out of the rain.

So under Smith's direction we have a carpenter named Robert Long employing 30 men exempt from military service for one reason or another constructing "shed-barracks." He transforms his payroll into a muster roll. He forms his employees into a volunteer company and goes to work with hammers and nails erecting these shacks on vacant lots.

But it's still not enough, so Smith seizes ropewalks—the long structures where ropes are made—and transforms them into barracks. The owners are not pleased. They serve Smith with written notice that they will hold him personally responsible for depriving them of their property and any damage incurred. Smith shrugs and continues his rounds. If the British take over Baltimore, none of that will matter.

Then there are the British deserters coming into town. The pay in the British army, like the pay in the British navy, is minuscule and the working conditions are harsh. But some of these people probably—indeed likely—are spies sent to check out the city's defenses. So Smith gets the committee to approve a plan to have the suspect characters "conveyed across the Susquehanna" and to give them $2 apiece and set them loose. Just get them out of town as quickly and quietly as possible.

Very quickly it becomes obvious that, as the Bible says, "men cannot live by bread alone." They need vegetables and meat and fruit. Free citizens are a choosy lot. They need a more balanced diet. But other supplies are in short supply. The people of surrounding farms normally bring their produce to market in Baltimore, but they have disappeared. They have heard that Smith is taking whatever he needs for the war—lumber, ropewalks, ships, horses and wagons, whatever. Smith must somehow convince the country people that their goods and wagons will not be confiscated. So he issues handbills and has them distributed. The handbills say clearly that the city "reposes unlimited confidence in the disposition of the good people of this and neighboring states who are not employed in a military capacity" and therefore "confidently calls upon them to bring to the city *for sale* such supplies as may contribute to the comfort of those whom, under Providence, the safety of the city is confided." The commanding general has given absolute assurance that "those who visit our city with the laudable intention of contributing to the comforts of its brave defenders ... shall be permitted to transact their business free from the danger of impressment of their wagons, carts or horses or of any species of interruption to themselves."[8]

It worked. Another problem solved. In this crisis, a reputation for integrity was a critical asset. Even people living outside of Baltimore knew and respected Sam Smith. If he said their property would be respected, they knew it would be.

Swanson, in *The Perilous Fight*, covered a lot of ground, duly noting that the concentration of thousands of untrained, undisciplined men in a confined area breeds a certain amount of trouble. "Some of them are bound to get drunk," he wrote. "They roar and they carouse in the streets, they break windows and get into fights in taverns."[9] Yes, they do. The Committee of Vigilance and Safety ordered the taverns and grogshops—"except those for the accommodation of travelers"—to close at 9 p.m. and stay closed all night. It is no reflection on the capacity of these patriots to assume that some of them can drink enough between sunrise and 9 p.m. to become "elevated," but even the Committee of Safety is not so bold as to shut off the liquor in the daytime. Instead, it increased the town watch. It also provided Smith with a detachment of military police. It identified three companies of men unfit for combat duty and assigned them to patrol the city every night.

To be sure, the challenge of whiskey was not the worst of Smith's headaches. Not all of the citizens of Baltimore were willing to dig trenches all day without compensation. Once Hampstead Hill had been fortified, Smith wanted breastworks built across the North Point road. So of course the committee kicked into gear. It undertook to hire laborers and to furnish them "with provisions and other necessaries." That list of "necessaries" of course included liquor. If the entire town was to be fortified, then by golly the workers themselves needed to be fortified.

Of course, Sam Smith—focusing on the town's eastern side—was not allowed to forget that the town had three other sides. Indignant citizens from those other sides came to see him and stamp their feet. Each and every one of them had become a military expert and thoughtfully considered that his home had become an objective for the British. Every man who helped dig a redoubt on Hampstead Hill wanted one in his own neighborhood, along with at least one 24- pound cannon, though two would be better.

Sam Smith was not oblivious or indifferent to their concerns. He simply did not have enough troops and cannon to fortify every neighborhood. But the complainants were reasonable people and Smith needed their support. He was also a politician and needed their votes. So he got underway some limited projects here and there that would never develop into finished breastworks or be supplied with cannon and garrisons. But the people would see something going on and they would be relieved. He knew it was all the product of frazzled nerves. His own nerves were no doubt doubly frazzled, but he never showed it. In fact, Smith appeared to be one of those rare individuals who thrived on crisis. Every new challenge got his blood pumping. Here I am! Bring it on!

Sanitation was also a rapidly growing concern. Thousands of men were living close to the land in a time when there were no porta-potties. Some of the out of towners simply squatted behind the nearest tree. After a while the noxious odors became, well, noxious. There simply was nothing much Sam could do about that except wait for a good breeze to blow the stink away.

But lesser problems are his to resolve. Captain Babcock who is superintending "the works" at Camp-look-out demands a horse. He is losing time walking from place to place. So he gets his horse and almost immediately needs laborers and mechanics. The committee permits him to hire 150 laborers at pay not to exceed a dollar a day. They have paper money now for the first time since the Revolution. The dollars printed during the Revolution—the disparagingly called "Continentals" lost value quickly. President Madison pushed through legislation authorizing the printing of paper money backed by the U.S. government to help pay for the war. But the laborers are not satisfied; they want more money. So the committee authorizes the superintendent to hire workmen "upon such terms as he shall think best." The committee is apprehensive about the cost of Babcock's elaborate plans. But Smith is in too deep to back out now. He assures the committee that the federal government will pay the tab. He has no authority to make such a promise, but then he has no real authority to do anything. He just plunges ahead.

Then it is called to his attention that some of the men called up for service have families but no money coming in. Their children are going hungry. A committee of relief is appointed "to ascertain … the situation and wants of the families of those called out on the present emergency … and distribute from time to time, with judicious care, such aid and comforts as they may think proper."[10] When your children are going hungry, any help is appreciated.

The men in the trenches are anxious and fearful. They are determined to defend their city, but they are aware they may pay a steep price for their loyalty. It is like a dull ache in the stomach. They know that some of them will be killed, that some will be wounded and crippled for life, and that some will linger in pain for days and then die. A lead slug or a fragment of iron in the guts hurts as badly in 1814 as it will 200 years later. But the wounds are ugly and the chances of surviving are less in 1814. For the wounded there will be little anesthetic—perhaps a little opium or a shot of whiskey. Neither will help very much.

In fact, anesthetic is not yet a word in a doctor's vocabulary. Sometimes the physicians introduce a means to "counteract" the pain and to "equalize excitement." That means they impose a blister to multiply the pain. They relieve the major pain by giving the patient a different pain to distract him. The doctors of 1814 have a formula they call "blister and bleed." They blister a man for pneumonia, for diarrhea and for paralysis. Or they bleed him, draining "bad" blood from his body. How they presume to differentiate good blood from bad blood is never explained. The ancient Greek physician Hippocrates advised young doctors—first do no harm. The 18th-century physicians apparently never got the memo. When former president George Washington caught a cold in the winter of 1799, his doctors bled him. He never recovered.

The prognosis for men wounded on the battlefield in 1814 is not good. A man shot in the belly may live, but nine out of 10 will die, and spend long, painful days dying. "A crushed arm bone or leg bone means being crippled for life," Swanson wrote. "It means knives in the conscious flesh. It means being tied to a board while a saw shudders through the bone. There will be no reprieve of blood plasma. There will be no sulfa to fight the infection in putrefied wounds. The surgeons will not boil either their knives or their saws; they will not wash their hands. They will speak with approval of 'laudable pus' and never suspect infection. They will go from one gangrenous wound to another and dabble in pus till their fingers are sore, and yet never suspect that their fingers are spreading death among wounded who might not die if their hands were clean."[11]

The men going into battle in Baltimore in 1814 were not confident in the medical care they would receive on the battlefield. They had no reason to be, and they generally regarded any wound as a death sentence. Still, they stood tall and awaited the enemy. They wouldn't have long to wait.

And while they waited, they took heart looking toward Fort McHenry where they saw something new—a giant flag. It flew from a pole just inside the parade ground. Measuring 30" × 42", it seemed to dominate not only the fort but also the outlying strong points and even the defenses on Hampstead Hill. It was certain to command the attention of the visitors anticipated any moment from Great Britain.

That was just the way Major George Armistead, commander of the fort, wanted it. During the invasion scare the year before, he had written to Sam Smith: "We, Sir, are ready at Fort McHenry to defend Baltimore against invading by the enemy. That is to say, we are ready except that we have no suitable ensign to display over the Star Fort, and it is my desire to have a flag so large that the British will have no difficulty in seeing it from a distance."[12]

He was to get his wish. Sometime that summer (1813) a committee of three high-ranking officers—General Stricker, Commodore Barney and Colonel William McDonald of the Maryland 6th Regiment—called on Mary Young Pickersgill, a widow who normally specialized in making house flags for Baltimore's far-flung merchant ships. They explained their needs and Mrs. Pickersgill accepted the order.

Recruiting her 13-year-old daughter Caroline to help, she spent the next several weeks cutting and measuring her bolts of cloth—15 white stars, each two feet from point to point … eight red stripes and seven white, each two feet across. Altogether she used some 400 yards of bunting.

Then came the job of piecing it together. Even the big upstairs bedroom in the Pickersgill house wasn't large enough, so on inspiration she borrowed the use of the malthouse in Brown's Brewery. Here she and Caroline continued working—often by candlelight—sewing and basting them together. "Mrs. Pickersgill's flag measured thirty-two by forty-two feet, one of the largest ever made, hand-sewn with an estimated 350.000 stitches," Ronald Utt wrote in *Ships of Oak, Guns of Iron*. "Some question whether a mother and her young daughter could have completed the task in the six weeks allotted, and Mrs. Pickersgill's three nieces and a slave, and a free black woman in her household, may have helped."[13]

That August the flag was delivered at a cost—meticulously calculated by Mrs. Pickersgill—of exactly $405.00. For a year it wasn't needed, but this hot, dangerous evening it blazed in the sunset—not an icon of might and power, but rather an expression of earnest purpose ... a mark of defiance about to take its stand against the strongest nation in the world.

That flag today is prominently mounted in the American History Museum of the Smithsonian Institution in Washington. It looks battle worn because it is battle worn. The edges are a bit ragged. It is the most beautiful flag you will ever see.

6

The Son Also Rises

In time of peril, like the needle to the lodestone, obedience, irrespective of rank, generally flies to him who is best fitted to command.—Herman Melville

Samuel Smith did not—like the goddess Athena—spring full blown from the head of Zeus. He was born on July 27, 1752, the first child of John and Mary Smith—all American names if there ever were any—in Carlisle, Pennsylvania. Four more children would come along in fairly quick succession. The Smiths were Scotch-Irish and were closely allied with other families of Buchanans, Steretts and Spears who always traveled with them. In subsequent years children of the four families would sometimes intermarry. Samuel Smith, the focal point of this work, married Margaret Spear in Baltimore some years later.

Carlisle was a military post in those days and today, a city of some 20,000, is home of the U.S. Army War College and the U.S. Army Heritage and Education Center (where this military writer has performed much research over the years). Carlisle is in the Cumberland Valley, a productive farming region. The Smiths had moved there with the other families from Lancaster, Pennsylvania, where they may have been intimidated by the Amish who were already claiming a lot of territory in that part of the world. In any event, the Smiths had always made decent money which they used to set up shop in Carlisle. Samuel's grandfather, after whom he was named, had owned a considerable amount of land, as well as a flour mill in Lancaster. In 1750, because of advancing age, he turned the family business over to his oldest son John.

Like his father, John Smith also had a knack for making money. He purchased land around Carlisle and opened a general store. He stocked manufactured items needed by local farmers and took payment in wheat which he began shipping to a new town to the southeast—Baltimore. Baltimore was a small burg in those days with a few houses and businesses, but it was about to ascend on a rapid growth track. There the Smith wheat was bought and shipped to other parts of the British empire. John Smith had a vision of prosperity in Baltimore. It was the beginning of something big.

In Carlisle, Samuel had been enrolled in a local school run by a minister—a not-uncommon situation in a world short of schools. His family was ambitious and wanted their eldest son to prosper. He was a quick pupil and learned to read and write and handle basic math, good things for a young man in business to know. In 1759 his dad abruptly moved the family and its business to Baltimore where they were already building a business reputation. They brought along a substantial amount of money they had earned selling their store and land in Pennsylvania which in Baltimore they invested in slaves and ships. There is no way to tell if the advantages of slave labor was an inducement to the family's move but it could have been. There has always been a clear advantage in having a loyal labor force that does not need to be paid—unless you happen to be one of the uncompensated workers.

Slavery never took root in Pennsylvania. When George Washington was president in the 1790s, Philadelphia was the nation's capital. The law in Pennsylvania stated clearly that any slave who managed to reside in the state for six consecutive months became free. Thus, Washington had to rotate his slaves back to Mount Vernon every six months to be replaced by others who took their place in Philadelphia.

In any event, the Smiths used the newly acquired slaves to build several wharves in Baltimore harbor, one of which was reputed to be 1,000 feet long. Smith formed a partnership with his brother-in-law William Buchanan, whose family also made the trek to Baltimore, as did the Steretts and Spears. Their long wharves were the only ones in town that reached the ship channel, which offered Smith & Buchanan a tremendous advantage. They did not have to hire swarms of barges to offload incoming ships. They also built warehouses, again employing slave labor, to store grain being readied for shipment abroad. Within a short period of time they were prominent people in Baltimore, and among the wealthiest.

The Smiths wanted young Samuel to continue his education so over a period of years he attended small private academies in Little Elk, Maryland, and Newark, Delaware. He became well versed in classical literature which was about the best one could expect from formal schooling in those days. At the age of 14 his formal education was done and Samuel began working as a clerk in his father's business. He worked hard at his job and learned the ropes of the family business as he grew into a physically imposing young man—almost six feet tall in a time when most men were maybe five foot five or less and built like a modern day linebacker. When he turned 19 his father sent him to England where he had arranged for Samuel to take a position with a large mercantile firm—Mildred, Roberts and Company—which the elder Smith had dealings with. Sam was sent to make contacts, learn how the English and European companies operated and drum up new business for the company—a fairly hefty lift for a 19-year-old. Clearly, the elder Smith saw great promise in his oldest son.

Accompanied by two slaves, young Smith traveled to Europe in 1771 aboard the *Carlisle*, a ship owned by Smith & Buchanan. The slaves are not identified by name in the record, but they were sent along to handle the young man's luggage and keep him from harm. Back in those days police work was in its infancy and young people in unfamiliar towns were vulnerable. Actually everyone was vulnerable. People of property in London in that era routinely travelled with armed guards in the middle of the day to protect them from roaming thieves. The slaves were presumably tough guys charged to look out for the boss' son as well as handle his luggage. In London, Smith sold the cargo from the ship and began making acquaintances among the merchants that had done business with his father's company.

At some point in London young Samuel made a pivotal decision. He decided to ignore his father's instructions and forbear the job with the British company. He headed off to Venice looking to make new contacts to do business with. "I may get some consignments from that part of the world," he wrote his father. "If I don't I shall have the pleasure of seeing a fine country & learning a little of the trade of different places."[1] He wrote numerous letters to his father during his European sojourn which, given the sluggish international commerce, probably arrived on the old man's desk in bundles.

Young Smith had some educational adventures—as in Venice when his ship piloted by a local who was supposed to know the local waters slammed into a sand bank and eventually sank. He sent his crew back to Baltimore, presumably including the slaves, and he continued his investigation of Europe. He visited different cities and ports, made contacts and learned where opportunities beckoned. He spent a good bit of time promoting the port of Baltimore as a viable alternative to Philadelphia. Within a short time, his efforts began to yield a growing number of orders for Smith & Buchanan.

He went on to Spain where he visited every major port and filled a notebook with observations on the economy of each city and the character of the men involved. In those days of rudimentary international relations it was vital to be able to do business with trustworthy people. He skipped Paris—he didn't see much opportunity there, at least not business opportunity—and made his way back to London. He concluded his trip in 1774 with a leisurely tour of English cities. He was mainly interested in purchasing large amounts of English goods—which no doubt brought him many new friends. While en route he got a letter from his father telling him he was now a partner in the firm. He sailed to Philadelphia and from there took a coach to Baltimore.

While he was in Philadelphia looking for a coach he was only a few blocks from Carpenter's Hall where the First Continental Congress was meeting, debating volatile issues that would soon change his life. He had to know about it, he was a curious young fellow, but he did not dwell upon that sort of thing in his missives and left no record of his opinions about the Congress. During his foreign adventure, despite his prolific letters, he did not write one word about the rising tide of rebellion in the colonies.

Smith was 22 when he returned home and already his foreign adventure was beginning to pay off big time. He was moving shiploads of wheat and flour across the Atlantic but perhaps even more importantly he had fostered an international network of trusted contacts. He kept up a steady correspondence with them, keeping them informed of market conditions in America while they returned the favor. But all around him events were racing out of control as the colonies began the arduous (and highly risky) process of breaking away from the mother country. The first major act of the new legislature was to break off economic ties with Great Britain, which pulled the rug out from under export-minded businesses like that of the Smiths. Newspapers kept tabs on which companies observed the ban and which ones continued doing business with Great Britain. The firm of Smith & Sons was never mentioned on the second list. "From the very beginning, the Smiths—father and son—had committed themselves professionally and personally to the American cause," Frank A. Cassell wrote in *Merchant Congressman in the Young Republic*. "When John Smith & Sons ceased doing business with London, the firm managed to maintain profits by expanding trade with the Mediterranean area and in the West Indies. They were soon trading wheat and flour for guns and powder which they smuggled past the British ships and resold to the fledgling rebel government."[2]

And Smith the younger further solidified his rebel credentials by enlisting in the Baltimore Independent Cadets, a militia unit made up of young and socially prominent Baltimoreans. He had no experience in military matters but quickly mastered the relevant skills. "With his quick intelligence, his flair for organization, and his youthful zeal, he won rapid promotion first to sergeant and then to adjutant of his company," Cassell wrote. "In January 1776 he managed to secure a captaincy in Colonel Smallwood's regiment, which had recently been formed."[3]

Smith had another opportunity to embellish his resume in 1776 when he was sent to Annapolis to arrest the governor, Robert Eden, who was the last proprietary governor of the Maryland colony. He was sent by the

Baltimore Committee of Safety. Eden was planning to sail to Great Britain and Smith tried to thwart his plan. He found the ship the governor planned to use and ordered his men to keep it in the port. But then the Annapolis Committee of Safety found out what was going on and got testy about the Baltimore committee infringing on its territory. Somehow Smith wiggled out of this imbroglio without getting arrested.

In July, word came about the Declaration of Independence and Smith was off with his unit to join General George Washington's army at New York City. Soon Smith and his troop were lined up against the British army which vastly outnumbered the Americans. In the Battle of Long Island on August 27, 1776, the senior commanders of the American forces were repeatedly outfoxed by the British generals who had more experience at that sort of thing. After two weeks in the field, Smith's troops had performed bravely and maintained cohesion, but they were forced to retreat. The only line of retreat was through a swamp and across Gowanus Creek. Smith and 250 other Maryland troops were the rear guard. Smith's unit was cut to pieces. Though exhausted and cut off from assistance, Smith never lost his cool. Smith and one of his sergeants stripped to the waist, pushed logs across the water for their soldiers to cling to and eventually managed to reach Brooklyn Heights and rejoin the American army.

However, the American position on Long Island was hopeless. Washington ordered his 12,000 troops to leave their positions and march to Brooklyn Ferry where a hastily assembled fleet of small boats ferried them to Manhattan. But somehow Smith did not get the memo. He presumed he and his troops were left as a rear guard. But Washington himself found them and led them to the embarkation point. That was Smith's first direct communication with Washington in a relationship that would continue until the great man's death in December 1799.

In these opening salvos of the revolution, American troops did not fare very well against the experienced British troops, but they never lost heart. In one particularly hot exchange, a cannonball struck the ground in front of Smith and bounced over his shoulder, beheading a sergeant standing directly behind him. The Americans were striving to maintain order while backpedaling before the combined might of British and Hessian regulars. At one point Smith was hit by a spent musket ball and temporarily lost use of one arm. (The record doesn't say which arm.) In the confusion, Smith managed to assemble his scattered forces along with a few strays and make it back to the main army. The record shows that the men from Maryland had done most of the fighting and paid dearly for it. One-fifth of them were dead or missing.

After the Battle of White Plains, Smith and the Marylanders now joined Washington's army moving into New Jersey. As always the

Marylanders comprised the rear guard fending off advance units of the British force. They also had to destroy anything the enemy might find useful. They were traveling light and never got enough food and rest. With his unit exhausted and down to less than a hundred men, Smith sought out General Washington and asked him to replace his unit. Washington denied the request telling Smith he could not find another unit "in which I could place the same confidence."[4] When told of this comment from the great man, Smith's troops raised a cheer and vowed to keep going as best they could.

Smith recorded an interesting exchange with an acquaintance, Colonel William Allen, a wealthy Philadelphian. Allen told Smith he disagreed with the Declaration of Independence and he intended to resign. If this was an attempt to persuade Smith to join him, it fell on deaf ears. Smith said he had not wanted independence when he joined the army but his loyalty was unshakable. "Whatever Congress determines, I will obey,"[5] he said. Smith also told Allen that upon reflection, he thoroughly agreed with the Declaration and its principles. Allen went into exile in Great Britain. Smith stayed to help build a new nation.

By December 7, Washington's army was across the Delaware River, just steps ahead of the British. Smith was bonded with his troops and eager for more action, but he would miss the victories at Trenton and Princeton. He was sent back to Baltimore to recruit men for a new regiment authorized by the Continental Congress. As an experienced officer of proven courage, Smith was elevated to lieutenant colonel and made second in command of the new Maryland regiment. Through the winter, Smith recruited and trained men. At the same time he realized his family's fortune was beginning to erode due to the British embargo and also the rapidly evaporating value of the new currency created by Congress—the much despised "Continentals."

But it wasn't all hard work. Smith found the time to persuade a beautiful woman named Margaret Spear to marry him. She was one of the Spear family that had long been aligned with the Smiths, and her father was also a wealthy merchant (or at least was until he ran afoul of the same forces undermining the Smith fortune). But there was no time for marriage, not then, anyway. Sam Smith was soon off with the Fourth Maryland to join Washington's army at Morristown, Pennsylvania.

The next big fight—and another major setback—for Washington's army was the Battle of Brandywine when the Americans sought to prevent the British from taking over Philadelphia which at the time was the nation's capital. The British outmaneuvered the American troops who were routed. The overall battle broke down into isolated skirmishes. Frantically Smith tried to rally his troops. They went looking for the main army. They encountered some British troops who they fired on. They drove the small British detachment away. By the middle of the afternoon Smith reached the top of a prominent hill where he could see scattered American troops milling around leaderless. Moving diligently about he managed to assemble a force of about a thousand men, but they didn't know where they were or where General Washington was. They encountered a farmer who refused to answer questions. Smith held a pistol to the farmer's chest. The farmer showed them the way to Washington's army, where they were soon reunited.

Washington then engaged in a series of maneuvers designed to keep the British out of Philadelphia, but it was useless. The British moved into town and Washington came up with another plan—to disrupt the flow of ships into Philadelphia thereby depriving the British of their supplies. At this juncture, Washington sent for Smith and put him in charge of Fort Mifflin on a small island in the Delaware River just below Philadelphia. The formal command belonged to a Prussian officer named Baron Henry Leonard Philipe D'Arendt. The Americans were always eager to employ officers from European armies who presumably knew more about military organization.

But D'Arendt was not there yet, so Smith finally had an opportunity to demonstrate his leadership. Fort Mifflin was a humble affair on a small patch of earth called Mud Island. Its name reflected what it was. "The keeping of the forts if of the greatest importance," Washington's order read, "and I strongly rely on your prudence, spirit and bravery for a vigorous and persevering defense."[6]

Smith led a force of 200 men to Bristol on the Delaware River and crossed to the Jersey shore. Slowly they progressed south along the river bank to Gloucester where he had his troops construct a large log raft, which they rode down the river to Fort Mifflin. At the ripe old age of 25 and with zero experience defending fortifications, Smith was tasked to prevent the British from supplying Philadelphia.

"Even Smith's untrained eye could see that an attack of any size would easily capture Fort Mifflin in the condition he found it," Cassell wrote. "In the first place, its design was imperfect. To be sure, the south and east sides of the fort facing the river boasted thick stone walls fitted with apertures through which muskets might be fired. Most of the fort's heavy batteries were located on these walls. But the defenses on the west and north consisted of only some ditches, a palisade, and three wooden blockhouses mounting a few cannon. Less than five hundred yards away from the vulnerable west wall, across a narrow channel, lay Province Island, unguarded and unfortified by the Americans. In British hands Province Island might prove fatal to Fort Mifflin. From it large caliber cannons could knock down the wooden walls and flatten the barracks inside.

Once this happened no part of the fort would provide shelter, and surrender would be inevitable. Furthermore, Province Island provided a handy staging area from which the British might launch an amphibious assault against the all-but-exposed rear of the fort."[7]

As Smith surveyed his new command, the story just got worse. At least a thousand men were required to man the fortification properly. Smith had 200 Continentals plus a few score militia. The militia were unfit for duty and Smith had them removed immediately. His own men lacked shoes, coats and blankets, and the fort's magazines were practically empty of powder and shot. There were insubstantial supplies of food and medicine. Worse yet, few of his soldiers had experience with artillery.

Washington wanted Smith to hold the fort until the river froze over and ships could not get through. Smith's requests for ammunition, food, clothes and gunnery experts were promptly filled by Washington's order. Smith had a little more than a week to get ready before the British fleet arrived. Working dawn to dusk Smith supervised construction of additional fortifications that gave his men better protection and assigned 60 men to receive instruction from the artillery officers. By the first week of October when more than 80 British warships sailed into Delaware Bay and began their way up the river, Smith's crew was as ready as conditions permitted.

The stakes were made clear on October 4 when Washington almost obliterated the British army led by General William Howe. The near-disaster underscored the importance to Howe in Philadelphia of having direct communication with the fleet that supplied his army with food and ammunition. He had to clear the river so he made that his highest priority. Smith got wind of the British focus on October 10 when he saw British soldiers cross over to Province Island and begin construction of batteries. Smith turned every one of his guns on the British positions and the survivors surrendered. Smith sent troops to seize the prisoners and destroy the fortifications but before the work could be completed British reinforcements arrived.

The Province Island batteries and Fort Mifflin engaged in an uninterrupted duel for six weeks. The British cannon were too light to force Smith's garrison to withdraw, but the fort sustained extensive damage, one blockhouse was destroyed, the barracks caught fire several times and several of his men were killed or wounded. It was a stalemate but dozens of small boats were ferrying supplies from the fleet to Philadelphia and Smith's forces were too occupied to do anything about it.

Amid the cannon duel D'Arendt finally arrived to assume command. The Prussian looked the part of a real officer but in battle he showed himself less than brave. His very presence angered Smith who had come to view Fort Mifflin as his arena of personal responsibility. He wrote to Washington asking to be relieved from that post and returned to his regiment. But the British launched a massive assault with 2,000 Hessians, only to be repulsed after taking heavy casualties. While the Hessians were attacking, the Province batteries opened up on Fort Mifflin and four British men-of-war sailed up looking to break through. Amid all the noise and smoke, the Prussian baron lost his nerve and, after hastily turning command over to Smith, hid out in the nearest shelter.

Then things got really interesting. The British warships should have been able to squash Fort Mifflin but the captains were unfamiliar with the river and promptly ran aground. Smith's big guns opened up on the stranded vessels. Two of the British ships managed to wiggle free and beat a retreat down the river but the *Augusta*, a ship of the line with 64 guns, caught fire and exploded. Shortly thereafter the crew of the frigate *Merlin* abandoned ship after lighting fuses in the powder magazines. Smith's command had managed to destroy two British warships.

After the battle was over, Baron D'Arendt reported that even though he had spent the fight in the deepest hole in the fort and was obviously unhurt, he had somehow sustained a groin injury. Smith told the doctor to treat this as a real injury and to get the Prussian off his island. D'Arendt disappeared and did not return.

Washington mistook all this as a major victory. He saluted Smith and two others for their leadership and ordered that each man be given an "elegant sword"[8] as a testimony to their gallantry. But the British had not quit; they merely took a break. Smith was trying to use the defeat of the British ships as a pretext to take Province Island, but he needed help from the Continental navy which was under the command of Commodore Hazelwood whose primary loyalty was to the government of Pennsylvania. Many residents of the colonies were having trouble thinking of themselves citizens of a unified nation. Hazelwood did not take orders from Smith or, for that matter, from General Washington.

By this time, rising water was taking over large sections of both Fort Mifflin and Province Island. All Smith needed was a little help from Hazelwood who finally sailed up as close as Fort Mifflin to Province Island and let go a volley or two. But he refused to do any more than that. Smith waded out in three feet of water for an angry exchange with Hazelwood, all to no avail. Smith finally told Hazelwood that if he did not withdraw, he would have his cannon fire on his ship. The lack of cooperation between Smith and Hazelwood let the British maintain control of Province Island and from there Howe would launch a major attack on Fort Mifflin.

Washington had been told by his spies that the British intended to attack Fort Mifflin with everything they had, but he did not know when.

On November 9, Smith sent a message to Washington that large numbers of British soldiers had arrived on Province Island and were vastly expanding the island's fortifications. He did not know that the British had stripped their ships of 10 large-caliber guns and moved them into the new works on Province Island. In addition they had built a floating battery within range of Smith's fort and added more batteries at the mouth of the Schuylkill River. Then the British had much more firepower at their disposal than Smith had.

At 7 a.m., November 10, the British opened up all their guns on Fort Mifflin. By the end of the day, more than 1,500 shells had hit the fort, tearing apart its vulnerable wooden walls and damaging many of the buildings inside. On the afternoon of November 11 when there was a momentary interruption of the cannonade, Smith went to the barracks building, which had somehow survived, and wrote a pessimistic report to Washington. He said the north and west walls had been knocked down, that the blockhouses were destroyed, and that many of the fort's guns were out of commission. He said that though casualties so far were light, they could not be expected to hold out longer than a few days more. As Smith handed the letter to a messenger, a cannonball crashed through the wall of the barracks, collapsed two chimneys, and then, nearly spent, struck Smith on the left hip. He collapsed under a load of bricks. He was nearly unconscious and his wrist was badly dislocated.

The other men in the room were stunned and were slow to react. Unable to walk and severely bruised, Smith managed to roll over and over until he reached the portal away from the smoke and breathed fresh air. The doctor set his wrist and then, of course, obedient to the medical wisdom of that time and place, bled him. Smith's injuries were considered serious and he was evacuated from Fort Mifflin.

For the next five days, Smith recuperated and watched from a distance as the British relentlessly pounded Fort Mifflin into rubble. Though he was barely able to move, the young officer tried to help the garrison by forcefully arguing that supplies and reinforcements should be sent to them. Commodore Hazelwood, of course, refused to authorize use of his ships for such an enterprise.

By November 16, the British had managed to get several men of war into the channel between Province and Mud islands. Smith could see the Marine sharpshooters high atop the riggings of the British vessels firing down on the fort. That night the garrison blew up what was left of the fort and rowed away.

The next morning, his arm in a sling, Smith rode to Washington's headquarters at White Marsh to report what had happened. Arriving just as the general and his senior officers had finished eating, Smith received a hero's welcome. In his report to Congress, Washington expressed disappointment that Fort Mifflin had fallen but called its defense a "credit to the American arms ... which will ever reflect the highest honor upon the officers and men of the garrison."[9] Washington also said that Hazelwood's conduct would be investigated.

Soon after the British fleet reached Philadelphia and seized control of the city. The American army withdrew toward Valley Forge which had been selected as its winter headquarters. Smith, still suffering from his wounds, joined his regiment on this melancholy march but soon received orders to return to Baltimore. He spent the next few months again recruiting soldiers for the Continental army—and possibly spending some quality time with Ms. Spear—but everything we know about Sam Smith, including his reluctance to experience the pleasures of Paris, suggests they kept their passions under wraps until their commitment was sanctioned by matrimony.

In the spring of 1778, Smith led his newly-recruited Baltimore troops into the Valley Forge encampment. The horrors of the preceding winter characterized by a critical lack of supplies had abated. After picking the local neighborhood clean, Washington had dispatched generals Nathaniel Greene and Anthony Wayne into New Jersey where they found the foraging more productive, even though they were competing with the British out on the land pursuing the same mission. The icy coldness of Valley Forge was real enough with temperatures approaching zero around poorly clothed men who were often without shoes. That period of time is now known as the "Little Ice Age" but global weather trends were poorly understood in the late 18th century.

Smith had missed the successful battles of Trenton and Princeton, and also the rigors of that brutal winter at Valley Forge, but with the spring of 1778, things were looking up. A vigorous training program had transformed Washington's motley crew into a tough and disciplined force.

Meanwhile, the British were not sitting still. General Henry Clinton had replaced Howe in February and was preparing to leave Philadelphia and move to New York. On June 16 the British embarked along with 3,000 Tories who did not want to remain behind subject to the tender mercies of their American countrymen. Two days later Clinton's 10,000 Redcoats with their 12-mile baggage train crossed the Delaware and headed north. Washington was determined to impede their transit.

As the American army broke camp and prepared to march, Smith got orders to join a special unit led by General Charles Scott that was assigned to closely follow the British army and observe its movements. Smith's group tailed the British so closely that on some mornings they extinguished the British cooking fires and captured camp followers. On June 26 the British camped at Monmouth Court House and Washington sent General "Light-Horse Harry" Lee with 5,000 men to attack.

The day of the battle Smith and his unit were stationed on the right wing of the American army. Lee had a grand plan to cut off and destroy the British rear guard, but the enemy anticipated his movement and reacted quickly. Somehow in the face of this unexpected resistance Lee lost control of his army. General Scott was not present and it was unclear who was in charge. The remaining officers put their heads together, and Smith persuaded them they had to turn around and march away if they were to save their troops.

Smith now commanded two regiments marching along a narrow path with a steep sand hill on one side and an impassable marsh on the other. His troops were spread out and vulnerable to attack. To further complicate the situation, units of the British army pursuing Lee's troops were marching parallel to Smith on the other side of the sand ridge. The British were apparently unaware of the Americans nearby and missed a clear chance to round them up. Riding at the very rear of the American column, Smith directed small groups of skirmishers to climb the hill and give warning should the British come their way. At one point a group of British cavalry opened fire on Smith's men who managed to drive them off. Before the British could attack in force, Smith's regiments were back with Washington's main army.

But they had no time to rest. Just as they regained the main force, the entire British army launched an attack. Under Washington's leadership, the Americans held the line and drove the Redcoats back. On Smith's orders, several companies of Americans pursued the British, capturing or killing many of them.

For Smith, this Battle of Monmouth was the final fight of the American Revolution. He remained with the army for the remainder of 1778 but saw no more action because the British retreated into New York City and declined to fight. But idleness never appealed to Sam Smith. He was so eager for more combat that he declined an offer to join Washington's staff. Washington had taken a keen interest in Smith ever since the Delaware River campaign of the year before when he kept Fort Mifflin in the fight longer than anyone thought possible. To be a staff officer for Washington would have been a signal distinction and opportunity for any young officer, but Smith told Washington he wanted to stay with his men. A bit later General Lafayette made Smith the same offer and got the same reply. That the two most illustrious leaders of the American army offered Smith positions on their staffs speaks volumes about Smith's reputation. His determination to be a fighter rather than a safe staff officer speaks volumes about his character and at least partially explains his reputation.

But Smith's dreams of achieving further military glory—assuming he had such dreams—never materialized. The war remained stalemated, and with the next winter just around the corner, Washington took his army into winter quarters. For the third time, Smith was ordered to return to Baltimore and recruit more men.

A few days after returning to Baltimore, Smith wrote to Washington resigning his commission. This did not some easy to the young officer who was fiercely loyal to the cause and his compatriots. But the war had involved a lot more than personal commitment and risk. The key problem was money. Continental officers received little pay and what they did get was the almost comical Continental currency that lost value daily. It had in fact taken six months of Smith's salary as a lieutenant colonel to pay for his trip from New York to Baltimore. Like many if not most officers in the Continental army, Smith had depended on his personal fortune to sustain him while in uniform. But by this time the firm of John Smith & Sons was in dire straits, beset by the British embargo of trade and the worthless currency. Smith concluded, probably correctly, that if he stayed with the army his personal fortune, and that of his family, would disappear.

He was also more than a little ticked off that he had not been promoted to bird colonel and given his own regimental command. The "Hero of Mud Island," as his friends jokingly called him, was not feeling very heroic. Smith delayed submitting his resignation until the spring of 1779 in part to fulfill his final assignment of recruiting another batch of soldiers. He also hoped that if he could not get a higher rank from the federal government, he might get one from the state of Maryland. "I want a regiment," he wrote to a fellow officer, "which cannot be without a settlement of rank."[10]

Torn between a desire to rejoin the army and his personal financial responsibilities to his family's company, Smith was under intense emotional strain. But one critical decision was within his power to conclude. For two years he had been engaged to Margaret Spear. Shortage of money be damned, Smith decided it was time to close the deal with Margaret. On December 31, 1778, the marriage took place in the First Presbyterian Church of Baltimore. It turned out okay. It lasted 60 years.

In May 1779, Smith finally wrote to George Washington resigning his commission. Washington responded graciously and complimented him on his conduct as a soldier. Smith apparently felt he had left something important unsaid. In July he wrote another letter to Washington. "I ever shall regret having been obliged to leave the service, to which I had devoted my life," he wrote, "and shall esteem myself happy, when I have it in my power to do an obliging thing for those who remain in it."[11]

Smith was later named a colonel in the Maryland militia and given command of the Baltimore Town Battalion. There was always a fairly good chance the British would do something unfortunate to the growing city. Smith drilled and disciplined his 800-man force. In April of 1781 the British blockaded the city harbor, forcing Smith to keep the militia on duty for several days. Eventually the British ships sailed away, but not before giving Smith some ideas on how the city could be defended. A few months later word came that the British general Lord Cornwallis intended to occupy Baltimore to complete his sweep through the southern states. This rumor incited Smith to again call the militia to duty, but soon came word of the British surrender at Yorktown—and the Revolution ceased, at least in military terms.

A less savory responsibility that devolved upon Smith was that of investigating and where appropriate arresting Tories. It was for Smith a real issue. During the brief British blockade in 1781 Smith had told the governor of Maryland that there were many British sympathizers in the city and that many militia men were reluctant to leave their homes for fear the Tories would burn them. He recommended that all Tories be rounded up and moved at least 30 miles away.

As military commander of the city, Smith was endowed with unusually broad powers which he used against suspected loyalists to the British crown with scant regard for due process or even common decency. During the Revolution feelings ran high about diehard British loyalists and the fellows in uniform were especially riled up. On one occasion, Smith at the head of a raiding party burst into the home of a man named James Parks in the middle of the night. After searching Parks' home and confiscating his personal papers, Smith put Parks in jail though he had no evidence of anything incriminating. Sometime later Smith and a magistrate interrogated Parks and once again failed to discern evidence of wrongdoing—however that was defined at the time. Three months later Parks was still locked up and was released only after his wife had tearfully appealed to the governor and a number of leading men in town had testified that Parks was harmless. Even Smith later conceded there was no reason to keep Parks locked away. This sort of thing did not resound to Smith's credit, though it apparently did not diminish his popularity in his home city.

While Sam was away at war, his father had devoted considerable time to the patriotic cause as a member of the Maryland legislature, letting his business interests wane in a tough time when strong decision making was called for. As soon as Samuel resigned from the army and returned home, his father retired and turned the company over to his son. He was only 27 years old and newly married, and he had exactly $100 in his pocket. That is to say 100 mostly worthless dollars.

After surveying the economic situation in Baltimore and seeking out whatever help he could get from members of his family—and the Buchanan, Sterett and Spear families—he moved aggressively into two specific areas of business: privateering and government supply contracts.

7

Acquiring Wealth

It's where the money is.—Willie Sutton (explaining why he robbed banks)

Like his father and grandfather, Samuel Smith had a knack for making money. Yes, he worked hard. All the Smiths worked hard. But the world is full of people who work hard from dawn to dusk and can't make ends meet. The Smiths had that elusive money-making gene that at times can seem almost mystical to the great majority of us who don't have it. Samuel Smith could make dollar bills proliferate like kudzu. He would start out in the morning with $10 in his pocket and by noon it would be $500. He thought that was normal. It can be argued that Smith's business activities contributed more to the American war effort, and incidentally to his own financial recovery, than did his services in Washington's army. When he returned to Baltimore, Smith found that John Smith & Sons, once the most successful mercantile establishment in the city, was nearly moribund. The main source of their revenues had always been trade, and the British were stifling commerce, depriving merchants of their foreign markets and sources of supplies, and the debased currency of the fledgling government made prudent investment impractical.

Some of the responsibility for the company's plight may be put on Sam's father John who, too old to fight in the revolution, entered politics instead. He had been a member of the constitutional convention that drafted a new instrument of government for Maryland and then was elected to the Maryland House of Delegates. This was important work but it took him away from company business at a most inconvenient time. But he saw time had passed him by and immediately stepped aside for his son as soon as Samuel formally resigned from the army.

Smith was 27 years old and newly married. But he was a Smith and that $100 in his pocket was all he needed. Privateering, or legalized piracy, was the rock upon which Smith and many other entrepreneurs would rebuild their fortunes. The United States had no navy in those days, but the government issued letters of "marque" to numerous privately owned and operated ships authorizing them to harass and plunder the British merchant marine. Baltimore schooners were the elite of this group. They were speedy and could outrun virtually any ship in the British navy or merchant marine. These raiders often brought financial windfalls to their owners while forcing the British to divert many of their best warships to defending their merchant shipping.

By the end of the Revolutionary War, Smith owned all or part of a dozen privateers. His biggest paydays came not from capturing ships but from the sale of wheat or flour cargoes that many Baltimore privateers carried in addition to their cannon. In the summer of 1779, after Smith retired from the army, Smith made more than $12,000 as his portion of a cargo carried to the French West Indies aboard a privateer. Smith and another merchant tripled their investment by the sale of cargo from a voyage in 1782. And so it went. That hundred dollars in his pocket had grown immeasurably.

To be sure, this was a risky way to make money. Even if there were no war, sailing vessels in the 18th century were vulnerable to bad weather or being preyed upon by other privateers or even real pirates. It was fairly common in those days for a ship to sail out of port on a promising venture amid a beautiful sunny day and never be seen or heard from again. Both the men who worked those ships and the investors who built them took their chances. Of course, the prizes taken by privateers often had their own cannon on board and fought back. Privateering offered the possibility of a big payoff, but it was a hazardous undertaking. In 1781–82 five vessels in which Smith had an interest were captured or disappeared, costing him thousands of dollars. But even losses such as these failed to tarnish the glamour of the successful ventures.

Fulfilling government contracts for food and other commodities offered less dramatic profits but also less risk. In terms of the Revolution, it enabled Smith to help himself while helping the American army. The central government of the aspiring United States was itself pretty much a hollow shell. It depended on the state governments of the former colonies to purchase needed goods, and they in turn depended on military contractors to supply food and other military supplies—such as uniforms and muskets. During the late war years, after Smith left the service, he was a contractor for both Maryland Virginia.

The Virginia contract involved bread, flour and wheat of which Virginia had a shortage and Maryland an abundance. The Virginia Board of War in 1779 arranged with the Maryland government to purchase unlimited supplies of wheat and wheat products. It then named Samuel Smith, who had gone to Williamsburg, the capital of Virginia back then, probably by boat, to solicit the business. Smith served as sole purchasing agent in Maryland. Operating on a healthy commission, Smith not only bought the supplies but also rented the vessels that carried them along the coastline from Maryland to Virginia.

Historian Cassell reports that the lucrative arrangement between Smith and the Virginia Board of War ended abruptly in 1781 when Maryland passed a law prohibiting the shipment of wheat or flour outside the state without special permission. Smith had actually obtained a permit for that activity but an aggressive port official in Baltimore seized large quantities of Smith's flour destined for Virginia and refused to let it leave. It seems odd that Smith permitted this official in his home town to interrupt his business in such a manner, but by the time Smith regained his property a few months later, Virginia had lost interest and the contract was terminated, probably because of the end of the war. (The Battle of Yorktown was in 1781 effectively ending the conflict though a peace treaty was not signed until two years later.)

Predictably, most of Smith's wartime contracts were with his home state of Maryland where he was known and respected. In late 1780, several Baltimore merchants went to the legislature asking for a subsidy to help them purchase cargoes of wheat and flour for shipment to the Spanish West Indies. Smith was one of those merchants, arguing that runaway inflation had destroyed their ability to secure cargoes for their ships. The state could gain, Smith said, by earning export duties on the sales. After a prolonged period of haggling, the state agreed to subsidize the merchants on provision that the state would receive half the profits of the voyages it helped finance. Smith was named the state's purchasing agent responsible for buying the wheat and flour. For his trouble, and it was probably not much trouble, he got 5 percent of the total deal. Smith's business was beginning to turn around.

As time went by other valuable contracts came from Annapolis to John Smith & Sons. Early in 1781 Smith's company became the state's representative charged with the supply and repair of gunboats that frequently engaged in firefights with British ships in the bay. Four months later the state government appointed John Smith & Sons as its agent for the procurement of military supplies for those troops still serving in the Continental army.

By shrewdly manipulating his inside contacts with the state government, plus the occasional windfall profit from his growing privateer fleet, Smith emerged from the Revolutionary War a wealthy man. His businesses generated huge profits, most of which he apparently invested in his company. He did use some of his income to acquire Tory property that had been seized by the state, eventually acquiring six lots in Baltimore and nearly 500 acres in surrounding Baltimore County. That was just for starters. Smith established a distillery in the city before the war formally ended. There is no evidence that Smith had a drinking problem but lots of other people did and Smith saw an opportunity to take advantage of it.

All things considered, the Revolutionary War worked to Smith's advantage. Thanks to the war, he was a hero twice wounded and honored by both George Washington and the Continental Congress. Also because of the war Smith had been able to expand his business in many areas and acquire numerous useful contacts throughout the Middle Atlantic states— which were no longer colonies. All of this together found Smith at the end of the war as a leading merchant with powerful political ties.

He had good reason to be optimistic about his future. He and the other merchants of Baltimore were looking at steady growth in the years ahead. The rapid economic growth of Baltimore in the pre-war years had been interrupted but not seriously impeded by the conflict. Unlike many other wars, it did not suffer significant physical damage or loss of life. Smith's father John had predicted when the family moved lock, stock and barrel from Carlisle, Pennsylvania, to Baltimore, Maryland, that because of its location, farther to the west than any other major American port, Baltimore would emerge as one of the principal economic engines of the Middle Atlantic region. The old merchant had lived to see his prophecy fulfilled as the agricultural riches of central Pennsylvania and western Maryland poured into Baltimore along natural waterways and a superior network of roads authorized by the state legislature but largely paid for by Baltimore businesspeople like Sam Smith.

Without question, wheat was the foundation of the city's prosperity during this period. The evolution of Chicago and Minneapolis-St. Paul lay off in the future. For now, the whole economy of Baltimore was geared to process, store and ship wheat. As the population on the frontier grew and wheat production increased, Baltimore's eager capitalists responded by building more flour mills, wharves, warehouses and ships. The boom economy in turn spawned rapacious demand for manpower. Men were needed as sailors, carpenters, iron workers, millers, clerks, and hundreds of other occupations. The city's population had grown from about 5,000 before the war to almost 15,000 by 1790. There had been only a few houses in Baltimore when the Smiths first showed up, but by 1790 there were at least 2,500 dwellings.

In times of rapid growth, people with ambition and a bit of luck tend to improve their living standards. Affluence was everywhere. This was in evidence in the harbor where the ships of many nations rode at anchor, or at the crowded market at Fell's Point, or along the broad, newly paved avenues adorned with spacious red-brick mansions. Foreign visitors were impressed by Baltimore's large public buildings, particularly the court-house which had been built over a vault-like passageway which carriages could roll through. Baltimore stood tall alongside Philadelphia and New York as one of the nation's premiere cities.

But with growth and prosperity come problems. Though the war with Great Britain was over, the evolving rivalry between Great Britain and France invariably drew the fledgling nation into its orbit. Great Britain still dominated the U.S. economy, and in the 1780s, French influence was also much in evidence. Some of the French influence stemmed from that country's support for the American Revolution without which the states would not have prevailed. The collapse of the French regime in Haiti sent a flood of French refugees into the states. The French expected the United States to support their continuing quarrel with Great Britain, but the new president George Washington would have none of it. He knew the United States was having birth pangs and lacked the resources to support another war.

Against that backdrop, both Great Britain and France imposed restrictive and discriminatory controls on American trade. They allowed import of only those goods that were not competitive with their own exports, and even then stipulated that with few exceptions their own and not American ships must carry the cargoes. These restrictions did not sit well with the United States, and even less well with the export-minded Samuel Smith.

At the same time other European merchants exploited the political weakness of the United States by flooding the U.S. market with manufac-tured goods that easily undersold the same products made in the United States which were less efficient and generally of poorer quality. Thus, amid the rapid growth and prosperity, dark clouds hovered over Baltimore and its merchant class. To survive in this milieu, American merchants needed skill, courage, energy and more than a touch of larceny to survive and prosper. It was a situation just made for someone like Sam Smith.

For starters, Smith fell back on the numerous contacts he had made during his prolonged European sojourn a few years earlier. John Smith & Sons, renamed Samuel and John Smith Company in 1784, after the old man finally retired, began shipping large quantities of lumber, wheat and flour to Italy and Spain in return for wine. Smith also engaged in shipping tobacco to Great Britain, a trade permitted and even encouraged under British law. Even then tobacco exerted its hypnotic spell on people, though it offers scant benefit and exacts a grim toll on human health.

But Smith also went a bit beyond legal commerce, undertaking a number of voyages that were expressly prohibited by the English and French restrictions. Smith paid bribes, forged papers and where necessary cleverly disguised cargoes. Employing unscrupulous techniques, Smith's vessels did robust business in both France and the French West Indies.

Smith was ever and always on the lookout for ways to make money and was not always too particular how he did it. Throughout the 1780s, his representatives in London arranged to buy safe-conduct papers from the Barbary powers of North Africa which engaged in rampant piracy on the Mediterranean and elsewhere. Smith's vessels were now free to operate in the eastern Mediterranean without fear of capture by the North African pirates, which gave him a distinct advantage over his domestic competitors.

Earlier Smith had struck a bargain with the powerful and influential Robert Morris of Philadelphia. Morris had managed to obtain from the French government a contract as the sole purchasing agent of American tobacco for France. On March 7, 1786, Smith wrote to Morris offering to act as a subcontractor for the financier in Maryland. Morris agreed and sent money with which Smith purchased Maryland tobacco and arranged for ships to carry the cargoes to France. For his trouble, and again it probably wasn't very much trouble, Smith received a commission of 2.5 percent. Within a few more years Smith was involved in yet another money-making scheme involving the Bank of Maryland. Along with a few other Baltimore businessmen, he obtained a charter for the new financial institution that the growing city economy direly needed. Smith bought many shares in the new bank and was a one of its first directors.

By the end of the decade, Smith presided over an extensive economic empire. Among his assets were 20 ships, a distillery, a retail store in Baltimore that sold some of the goods he imported, substantial landholdings in Maryland, warehouses, wharves, houses, some domestic slaves, and investments in a number of local businesses. He had done very well economically and was likely one of the wealthiest men in Baltimore. Not too bad for a guy who returned from the war with one dollar in his pocket.

The reference to "domestic slaves" requires some elucidation. At the time, the United States—or most of it—permitted slavery. There was an evolving anti-slavery movement, mainly in New England, but it had yet to take root in southern states like Maryland and never would until the Civil War settled the matter. Samuel Smith did not manage a plantation with whip-cracking overseers. But he and his wife Margaret at times had as many as eight slaves engaged in domestic activities such as maintaining their domiciles and caring for the horses that pulled their carriage when they went somewhere. In the pre-electric age, keeping a household going required a lot of labor. There were no washers and dryers, electric ovens, vacuum cleaners, etc. The treatment of slaves varied greatly from house to house. Many slaves were permitted to work for outside employers when not engaged at home, by which many of them earned enough money to buy their own freedom.

Smith's record on slavery is somewhat equivocal. Overall, he was action oriented and less inclined to thoughtful analysis of complicated social issues than a man in his position should have been. In terms of slavery, he was a man of his own times. On the other hand, in 1807, when Smith was a member of the House of Representatives, he voted in favor of President Jefferson's bill to ban the import of slaves, which passed and went into effect on January 1, 1808. He obviously did have second thoughts about slavery. In 1828, Smith served as vice president of the Maryland State Colonization Society which was dedicated to "returning" slaves to Africa. Many years later President Abraham Lincoln was touting the same concept. Of course, very few of the slaves in America had ever been to Africa so "returning" them there was to them completely nonsensical. Even so, several thousand slaves were actually shipped to western Africa where they founded a nation—Liberia—which is still extant.

One indication of Smith's prestige within Baltimore during the 1780s was the large number of civic responsibilities the city government asked him to assume. Like most growing cities of that time and place, Baltimore made its success with aggressive trade. And owing to their wealth and power, merchants dominated virtually every aspect of urban life. The more prominent a merchant became, the more responsibility he was expected to assume. Thus Smith served on committees and welcomed important visitors. That sort of thing that must have distracted him from his primary objective which was making money.

Sometimes it was probably exciting for him—like the time he joined other citizens in greeting the French army commander Jean-Baptiste Donatien de Vimeur—the Count de Rochambeau. He probably did not meet Rochambeau during the Revolution though the Frenchman was very much a critical player. Rochambeau showed up at the head of an expeditionary force in 1780 and helped Washington corner the British at Yorktown. The count may have heard of Smith but Smith was back in Baltimore in 1780. On another occasion Smith received the American general Nathaniel Greene who Smith probably did know personally.

A bigger deal was Smith's appointment as one of the wardens of the Port of Baltimore in 1783. Only the most respected merchants in town received these appointments. Collectively the port wardens supervised the upkeep of the harbor, making sure that the ship channel was clearly marked and kept free of obstructions. And probably just to keep Smith from getting bored, the governor of Maryland added another responsibility to his already considerable pile—brigadier general of the Maryland militia, the highest military post in the state. Maryland like most former colonies was in awe of high-falutin' titles. From that point on, he would be known as General Samuel Smith. Even when he was a member of Congress and later a senator, he preferred to be known as General Smith.

Smith's private life seemed at least on the surface to be as successful and productive as his business life. By 1783, Margaret had presented him with three children: Louis, St. John and Elizabeth. During the 1780s, the family lived in a large, two-story brick mansion on Gay Street near the homes of relatives and the various clans that had migrated from Carlisle to Baltimore with the Smiths. Nowhere in the record does Sam Smith come across as a seriously religious person, but he kept up appearances. He and Margaret regularly attended services at the First Presbyterian Church where they had been married.

John Smith, William Buchanan and William Spear had been part of the group that founded the church in 1760, and Samuel was now counted among its leading members. Sam and Margaret were not highly active socially, but on occasion they did host grand dinner parties for the city's elite. In 1785 a young Englishman named Robert Hunter was the guest at one such event at their Gay Street house. Years later he recalled it began at 3:00 p.m. in a second floor drawing room. There Samuel and Margaret, "a genteel and elegant woman," presided over a "most agreeable company." In the early evening the guests were treated to violin music and at 10 p.m. they were finally led downstairs to the dining room where they shared an "elegant dinner."[1] The Smiths also owned a townhouse on Water Street that they built in 1796. They owned many plots of land in the city and no doubt many of them had houses that the Smiths rented out or used to accommodate their extended family, in-laws and friends.

The Smiths lived in a time when there was no progressive income tax—indeed no income tax at all. Situated where he was, Sam Smith was deliriously wealthy. "Fifty years old, with a martial bearing and quiet dignity, Smith was proud of his accomplishments," Cassell wrote. "By his own estimate he owned over $400,000 in land and stock. This did not take into account, however, his half share of S. Smith & Buchanan, which made an annual profit of at least $200,000."[2]

He had built several houses but in 1799 he laid the foundation of what would become a truly magnificent mansion that Smith dubbed "Montebello," named after Marshal Lannes' minor victory over the Austrians at Montebello in 1800, about the time the mansion was completed. It was situated on an estate of 473 acres called at the time "Black Heath." It appears that General Smith was his own architect in that he was ever eager to put his personal imprint on the world around him in any number of ways. With its marble-paved, columned porch, its huge central bay, and its furnishings collected from all corners of the world, Montebello was a testament to its owner's affluence and taste. The dark-paneled study held other clues to Smith's personality. Behind busts of Benjamin Franklin and Thomas Jefferson stood shelf upon shelf of the world's great literature. Perhaps reflecting his early training, Smith's collection was heavily weighted with Greek and Roman authors as well as more recent French novels. And of course English works were also much in evidence. In addition to John Locke were volumes by Fielding and Pope. The library indicated Smith's wide-ranging intellectual interests and showed that, despite his brief formal education, he never lost the taste for learning.

By 1800, General Smith and his wife Margaret, described as "a beautiful and imperious woman," and their growing family were ensconced at Montebello. "The sites of the houses are well selected," wrote William Wirt, "always upon some eminence, embosomed among beautiful trees, from which their white fronts peep out enchantingly; for the houses are all white, which adds much to the cheerfulness and grace of this unrivalled scenery."[3]

The structure was well thought out and meticulously planned. "The detail, inside and out, was most delicate and knowingly used; there are none of the devices commonly employed to impress the visitor," wrote J. Gilman D. Paul. "Instead the designer depended for his effects on subtle touches such as the harmonious relation of the rounded ends of the high rear part of the house to the reentrant curves by which the porches flank the one story section."[4] Perhaps the most interesting room was the oval dining room, constructed with a reckless expenditure of masonry which was more elaborately finished than other similar houses. Smith filled it with French furniture of exceptional workmanship, a fine marble mantelpiece from Italy, and on the walls two handsome portraits of the general and his wife by the famous artist Gilbert Stuart.

"All these well thought out details were not lost on distinguished visitors from Europe who were entertained there as General Smith became more and more deeply involved in national and state affairs," wrote Paul. "The chronicle of his occupancy of Montebello is a happy and interesting one. As years and honors were laid on him, he seems to have made a truce with the forces of mental and physical disintegration, for at the age of eighty-three, he was called upon by the despairing citizens of Baltimore to suppress the great Bank Riot of 1835. Shortly after this he was elected Mayor of the City, holding this office almost until his death in 1839."

Upon Smith's death, his son John Spear Smith, first president of the Maryland Historical Association, took over Montebello, living there with his mother Margaret Smith until her death in 1842. He wrote of his affection for the estate in a letter dated May 1839 to his daughter Mary: "It is hard to be kept in town this beautiful weather, and that too when

Montebello is in all its glory—strawberries ripening, flowers in bloom, the lawns fresh mowed."[5]

Montebello should be remembered as an artifact of its time and place. It was large and elegant but did not have running water or electricity. Bedrooms were adorned with chamber pots which had to be emptied every day. After dark the only lights were candles and the occasional lantern burning whale oil. The vast grounds, and the house itself, were maintained by slave labor without aid of modern machinery.

But we're getting ahead of ourselves and our story. We know that Sam Smith knew how to make war and how to make money and how to make babies. But what other abilities did he bring to the fore?

8

The Political Life Beckons

I belong to no organized political party—I am a Democrat.
—Will Rogers

One field of endeavor that had never seemed to have charms for Samuel Smith in the 1780s was politics. He had made his name as a warrior and a career as a businessman, and he had hobnobbed with politicians from George Washington on down, but he had never evinced any interest in the political life—though his father John had served in both the Pennsylvania and Maryland assemblies and was currently in the Maryland Senate. Even the raging debates about ratifying the Constitution had not evoked an interest in politics, though he supported the Constitution because he believed it would benefit business.

It could have been that his commitments to his business and as port warden and also his growing family was more than enough to keep one man busy, but by 1790 he seemed inclined to try something new. He had recently reorganized his business by taking on a new partner, his cousin James Buchanan, son of John Smith's first partner and brother-in-law. The new firm was S. Smith & Buchanan and in the early years it seemed a fortuitous arrangement. Buchanan took over much of the business responsibility, freeing Sam for greater things.

Whatever his reasoning, he permitted his name to be entered as a candidate for the Maryland House of Delegates for the fall elections of 1790. Probably because of his stature, no one materialized to oppose him. A year later he won reelection, again without challenge. During his two undistinguished years in the Maryland House, he pretty much spoke for his wealthy merchant colleagues. On one occasion he vigorously opposed efforts to secure relief for insolvent debtors, though they often ended up in debtor's prisons. There is no record of Smith ever being inclined to charity though he supported state-subsidized improvement to Maryland's roads—again reflecting his business orientation. Thus it was only natural that his friends would nominate him for a seat in Congress representing the 5th

Maryland District—Baltimore and Baltimore County—when it opened up.

In those days, the outcome of congressional elections depended more on personal connections than political parties which did not yet exist. But there were hints of parties to come despite President Washington's warnings against them. Through a personal connection, Smith became close to Alexander Hamilton, the first secretary of the treasury, who was known as a Federalist though no such party existed at the time. Of course, Smith already had a rapport with President Washington. So in November 1792 Smith boarded a ship, possibly one of his own, that took him to Elkton, Maryland, at the northern tip of the Chesapeake Bay, where he connected with a carriage to take him the rest of the way to Philadelphia which was where Congress convened in the 1790s. There was no I95 in those days; it took a long time to get from Baltimore to Philadelphia. (This author posits that President Washington also took a boat to Elkton, to avoid all those hours jostling in a carriage all the way from Mount Vernon to Philadelphia, though I can find no record of it.)

Smith made his way to the red-brick building adjacent to Independence Hall where the national legislature met. The House of Representatives on the first floor was dimly lit and heated only by a few stoves along the walls. The congressmen sat on long benches covered in red felt and arranged in a semicircle before the speaker's platform. As a new member, Smith would have been assigned a seat far from the stoves. He was sitting among the founding fathers and was known by all, at least by reputation. The business before them was the war between England and France that they all knew would affect them. Both England and France sought to stifle trade between the other and knew the fledgling republic had no navy to defend its interests. U.S. ships were routinely stopped and sometimes seized for carrying goods proscribed by whichever nation was calling the shots that day. Merchants were most directly affected and Smith was one of the few merchants in Congress.

The Washington Administration wanted more money for defense which was opposed by budget-minded members. Some members objected to the pay differential between officers and enlisted men. Smith rose from his seat and declaimed that officers would leave the military if they were not justly compensated, and he ridiculed the notion that all should be paid at the same rate. "Gentleman might speak of equality," Smith said sarcastically, "but in practice, the thing is impossible."[1] The army bill eventually passed with Smith voting aye.

The loyal opposition, led by James Madison of Virginia, remained opposed to military spending which they felt would lead to a large military establishment and an executive department swollen in power by vast patronage. Madison suggested a better alternative was to wield economic influence against Great Britain which depended on the United States for a variety of products—such as tall trees to convert into ship masts. The British had long since cut down their own forests. Smith took the floor and made a case that any embargo of American goods would hurt U.S. exporters more than Great Britain. "It is not what Britain may suffer by the system proposed," Smith said, "but the disadvantage which will be the consequence to the United States that ought to be taken into consideration."[2]

But before Congress could vote, the British raised the stakes, issuing a new order-in-council declaring all neutral ships found carrying produce or goods belonging to France or her colonies to be liable for seizure. The order had been delayed long enough for the British navy to reach the West Indies and surprise unsuspecting American ships trading with the islands. More than 250 American ships were captured.

This news took Smith by surprise and made him angry. "I do believe that the temperate will not be able to keep peace with G.B.," he wrote to a friend in Baltimore, "her insolence & her cruel depredation of our property would Influence even the most moderate."[3] He seriously considered supporting a declaration of war but thought twice about it since the nation was virtually unarmed and unable to challenge Great Britain.

In combat and business competition, Smith's temper was taken in stride. He was easily riled up and quick to take action. In Congress his temper got attention. He blamed "Maddison's party" for preventing passage of the army and navy bills in the Senate, something they had been unable to do in the House. The more he thought about the behavior of Madison and his allies, the madder he became. In private letters he claimed Madison had deliberately delayed many important bills from reaching the House floor by prolonging debate on his resolutions.

He also was beginning to conclude that Alexander Hamilton did not share his views about dealing with Great Britain. Sam considered British attacks on U.S. commerce intolerable and suspected the Washington Administration's zeal to protect mercantile interests did not equal his own. On March 27, Smith took the floor to challenge the administration. The issue was a motion by an anti-administration legislator to sequester all debts owed by British citizens to Americans. Madison hoped the House would accept the measure as a viable substitute for a military buildup. But Smith backed the bill as a useful addition to other military preparations. The total debts involved exceeded $20,000,000 which would easily reimburse those Americans whose ships had been captured in the West Indies. (Possibly some of those ships were Smith's. Much of Smith's virulence against Great Britain was without doubt due to the losses his firm suffered from these and other actions against shipping on the high seas.) The debt seizure bill never came up for a vote. Even in the early days of the republic, wily politicians were learning that it was much easier to kill someone else's legislation than to get your own enacted.

While these and other measures were pinging around in Congress, Chief Justice John Jay—the nation's first chief justice—was in London trying to resolve various issues between the United States and Great Britain. It was the general opinion among the legislators in Philadelphia that nothing should be done until Jay's mission was completed. Perhaps Jay could persuade the British to modify their policies that were causing so much consternation in the United States and forestall the drift toward war.

Smith returned to Baltimore in early May. Although he was an active participant in Congress, he had not emerged among the leading figures. Neither Hamilton nor Madison had asked him to help develop policies and strategies, nor had the president invited him to dinner which was an unofficial signal that he had friends in high places. He had come to Congress as an unofficial ally of Washington and Hamilton, but already he was veering toward independence. His recurring theme was as champion of trade and uncompromising devotion to commerce. This explains his growing rift with the Federalists who believed war was an unrealistic option. Thus commences Smith's slow but inexorable shift toward the opposition.

But before returning to Philadelphia for the second session of the Third Congress, Smith had to deal with the whiskey rebellion in western Pennsylvania and Maryland. The farmers out in the hinterland depended on bourbon to generate real income because it could be transported long distances without refrigeration, and they resented federal tax collectors demanding some of their hard-earned cash. President Washington convened a substantial army and with Alexander Hamilton in tow set out to suppress the rebels. Smith was in church with Margaret when he received word that a large body of rebels was moving on Frederick, Maryland, to seize the state arsenal. Smith convened the Baltimore militia and gave them a rousing speech, calling the rebels "lawless banditti who set themselves up to govern.[4] Shall we permit them to seize our arms and give us laws, or shall we keep them and give laws to ourselves." He called for 300 volunteers to accompany him to Frederick, and three times that many stepped forward. It took them nine days to walk to Frederick, and by the time they got there, the rebellion was kaput.

But the adventure made it clear to Smith how unprepared the militia were. Smith had trained them for 14 years and made them into one of the best fighting units in the eastern United States. But the stingy state legislature had left many of the men without shoes, arms or adequate clothing. By the time they got to Frederick, they were in no condition to fight. While he was gone he had been reelected to Congress for a second term.

He addressed his colleagues in Congress about the woeful state of the militia. Many of his men did not know how to load a gun (which was a rather complicated process in those days) or even to fire it (which was also complicated by today's standards). Smith proposed legislation that provided for a nationwide militia of 100,000 men that would always be ready and able to fight. It was voted down because many of Smith's colleagues feared it would give too much power to the federal government. Then as today, fear of too much power in the nation's capital was grist for the political mills.

Smith also stood to the fore combatting excise taxes on domestically produced products. The Federalists supported this tax as part of their campaign to reduce the national debt. In a powerful speech, Smith condemned the excise taxes as harmful to the country and all but declared his open opposition to the Washington Administration. When Smith got wound up, he was a veritable fountain of indignation. Before imposing the taxes, the government had followed a policy of encouraging domestic manufacturing by placing extra duties on many imported articles, but now Smith said that investment was being destroyed by the new policy of taxing industry. He said the government was guilty of "bad faith."

Smith said there was "deception upon deception in the management of this business."[5] To express his opposition to the excise taxes was routine legislative business, but Smith was making a personal attack on his opponents. That sort of thing just wasn't done in those days. Smith tried to walk his comments back the next day but it was too late. Eventually the tax bill passed with Smith and the anti-administration bloc voting against it.

Matters came to a head when Chief Justice John Jay returned from London with the treaty he and others had negotiated. Many people, including Smith, were incensed about it because it did not really address the country's grievances—such as the impressment of American seamen into the British navy or the agitation of Indian nations on the frontier. When the treaty reached Philadelphia, even many Federalists—who essentially wanted peace with Great Britain at any price—were astonished at its terms. Nearly everyone could find something in the treaty to complain about which, in the words of Cassell in *Merchant Congressman*, "virtually created two national political parties in the United States."[6] Washington had done all he could to discourage this happening, but it was to no avail. And Smith had done as much as any member of Congress to make it happen.

In Baltimore, a large public meeting on July 28, 1795, approved resolutions denouncing the treaty and authorizing an address to President Washington expressing "disapprobation of said treaty and requesting that it not be ratified." Washington shared the general disaffection for the treaty, but knowing his fledgling nation was ill-prepared for war, he was determined to avoid a direct confrontation with Great Britain. Despite his misgivings, he proclaimed the treaty as law as soon as the Senate voted its acceptance.

Smith had hoped against hope that Jay could resolve some of the thornier issues with the British, but after reviewing the language of the treaty, he found it deficient. He introduced a resolution in the House that it should be the policy of the United States not to allow foreign ships to bring into the country goods or produce not grown or produced by the nations sending the goods or produce. This would have been a bold slap at the British and stirred up an international confrontation. Smith led the debate, a somewhat presumptuous action by one House member, but he never ducked a fight. In the end, the Federalists—employing legislative legerdemain—put Smith's resolution aside while everyone became embroiled in a more fundamental fight—whether to approve funding to enforce the treaty. The Federalists insisted that the treaty had been negotiated in good faith, approved by the Senate and signed by the president—and that was the end of it. The opposition was basically trying to create another roadblock for treaties. Smith was walking a tightrope trying not to alienate either faction, but a large group of Baltimore merchants signed a petition asking him to vote for the treaty funding. It was a hot issue of the sort that can easily incinerate political careers. Several Federalists warned Smith he would not be reelected in the fall if he didn't back the treaty.

Smith had a lot to chew on. It was an important issue for business executives like himself and also an explosive issue for politicians also like himself. Smith returned to Philadelphia, taking the boat ride to Elk's Neck, and on April 22 delivered a long, highly emotional address about the Jay treaty. He said there was "so little good contained in it, and so much evil to be apprehended from it" that he wished the president had never signed it. Nevertheless, he said he would vote for the appropriations bill because the treaty was not unconstitutional and failure to approve it would cause the British to renew their seizures of American vessels.[7] On May 1, the bill finally passed the house in a 51 to 48 vote, with Smith voting aye.

But the win left a bitter taste in Smith's mouth. He never took such affronts lightly. The Federalists were going all out against him despite his vote. Clearly, he was not a team player. They refused to believe that some of Smith's efforts to modify some of the more offensive aspects of the treaty were sincere. The Republican opposition was also confused about Smith's motivations. "Like the Federalists they had trouble understanding a man who based his actions on economic rather than political interests,"[8] Cassell wrote.

Inadvertently, perhaps, the Federalists had forced Smith into the enemy camp. Washington and Hamilton could have salvaged that grave error but for whatever reasons did not become involved. Now in his quest for reelection to a third term, Smith had to reach out for support from people other than the merchants, bankers, ship owners and insurance men he had heretofore depended upon. Nonetheless, for all their bombast the Federalists did not actually challenge Smith at the polls and he won reelection in 1796—the last year of Washington's second term as president.

One casualty of the fracas over the Jay treaty in Baltimore was an end to the long standing peaceable politics of the city. Politics "was no longer a gentleman's pastime," Cassell wrote. "Politics in Baltimore had become a deadly serious affair where only tough professionals could hope to succeed. The easy path for Smith after his unhappy experiences in April of 1796 would have been to retire gracefully and resume his station at S. Smith & Buchanan." But Sam Smith was not a graceful man. "Instead he preferred to try to keep his position, which meant that he had to make the difficult transition from gentleman-politician to being a brass-knuckles, nuts and bolts politico."[9]

Smith had a deep well of support to draw from. For example, he could depend on the Maryland militia in his political battles. The men in the street were naturally sympathetic to anyone opposing the merchant establishment, even if he was himself a merchant. The officers in the militia were as devoted to the general as the common soldiers. For the most part the officers were well-to-do business men, but they were also friends of Smith and owed their commissions to him. As party strife in Baltimore increased after 1796, the officer corps took a more active part in politics, meshing the structure of the militia with that of the Republican Party. Smith's two military aides, John Barney and Isaac McKim, soon emerged as leading figures in the Republican Party, and the same is true of many lower echelon officers.

The political schism in Baltimore was also evident among the powerful merchant class. The majority remained bound to the Federalists, but a smaller faction followed Smith toward the Republican Party. These were mainly Smith's business associates and relatives. These men made up in influence what they lacked in numbers. Together with the militia, they enabled Smith to become recognized as the most powerful political power in Baltimore.

There was a certain amount of incoherence in this arrangement. A Republican merchant was almost a contradiction in terms in those days, but somehow Smith became a leader of the Republican Party both in Maryland and on the national level. It was a marriage of convenience. The party would help Smith politically and in return he would bring Baltimore's votes to the Republicans. From a distance it probably seemed like a fragile alliance, but it was to prove more than solid enough when the British armada sailed up the bay in 1814.

For the time being, Smith was slowly learning that the twists and turns of politics could make mere warfare seem a comparably simple undertaking. One of the unforeseen consequences of the Jay treaty was the enmity of the French who soon began seizing American ships and crews on the high seas. The Republicans had long nourished a soft spot for France in the nation's dealings born largely of gratitude for France's support in the Revolution and also because the Republicans were led by Thomas Jefferson who was always pro–France. John Adams had narrowly won election to the presidency after Washington retired, but Jefferson came in second and was widely expected to come in first in the election of 1800.

Smith was soon caught up in a budget battle over military spending. The Republicans were trying to reduce spending on the army and navy and Smith and his allies were attempting to increase the military budget. In this he came into conflict with Albert Gallatin who was to hold a variety of government offices over the years and in all of them he was engaged in conflict with Smith. Gallatin wanted to reduce the military to save money. There also appears to have been a personality clash between Smith and Gallatin as they would invariably find themselves at odds over a variety of issues, sometimes, it would seem, out of habit.

Gallatin contended the most important challenge was to reduce the public debt—which was to become a recurring theme over the centuries called on by different parties and politicians. In response, Smith delivered one of his most significant speeches on naval and commercial policy. Since 1789, he said, revenues collected from import duties amounted to $75,000,000 of which only $700,000 had been allocated to the navy. "Go where you will," Smith said, "and you will see wealth, independence and happiness arising from the prosperity introduced by commerce."[10] Thus, we needed a strong navy to defend the nation's maritime interests. But he was unable to persuade politicians from the western regions that they benefited from this commerce and that a viable navy was needed to defend it.

In May 1797 President Adams sent a delegation to France to seek a peaceful resolution to the differences between the two nations. It could not be foreseen at the time that the French government would soon give way to the rise of Napoleon which in turn would lead to a prolonged military conflict with Great Britain. Everything came to a halt when it was revealed that three minor French functionaries, hereafter known as X, Y and Z, had demanded from the United States a huge bribe of £50,000 before talks could even begin.

This event, known to history as the XYZ Affair, did not go down well in Washington. When the Americans refused, the French broke off negotiations. The whole business left the pro–French Republicans in Congress

"overwhelmed by confusion." Smith was often outraged but never confused. Misinformed, perhaps, or even wrong, but never confused. He
threw his weight behind a massive defense spending program backed by
the Federalists. "It must be in the view of every gentleman," Smith told his
fellow Republicans in the House, "that we are to be involved in war."[11]

At the time the Federalists were also engaged in one of the most sordid legislative acts in American history—the infamous Alien and Sedition
Acts—which was a concentrated act of political repression. A major thrust
of the acts was to discourage immigration by lengthening the residence
period required for naturalization from five to 14 years. Another was the
Alien Enemies Act that permitted the president, in time of war, to arrest,
deport or imprison aliens who were citizens of an enemy nation. Many
could see the reasoning of that provision. But the Alien Act also allowed
the president to expel any alien he judged dangerous regardless of whether
the United States was at war; it ran into a buzz saw of opposition from the
Republicans. Smith announced he would oppose that provision because it
was "in direct contradiction to the letter of the Constitution." He pointed
out that many long-term residents of the United States would be vulnerable to persecution. He said the bill was "a step toward despotism."

Two outspoken voices spoke against the act—Smith and Gallatin—
on the same side for once. Smith offered an amendment that would have
mitigated the law's most offensive feature, which was to authorize persecution of anyone saying bad things about government officials, but his
measure failed. Smith's stand against the Sedition Act reunited him with
the Republican Party. But for the time being it brought him nothing but
grief. The Federalists recruited a promising young man, James Winchester,
who had been a Republican but was now a Federalist, to run against Smith
in the election of 1798. If Smith could be defeated, the Federalists could
remove a formidable opponent from the House of Representatives and
deal a serious blow to the Baltimore Republican Party which Smith led.

The election of 1798 was a real election—the first Smith had been
forced to deal with. He had a real opponent who was backed by tough
politicos with money. On July 30, a Federalist newspaper reported that
"a number of respectable merchants and other gentlemen" of Baltimore
had arranged a dinner supposedly to honor Federalist senator John Eager
Howard, one of the recognized party leaders of Maryland. In fact the dinner turned out to be nothing less than anti–Smith rally. Federalists at the
event said Smith had not been invited to demonstrate how much his conduct had been disapproved. Some Federalists were quoted saying the dinner had been a great affront to Smith. Smith was also accused of saying the
government should have just paid the XYZ bribe. Smith at first denied saying it and then said later that he was speaking hypothetically. In his third

comment, in an open letter to Baltimore newspapers, Smith said that the source of the report was his avid critic John Eager Howard.

The Federalists kept the charges and allegations coming, one after another. On one occasion, as reported elsewhere, some of Smith's tough fans broke up a Federalist meeting and beat up several of Winchester's followers. The voting took place in the first week of October and Smith won by a narrow margin—200 out of the 3,500 votes cast. A lot of Smith's support came from his friends in the militia and also he spent $6,000 of his own money which was a small fortune in those days.

But he had won and in politics that is what matters most. There's no point spread in politics. The years 1796 and 1797 had been turbulent for Smith, but in a good way. He had acquired greater prominence. His opposition to the Alien and Sedition Acts had earned him points with the leadership of the Republican Party. But it was the narrow victory in the election that sealed his position. He had proven his mettle by winning an election dominated by the Federalists who had thrown everything but the kitchen sink at him. Smith's success had given the Republicans control of Baltimore and thus ordained him a leader of the party. Thomas Jefferson opened a friendly and confidential correspondence with Smith as they both looked ahead to the elections of 1800, hoping Smith's win would lead to a national victory.

But while his political fortunes were looking up, his business fortunes were going the other way. The predations of the French on American shipping continued. Smith and other merchants found that their business with the West Indies, Europe and the Mediterranean were becoming unduly hazardous. Soaring insurance rates and dwindling supplies of money and credit combined to bring on a serious recession in the city. Ships lay idle in the harbor while warehouses bulged with goods that could neither be sold nor exported. Thousands of unemployed seamen wandered the docks in a time when there was no such thing as unemployment insurance.

While worrying about business, Smith was focused on the coming presidential election in which Thomas Jefferson was challenging Adams. The campaign was especially bitter in Maryland where popular dissatisfaction with the war and the Alien and Sedition Acts had put the Federalists on the defensive. The Federalists came up with a scheme to alter the method of choosing presidential electors. By eliminating the district system and allowing their majorities in both houses of the Maryland legislation to appoint electors, they could get all of Maryland's electoral votes. It was well-nigh impossible to concoct a scheme like that in Maryland without Sam Smith learning about it.

Smith concluded the only remedy was for him and other Republicans to win control of the (lower) House of Delegates. Thus, Smith launched a round of vigorous electioneering. Confident of his own seat in Congress, he became a "political preacher" traveling around the state and debating Federalists in local forums—trying to influence local elections for state delegates. He focused mainly on Anne Arundel, Frederick and Baltimore counties where most of the voters were. Smith's success as a stump speaker prompted Baltimore's Federalists to launch a newspaper attack against him in late September and into October. Their ads said Smith was "insidious" and "ambitious" and that his opposition to the Federalists bordered on treason. They even ridiculed Smith's use of Aesop's fables in his campaign speeches (which must have been amusing).

Of course Smith spent a good bit of time with local groups of Maryland militia which spurred Federalist publications to new levels of wrath and indignation. They sought to limit Smith's influence by inflaming traditional rural sympathies against Baltimore. Maryland farmers were warned that Smith was a conniving big city politician "publicly interfering in your actions." Smith declined to respond to these insults, preferring to condemn John Adams as a monarchist who had once said America would never be happy until it had a hereditary chief magistrate and senate—like Great Britain. (Adams had in reality expressed that thought, or something similar to it.)

It was another win for Smith. Once again the voters endorsed him and whatever it was he said. Maryland Republicans gratefully acknowledged Smith's effectiveness throughout the state. One party leader noted that Smith's "industry and zeal" greatly contributed to the Republican victories in Harford, Cecil and Kent counties. Thomas Jefferson personally sent his congratulations to Smith "on the triumph of Republicanism in the city and county of Baltimore."[12]

The electoral vote at stake in Baltimore was virtually uncontested by the Federalists. James McHenry grudgingly admitted that Sam Smith had built a powerful and unbeatable political machine. He said it was foolish to labor on behalf of Federalist candidates "not from any indifference to the good old cause, but from a kind of conviction that our labor would be lost."[13]

The Baltimore election returns justified McHenry's pessimism and again demonstrated the general's political dominance within the city. The Republican electoral candidate defeated his rival by a margin of five to one. Outside of Baltimore the Republicans enjoyed similar success. No less than five of 10 presidential electors chosen were Republicans, one more than the party elected in 1796 and two more than the Federalists had predicted before balloting began.

The election of 1800 was the famous one in which Thomas Jefferson and Aaron Burr tied in the Electoral College. This was back when the Electoral College actually did what it was supposed to do—elect the president—but there was no provision for a tie vote. Burr had written a letter to Smith—whom he had known for several years—disclaiming any interest in the presidency and asking Smith to be his spokesman in Washington. Smith had never wavered in his support for Jefferson, and he may have had misgivings about Burr, but he immediately had the letter published in an effort to undercut Federalist efforts to defeat Jefferson.

After the final election totals came in, Burr again wrote to Smith restating his lack of interest in the presidency. But then on December 28, 1800, Burr wrote another letter to Smith, this one seemingly hinting that he might after all accept the position. After this missive, Burr invited Smith to meet him in Philadelphia. It is a given that Smith went to this meeting with Jefferson's knowledge. This time Burr sounded like he was an active candidate, leaving Smith "mortified." But it was still ambiguous, and Burr's other associates insisted their friend had no interest in the top job.

In the months preceding the actual vote in the House, Sam Smith had established himself as a center for negotiations. Enjoying the friendship of both Jefferson and Burr, with a reputation as a political moderate, it seemed only natural for him to continue in this role during the critical House deliberations. It was a difficult situation and everyone was under great pressure. Nevertheless, Smith's role as a conduit between the two sides gave him a chance to shape the settlement. Everybody was trying to cut a deal. If they gave their support to Jefferson, what would be his stance on the public debt, spending on the navy and commerce in general? Smith suspected a sinister conspiracy between Burr and the Federalists, but he tried to thread the needle. He predictably left some people thinking they had an agreement from Jefferson about this and that, when in fact Smith had never raised their issues with Jefferson.

There was much at stake in this drama. Without a settlement, the struggling in the House might have continued and extremist elements among the Federalists might well have tried to impose some unconstitutional solution. The confidence of the American people in their institutions of government might have been shaken and civil strife might have resulted. Smith was doing some serious wheeling and dealing. He conveyed the impression that Jefferson agreed to various demands when in reality Jefferson had done no such thing. Jefferson insisted later that he had not entrusted Smith to make any deals. It was all smoke and mirrors.

The real story is that whatever Smith said and did, he got the Federalists to step back and ratify Jefferson's election. This was even more impressive than winning a close election. He emerged as a major playmaker on the national stage, not just in Baltimore and Maryland. Without question, he had the ear of the new president.

9

Tom and Sam's
Excellent Adventure

Laissez les bon temps, rouler! [Let the good times roll]
—Cajun mantra

Sam Smith was on a roll. Thanks mainly to him, his family was prospering. Five of his sisters and a brother had survived to adulthood (a rare achievement in those days—and one his own immediate family would fall far short of). Robert Smith, already a well-known lawyer and politician in Baltimore, was poised for even greater things. All of Sam's sisters had married well and were raising families of their own. Sam and Margaret's homes—the one in town and the bigger one northwest of the city, Montebello—rang to the hectic noise of little children when the family convened. But Sam's own family was less fortunate than that of his father. In 1797 Margaret had borne the last of 12 children, Anne, who died five years later. Only six of the 12 reached maturity and the oldest, Louis, his father's favorite, died in 1805 of tuberculosis while visiting Europe.

Sam was grateful for the children and grandchildren who survived. He helped them find good jobs in the government and handled their financial affairs. He had deep pockets and was happy to invest in his progeny. There was no conspicuous rebellion as characterizes many wealthy families—at least in TV dramas. By and large they were all serious people who did not disgrace the family's good name.

Sam had a genius for making money and also for being where the action was. In March 1801, for example, he was in Washington for Jefferson's inaugural—the first to be held in Washington. (Washington and Adams were inaugurated in Philadelphia.) Along with several hundred other people Sam crowded into the Senate chamber of the Capitol building which was still unfinished. It was a coming of age for the Republican Party taking the Presidency for the first time. (It was a totally different Republican Party that took office in 1861 when Lincoln was elected, and that one was a totally different Republican Party than that which took office in 2017.)

It is a basic rule of politics that people in office get credit for whatever good is happening and take the blame when things go wrong—though at best there is a fuzzy line between decisions made in Washington and the world outside. In 1801, the economy was booming in every part of the country. The vast American hinterland was opening up to development and throngs of settlers were moving west. It was a legacy of British rule that most land in the east belonged to the ruling class. Most farmers were tenants who did not own their own land. But they owned their own wagons and oxen and could pack up and move toward those western mountains, laying claim to undeveloped land. That scenario was built for freedom and opportunity, and people took advantage of it. Of course, they had to fight the Indians tooth and nail for every acre, but freedom has never come cheap.

To be sure, people with money tried to lay claim to vast tracts of the undeveloped land to the west. George Washington ended up in protracted litigation over land he had claimed before the Revolutionary War, and to this day the *Samuel Smith Land Grants* are a continuing issue in the courts of southern West Virginia. Actually, Smith knew he had lost any claim to ownership of the western lands he had purchased because people in his employ had neglected to pay the requisite taxes and other fees when they came due. At least Washington actually visited his land holdings in what is now West Virginia and met with illegal tenants trying to persuade them to pay up. There is no record that Smith ever visited his land holdings which back then were part of Virginia.

The Republicans of 1801 not only had a prosperous economy to claim credit for but even better there was no viable alternative party to challenge that conceit. The Federalists were on their last legs—disoriented and fragmented. Jefferson's party controlled both houses of Congress and the United States was at peace with the world. Even France and Great Britain were at peace so they weren't preying on American shipping. What could go wrong?

A few days after the inauguration, Smith received word that President Jefferson wanted to make him secretary of the navy.[1] "If you can be added to the administration I am forming," Jefferson wrote, "it will constitute a magistracy entirely possessed of the public confidence."

Jefferson had a way with words, of course. "We hold these truths to be self-evident that all men are created equal," Jefferson wrote in another context, "that they are endowed by their creator with certain unalienable rights." Unless of course some of the men have dark skin and as for women, well…

In any event, Smith was himself a slave holder and knew better than to lap up Jefferson's inspired rhetoric. Jefferson gave two reasons for Smith to be navy secretary. Smith would be the "only" representative of commercial interests in the cabinet, and he was one of the few Republicans qualified to administer the department. As Jefferson said in his letter, "knowledge of naval matters" in America was monopolized by the Federalists who Jefferson was loathe to appoint to office. Therefore it was Smith's "moral duty" to take the job.

Smith declined the offer citing the "disapprobation" of his constituents. That must have sent the erudite Jefferson to his dictionary. After going back and forth with Jefferson a while, Smith agreed to serve as navy secretary briefly, which he did, but without pay. In reality, there was pitifully little navy in those days to worry with. When later he insisted he had other things to do, Jefferson appointed Smith's brother Robert Smith to the position. Robert knew next to nothing about the navy but he was happy to be in the cabinet. In truth, it appears it wasn't "disapprobation" that made Smith forego the navy secretary's slot. Smith wanted a major diplomatic post. In October 1802 when word came that the American ministers in England and France intended to resign, Smith nominated himself for one of the posts. He didn't seem to care which one. He just wanted to be a diplomat.

The answer was neither one. This is a telltale

Major General Samuel Smith organized Baltimore's defenses, including Fort McHenry, and led the Americans to victory over the British on both land and sea. He served in Congress for 40 years, sometimes as congressman and sometimes as senator. He was probably the most successful shipping magnate in Baltimore (1817–1818 painting by Rembrandt Peale, Baltimore City Life Museum, item ID BCLM-CA.681, courtesy Maryland Historical Society).

detail of Smith's otherwise soaring career. No one who knew him well—friend or rival or enemy—thought him fit for a diplomatic post. He could knock heads in battle, win stiff competitions in business and prevail in the rough and tumble of politics, but diplomatic he was not. It was well known all over Washington and Baltimore that Smith craved a diplomatic post, but it never happened.

Like other members of Congress, Smith was embroiled in an endless parade of legislative activities that rarely produced a satisfactory conclusion. It wasn't necessarily all his fault that he had few legislative achievements to his name. Many leaders of Congress then and now shared Smith's dearth of legislative victories. But the very nature of the give and take of the legislative process made progress difficult, and in the end, no one ever got exactly what he wanted. These first American legislators were learning, as subsequent generations have learned and relearned again and again over the years, that it is much easier to kill legislation than to pass it. For a man accustomed to getting things done, it was a dreary education in the world of maybes, as the holy grails of legislative success—bills that actually became law and did what their authors wanted them to do—eluded grasp time after time.

But then once again Smith managed to pull a rabbit out of his hat. In the fall of 1802, the Republicans gained control of the Maryland legislature and as one of their first actions elected Smith to a full term in the U.S. Senate. (Back in those days senators were selected by state legislatures, not direct votes of citizens. Direct election of senators was provided by the 17th Amendment ratified in 1913.) Smith did not record his emotions. It surely flattered his vanity and confirmed his standing among his peers, but at the same time he must have rued leaving the House where he had served effectively for more than a decade. He was party leader in the House and chairman of the Committee on Commerce and Manufactures, one of only five standing committees at the time. As a new member of the Senate he would be lowest in seniority and once again would have to start at the back of the pack.

Of course, it was contrary to Smith's nature to be in the background anywhere for long. His name guaranteed prominent treatment. Everyone wanted to bask in his aura. He backed Jefferson's purchase of the Louisiana territory in 1803, which essentially doubled the size of the country, but the true significance of that achievement would not be fully appreciated for many years. No one really knew what lay between the Mississippi River and the Pacific Ocean. The following year Jefferson sent Meriwether Lewis and William Clark with a couple dozen other people, including a Shoshone woman named Sacagawea. She helped them communicate with the various Native American tribes they encountered along the way. All of this is today basic American lore, but it bestirred scarcely a ripple at the time. They had no CNN to explore newly acquired territories.

Of much greater immediate importance were the war clouds gathering on the horizon as Great Britain and France were soon shooting at each other again on the outset of the Napoleonic wars that would drag on for more than a decade. Once again the French and English were wreaking havoc on American shipping which tended to underscore the fundamental flaw in Smith's romance with the Republicans. Smith believed, and believed strongly, that his country needed a viable navy to defend its international commerce. But he was unable to persuade his fellow Republicans to his point of view.

Smith had become a regular at the White House having dinner with President Jefferson and other dignitaries from time to time, and that status is one perk that generations of Washington climbers have eagerly sought. But the fact remained that Smith's first love—his first priority—was commerce and trade. In this he never wavered. It's just too bad there was no U.S. Chamber of Commerce in those days—Smith would have had a fancy room named after him.

However, Jefferson and his political organization were, if not actively anti-business, at least indifferent to business interests. Jefferson advocated an odd philosophy he called "agricultural fundamentalism," the notion that yeomen working farms were the ideal citizens of a viable republic. He believed farm life encouraged and sustained solid democratic values. Of course, Jefferson himself was a farmer but he had slaves to do all the dirty work. Most people who extol life on the farm have never actually worked on a farm where the labor begins before sunrise and continues until after dark. The cows must be milked twice a day even in the winter. The cows never take a holiday. Smith was a city boy most at home on a ship at sea and raking in large piles of cash. It was a curious trend of circumstances that had brought him to the Republican table, and he found the ground once again shifting below his feet. The amazing thing was that he, Jefferson and many others thought he would fit right in with the Republicans.

Smith came close to a break with Jefferson in January–February 1805 when the administration moved to curtail American trade with the rebellious French colony of Haiti in the West Indies. The slaves of Haiti were striving to drive the French out, and Americans had been taking advantage of the situation engaging in trade with Haiti in defiance of a French proscription of such commerce. The French could control neither the uprising nor the trade. Then as always Jefferson was pro–French so he backed legislation to discourage American commerce with the island. When the bill reached the Senate Smith tried to block it. "For a few days Smith verged on the brink of a complete and irreconcilable break with the administration," Cassell wrote. "Many wondered how Smith could remain in the Republican Party after such an open disavowal of a presidentially sponsored bill."[2]

The president made his bill a test of party loyalty and it passed after prolonged and often heated debate. Of course, Smith did not accept his defeat gracefully. "It appeared that our executive were more anxious to restrain our commerce, lest our merchants should by some means injure the French government, than they were to demand from France the millions they had wantonly robbed from our merchants,"[3] Smith was quoted as saying though it sounds like a mouthful, even for Smith.

On March 4, 1805, Jefferson was sworn in for his second term. On the surface at least it seemed his first four years had been a rousing success. The country was more populous, more wealthy and more united than it had been four years earlier under President John Adams. The physical size of the country had doubled with the Louisiana Purchase and the Republicans owned both houses of Congress as well as the White House.

But there were war clouds on the horizon and the resumption of conflict between France and Great Britain signaled an end to Smith's cozy relationship with the Republican Party. As the toll of American shipping taken by both the French and English began to rise, Smith's unhappiness with the Jefferson Administration began to boil. For four years he had somehow reconciled his roles as both merchant and Republican, but the chasm between the two was getting ever larger.

For the time being, the transfer of the national capital from Philadelphia to Washington had saved Smith a good bit of travel time. He could get from his home in Baltimore to Washington in his carriage in less than a day. The trip to Philadelphia had been more complicated. But Washington did not have much to offer in terms of lifestyle. There were a few government buildings, including the White House and the Capitol, and a few boarding houses where politicos like Smith rented rooms when Congress was in session—four or five months a year. But no fine restaurants or theaters. Eventually Smith built a house near Capitol Hill where he and Margaret could live together when Congress was in session.

Beyond that there wasn't much to commend Washington for living. There were about 7,000 residents, including Georgetown. There were no streets, just dirt tracks that turned to mud with each serious rain. Carriage accidents were frequent and sometimes fatal. Margaret Smith had nearly died in one when she came to visit her husband in 1802. But the halls of Congress were magnificent—opulent and well furnished. Each senator sat in a mahogany chair behind a writing table piled high with reference works and copies of pending legislation. The desks were arranged in a semicircle around a canopied platform from which the president of the

Senate presided. As a senator Smith was entitled to writing paper, free use of the mails, and subscriptions to 18 weekly newspapers of his choice. Back in those days, a handful of newspapers made one unusually well informed.

But there was socializing to break up the monotony. Smith was a much sought-after guest at dinner parties, some hosted by President Jefferson and others by cabinet officers and diplomats. At least one prominent lady commended Smith for his "pleasantry and wit." Sam and Margaret themselves also entertained once they acquired a house of their own and they did not spare expenses. Smith estimated that between June 1803 and July 1804, his expenses in Washington had exceeded $10,000 and much of that went to entertaining. And when Washington became too boring, Smith and his wife could easily retreat to nearby Baltimore which had more than 35,000 residents in 1805 with lots of theaters, restaurants and assorted retail shops.

The first session of the Ninth Congress convened in December 1805. Smith was on edge, worried about growing harassment of American shipping by both the French and English, and he was also worried about his relationship with the Jefferson Administration. But the Republican majority in the Senate put his mind at ease by choosing him as president pro tem, an honor that both surprised and embarrassed him. Also, the president and his administration continued to respect Smith's requests for patronage—giving his friends government jobs—which enabled him to continue building his position in Washington.

But the British were capturing American ships willy-nilly, provoking many merchants to complain to Congress and demand relief. They always came to Smith because he was one of them and they knew he sympathized with their cause. Smith was sympathetic but expressed doubt that the Jefferson Administration would do anything about it. "It is indeed a mortifying thing," he said, "that we cannot in an effectual manner resent the Insults and Injuries of G.B."[4] He told friends that nothing would be done because of the "agriculturalists" who controlled the government and who "have no idea of honor, dignity, or use of National Character." What he may have failed to grasp, within the Washington scheme of things, was that "agriculturists" turned out to vote in greater numbers than seamen, and not just because seamen were often at sea. In 1805, the United States was a nation of farmers and they were the mainstay of Jefferson's political power.

But there is evidence that Smith's constant nagging was having an impact on the Jefferson Administration. In January 1796 Secretary of State Madison distributed a report refuting the British justification for infringing on the rights of neutral commerce and impressing American seamen. In his annual address to Congress, Jefferson asked for an increase in the navy and a reorganization of the militia system to make it more efficient. But when Smith championed legislation to expand spending on the army and navy, the Republicans deserted him in droves. It was typical Washington doubletalk.

Over a period of time Smith grew increasingly frustrated with the Jefferson Administration's lack of support for a stronger stand against Great Britain, and he was not the only one. Republican senator George Logan, who had been one of Jefferson's closest friends in the Senate, was heard to say, "I have no confidence in the President. He will not negotiate unless we resolve it is necessary—He has shamefully neglected the interests of this nation by not making a treaty with Great Britain years ago."[5] Eventually, Jefferson knuckled under to clear sentiment in the House and Senate and agreed to send a mission to Great Britain.

But Jefferson did not appreciate being compelled to do things like that. All of a sudden, or so it seemed to some, the wonderful harmony between the president and Congress had gone south. The Republican Party was at odds with itself as Congress was in open rebellion against the policies of the president.

Smith was at his wits' end. More than ever, he wanted the U.S. government to stand up to the British who were blockading virtually every American port and seizing American ships and sailors within sight of land. In 1805–06 he had disagreed with every facet of Jefferson's foreign policies and was a leader among those in Congress trying to circumvent the administration at every turn. He had avoided any personal confrontation with the president, but a series of unpleasant confrontations was making his position untenable. He had hoped Jefferson would appoint him to the diplomatic mission that would go to London in quest of more reasonable policies, and Jefferson had hinted that he would, but it never happened.

Instead, Jefferson nominated William Pinkney, a Maryland Federalist, to join James Monroe in London to conduct the negotiations. This time the message was unambiguous. Jefferson had not only passed over Smith, but he had picked one of Smith's political enemies in his home state for the slot. Smith said the Pinkney choice had put new life in the Federalist Party in Maryland, which was probably a fair assessment. By April of 1806, the long-standing friendship between Jefferson and Smith had apparently ended.

The Smith-less delegation to London came home with a treaty that Jefferson said was so bad he would not even transfer it to the Senate for review. When Smith finally got to see a copy, he thought it was even worse than the one that got John Jay in so much trouble. Thus, the effort to conciliate Great Britain had come to naught, and in its aftermath there was a timid effort at reconciliation between Jefferson and Senate Republicans, including Smith.

Whatever animosity remained was obviated when news of the *Chesapeake* arrived. The *Chesapeake* was an American frigate that had only recently begun service. It was confronted by the British warship the *Leopard* off the American coast. The captain of the *Leopard* demanded that the *Chesapeake* heave to and surrender several sailors believed to be of British origin. When the *Chesapeake*'s captain refused, the *Leopard* opened fire, killing several Americans. A British boarding party then took in tow several seamen it claimed were British deserters. People all over the country were outraged and none more so than Smith. At a large public meeting in Baltimore, the crowd challenged Smith to demand justice. In a letter to Madison, Smith said the people would support any action the government wanted to take, including declaring war. "Either England must be made to pay reparations," he said, or "we must go to War."[6]

In the next few months were there intense negotiations about what to do and the administration repeatedly solicited Smith's advice. He was asked about a possible U.S. invasion of Canada. He said the war would of necessity be a maritime affair to be carried out by privateers, such as his own ships, because the U.S. Navy was in its infancy. He expected a British blockade of U.S. ports but said speedy "schooners," mostly made in Baltimore, could easily avoid British ships. He said he did not think the U.S. Army would have much trouble conquering Canada—a forecast that would not hold up when the shooting started. At the end of August, for the first time in more than a year, Jefferson wrote to Smith thanking him for his assistance and assuring him that many of his proposals would be acted upon. He did not say which proposals.

Congress was ready to do whatever the president suggested, but instead of declaring war Jefferson finally opted for a total embargo of American shipping. Smith was asked to guide the embargo bill through the Senate which he did with impressive speed. On the same day it was introduced, the Senate passed the embargo bill by a vote of 22 to six and sent it to the House of Representatives. Rarely had the Republican majority in the Senate demonstrated such solidarity.

Jefferson's embargo was intended as a substitute for war. He was proposing to keep American ships and goods at home until France and England would be so badly hurt economically that they would change their policies, at least as they affected American trade. That Samuel Smith, the outspoken champion of mercantile interests, would support a law virtually ending all American commerce for an indefinite length of time seems paradoxical, but there were persuasive reasons for his action. Smith was a true patriot who resented the *Leopard*'s attack on the *Chesapeake* as a blow to American honor. He had in fact been perfectly willing to go along with a declaration of war against Britain, a far more dramatic action than an embargo. Furthermore, he was very much aware that his constituents in Maryland wanted England punished and were willing to accept an embargo instead of war.

Smith had personal as well as political reasons for approving the plan. His company, S. Smith & Buchanan, was losing ships at an alarming rate to the royal navy and the French privateers, who between them were rapidly strangling all neutral commerce. The embargo at the very least held out the promise of ending this discouring situation. Privately, Smith told his fellow senators that the embargo should bring quick results because the French and British sugar islands in the West Indies were dependent on American food. England and France would soon have to accept American demands or face the possibility of mass starvation in their colonies.

So it seemed to Smith who should have known better. The embargo—like most Washington schemes—came to naught. There were many loopholes that unscrupulous people took advantage of. There was large-scale smuggling from every port and also by land. Smith found himself caught up in variety of legislative "fixes" that never fixed. By the summer of 1808 it was clear the embargo was impeding neither Britain nor France. Even Jefferson came to believe it was all a great mistake. "Should neither peace nor a revocation of the decrees and order in Europe take place," he wrote, "the day cannot be distant when that [embargo] will cease to be preferable to open hostility."[7]

But still Jefferson blanched at the prospect of war and kept the embargo going as long as he could. When the second session of the Tenth Congress convened in November 1808, the high spirits and vigorous chest-thumping nationalism of the year before had dissipated. The war fever had subsided. Smith led the effort to defeat a proposed resolution calling for an end to the embargo, but that was not a permanent solution. Jefferson became increasingly irrelevant as his second and final term neared its end.

In February, Smith sat silently in the Senate chamber while his colleagues discussed ways to get rid of the embargo. The repeal bill passed on February 14. Smith voted for it. It was at best a pathetic effort for the nation to conceal the grim fact that its grand scheme had failed and the nation was simply too weak to stand up to Great Britain and France. Even the provisions authorizing privateers to operate against Great Britain and France were allowed to expire. And thus a once promising administration limped to a pathetic end. Jefferson returned to Monticello where his slaves continued their unrequited toil on his behalf, trying to keep the plantation going despite the inspired leader's irresponsible lifestyle.

(The great champion of virtuous life, Jefferson continued to father children by his concubine Sally Hemings, who was half-sister to Jefferson's late wife Martha. Martha's father routinely fathered children by his slaves, a common practice during slavery days. By the time Jefferson died, he was bankrupt and his property, including most of his slaves, was sold off to compensate his creditors. But Sally had earlier cut a deal with Jefferson that she would not be sold, and neither would her children by Jefferson. She was never officially freed, but she was allowed to live as if she were free in Charlottesville accompanied by her sons that she had by Jefferson, Madison and Eston, who were legally freed by Jefferson's will.)

To be sure, repeal of the embargo settled nothing. As Smith had predicted, the British and French continued their rapacious ways and American trade was crippled. American ships were still seized and American sailors impressed. The embargo had left the Republican Party more seriously divided than ever before. In New England, the Federalist Party had been brought back from the brink and resuscitated. In Congress the embargo issue had shattered the Republicans—as demonstrated by the fact they could not agree on a candidate for the presidency. The presidential election of 1808 found three Republicans on the ballot.

As ineffectual as the embargo had been, Samuel Smith continued to view it as the only feasible policy short of war. For him the end of the embargo restored conditions to those in the spring of 1807 when he had been on the verge of a break with the administration because of its inability to defend American commerce. A new president, however, James Madison by name, was entering office and General Smith could only hope that the incoming administration would be able to achieve what the outgoing one had not.

10

Madison Takes Over

If you want a friend in Washington, get a dog.—Old
Washington saying

Some attitudes are apparently hereditary and such appears to have
been the case in the animosity of Sam Smith's younger brother Robert,
who was secretary of state under President Madison, for Albert Gallatin,
Madison's first choice for that job. However, Sam despised Gallatin and
orchestrated an anti–Gallatin campaign that made it clear Gallatin's nomination would never be confirmed. Madison's appointment of the younger
Smith to the post may have been an effort to mollify Sam but it most assuredly did not mollify Gallatin.

Robert Smith had a lot going for him besides his family tie to Sam.
He had served in the Continental army and attended Princeton and then
trained as a lawyer. He was soon one of the most successful attorneys in
Baltimore and in 1789 he had been chosen one of Maryland's electors. This
was back when the electors did what they were supposed to do—elect the
president. During the 1790s, he served in both houses of the Maryland legislature and on the Baltimore City Council. And then Madison appointed
him secretary of state. Robert Smith's relationship with Sam Smith was
surely a factor in his connections, but it was clear he was a talented young
man in his own right.

Madison must have been in a mischievous mood when he appointed
Robert Smith as secretary of state. Gallatin had been plotting against Robert Smith ever since Sam Smith served as acting secretary of the navy. In
that post, he had advocated more spending on the navy which antagonized
Gallatin who was obsessed with reducing the national debt. As secretary
of the treasury, Gallatin had twice asked Jefferson to fire Robert Smith, but
Jefferson did not wish to participate in Gallatin's personal vendettas and
thus declined.

So now both Gallatin and Smith were in Madison's cabinet and the
sparks began flying, but it wasn't just Smith who resented Gallatin's hubris.

Other members of Madison's cabinet also resented Gallatin because his unremitting efforts to reduce the deficit threatened all of their budgets. On at least two occasions, Gallatin threatened to resign if Madison did not support his budget-cutting efforts. Madison talked him down. Gallatin and Robert Smith were also at opposite poles on what to do about the British and French. Robert Smith echoed his brother's stand that firmness was called for. Gallatin opposed anything that would call for more spending. He apparently had no objection to war, per se, just the spending made necessary by war.

Madison had made an obvious mistake in inviting both Gallatin and Smith into his cabinet and he further complicated the error by favoring Gallatin. Former president Jefferson, from his refuge in Monticello, could see the problem was a direct result of Madison's reluctance to impose leadership on his cabinet. He reminded Madison that he and Alexander Hamilton had co-existed on Washington's cabinet for four years because Washington established his authority over them.

Of course, the brotherly relationship between Sam and Robert aroused suspicions. Many suspected the Smith brothers were coordinating a conspiracy to undermine the Madison Administration. Some suspected the conspiracy was directed at unseating Gallatin since Sam had long been a rival of Gallatin. Sam Smith was extremely popular in Baltimore, and indeed in Maryland, but he and his brother had active opponents in Congress from other states eager to bring them down. That is the nature of politics. People adopt extreme positions and go to battle not because they believe their own propaganda but because they love the fight. That's what they do. It's rather like a sports event but they had no football to distract them in those days.

But changing political pressures had made Jefferson and Madison less dogmatic in their thinking and the Republican Party itself was changing as younger members displayed less sympathy for the old guard. Gallatin was finding his crusade against the federal debt to be losing adherents. People were in reality becoming less doctrinaire than they appeared to be. But people are what they are. Gallatin could no more rise above his phobia about government spending than Sam Smith could put aside his devotion to commerce and trade. And both of them found increasing difficulty persuading colleagues to embrace their causes.

There were cosmic forces eroding the glue that held the Republican Party together in those stressful days. It wasn't a nefarious conspiracy but the absence of one that was working its mischief. Political activists need a cause. But there was no domestic opposition to the Republicans who in any event were up against an insoluble international crisis. That crisis was caused not by unfair trade practices of the English and French but the military ambitions of Napoleon Bonaparte. There was a war on between France and Great Britain and the Americans were pawns in that war. Madison's quivering backbone was another factor as the party disintegrated into chaos. The result was a hodgepodge of shifting alliances and factions arising around disparate issues. "We are all at odds and evens," Smith lamented to a friend, "and never can get together again."[1]

Matters came to a head in the winter-spring of 1811 over the question whether the Bank of the United States should be granted a new charter. The brainchild of Washington's secretary of the treasury Alexander Hamilton years before, it had originally been chartered for 20 years. But Hamilton was no longer on the scene—killed in a duel with Vice President Aaron Burr in 1804. The bank had come to represent all that Republicans distrusted about government—mainly centralization of power. But Gallatin had found it indispensable. Some 20 years earlier Madison had opposed the bank, and as a member of Congress he fought to prevent its creation, but by now Gallatin had won him over. Still, the Republicans regarded the bank as a monster to be slain.

Philosophically Smith should have been pro-bank. As a merchant he knew that banks were essential to the orderly working of a free enterprise economy. On the other hand, he had vested interest in the banks of Baltimore and Maryland and sat on the boards of each. In the final analysis, however, it wasn't the concept of a national bank that Smith found offensive but rather the operation of the one they had which had been active in politics. He had managed to have the bank charter revised to eliminate its abuse of power. But the majority of Republicans still opposed the bank. To pacify his colleagues, Smith arranged a motion to continue the bank under its old charter until June 30, 1812, giving Congress time to carefully review the issues involved.

This was the kind of situation guaranteed to get Smith seriously worked up. After Congress adjourned in the summer of 1810, Smith returned to Baltimore to find the local branch of the Bank of the United States engaging in heavy-handed blackmail. To force local merchants to support its re-charter, the Bank of the United States deliberately caused a recession by tightening its lending and withdrawing the funds it normally kept on hand to keep business operating. Smith went ballistic as he was often inclined to do when under stress. Smith challenged the president of the branch bank, asserting that it was controlled by foreigners and loaned its money only to federalists. In a testy exchange of letters, the head of the local branch forced Smith to retract his charges which he could not prove.

Smith then tried to get the Madison Administration to withdraw all federal funds from the bank and deposit its money only in local banks. Smith hinted that if this were not done he would rally members of Congress to shut the bank down. Smith's letter was replete with scorn and insults—unlikely to persuade people to his side. As so often happened, Sam Smith's temper got the better of him. Madison did not bother to respond to Smith's fiery letter.

When Congress reconvened, the House was unable to enact bank legislation, leaving the decision up to the Senate. With so much at stake, both sides poured in rhetoric and money to help determine the outcome. Gallatin worked closely with lobbyists from the bank while word was quietly passed along that Madison supported the re-charter. Meanwhile, several states weighed in against re-charter, ordering their senators to oppose the legislation. Smith played his cards close to his chest for a while. The Maryland legislature had instructed him to favor renewal of the bank's charter, and his job depended on the state legislature.

But Smith was by this time livid about the bank, and it involved more than his animus for Gallatin who was the bank's most outspoken champion. Following his earlier confrontation with the Baltimore branch of the bank, he was convinced that the branches of the Bank of the United States not only did irreparable harm to local communities, but that they performed no useful function that local banks did not provide. He insisted he was not opposed to the existence of a national bank but insisted it must be free of foreign influence and without power to establish branches.

At some point in a prolonged floor speech, Smith took a direct shot at Gallatin for using his official position to support the bank. This approach helped fuel belief that there was a "Smith faction" led by Sam Smith in opposition to the Madison Administration. However, despite Smith's well-documented distaste for Gallatin, there were solid reasons he opposed the bank bill. He believed the bank was bad for his own financial interests, bad for Baltimore, bad for Republicanism, and bad for the country. Other than that, apparently the bank was okay.

One cannot reasonably say, as some critics did, that Smith defied his party to oppose the bank bill. There was in effect no discernible Republican position on the bill. In the House, a majority of Republicans had opposed the charter. In the final Senate vote, Smith and 16 other Republicans voted nay; 10 Republicans and seven Federalists voted yea. The tie was decided by Vice President George Clinton, a Republican, who voted nay.

But in his obsession with issues on his desk, Smith was losing sight of the bigger picture. War was on the horizon and would begin within 18 months. Smith's claims that state banks could act as efficiently as branches of a national bank were way off the mark. Because it had not been chartered, the United States lost its most important financial asset on the eve of the War of 1812. It takes a lot of money to fund a war. One could argue that Smith should have known better. But President Madison most assuredly did know better and yet he made no effort to defend the bank. Gallatin sent Madison an imprudent letter demanding major changes, else he—Gallatin—would resign. Madison did not take the bait. Rather he wrote to James Monroe offering him the secretary of state post. Monroe eagerly accepted. That left Madison with only one problem—getting rid of the current secretary of state Robert Smith, Sam's brother.

On March 12 or 13, 1811, Madison notified Robert Smith that he was fired for incompetence and disloyalty. On balance, Smith was competent enough, especially since Madison insisted on being his own secretary of state. The disloyalty stemmed from Smith's unfortunate habit of revealing cabinet secrets to his brother, Sam. Of course, Robert had been doing that since he took office years before. It was typical of Madison that along with the accusations of incompetence and disloyalty, he offered Robert Smith the post of minister to Russia. This was a clear sign that Madison was not ready to totally eradicate Samuel Smith's standing in the administration if not the Republican Party. To be sure, one reason Madison had appointed Robert Smith in the first place was to secure Sam's loyalty and support. Since that had not materialized, Madison saw no need to keep the arrangement any longer.

Monroe accepted the post at the State Department. With Robert Smith gone, Gallatin agreed to stay on at Treasury. As for Robert, he at first accepted the Russian post, but then decided to accept it would validate Madison's allegations against him. He not only rejected the appointment but also boycotted a dinner the president had arranged to honor him.

As for Sam Smith, he could see what Madison was doing, but he advised Robert to take the Russian post. (Sam himself would have given his eye teeth for a diplomatic post.) Like Madison he did not want to see the controversy blown up into a big deal. There was nothing to be gained from that. The president like any president had the right to dismiss a cabinet officer, with or without compelling reasons. In a letter to his daughter who was living in England, Sam said Robert's dismissal "came upon us like a thunderstroke," although, for some reason, the Federalists in Congress seemed to know about it in advance. The motive for the action, Smith guessed, was to "prepare the way for Mr. Monroe to be successor to Mr. M[adison]." Smith also conjectured, probably correctly, that Gallatin also had a hand in it.

Robert Smith heard his brother's words of caution but he had the same family temper that did not come with caution. He decided to take his case to the public. He informed his brother that he intended to publish an exposé of the Madison Administration. Robert confidently predicted that his information, once known, would "lead to the injury of Mr. Madison to my advantage."

He was eager to see Madison's "overthrow," though he seemed to have minimal understanding of the complexity of driving a president from office. Sam tried to dissuade his brother. He acknowledged that the president's star was at low ebb but that a favorable change in the foreign situation could revive his fortunes so that "his conduct and wisdom will be immortalized." If that happened, Sam said, anyone who had taken shots at the president will himself be blamed.

Sam said also that whatever happened with regard to the English and French, Madison's repute in the south and west would remain strong. There was simply nothing to be gained, Sam said, by washing the administration's dirty linen. He also advised his brother that whatever he wrote about Madison would be answered by a "thousand able pens" who would "reflect on the course you take of disclosing the proceedings of the Cabinet."

Robert would not be dissuaded. He released the text of his revelations to the Baltimore newspapers. Titled *Robert Smith's Address to the People of the United States*, it was a screed that invited ridicule—which was quickly forthcoming. One Republican described the pamphlet as "singular" because it was "one of the rare instances of a man's giving the finishing stroke to his own character in his eagerness to ruin his enemy." Sam had warned him to no avail. Those "thousand able pens" tore Robert's work apart, leaving the author an altogether pathetic and ridiculous figure. Sam told his son that Robert's *Address* had permanently ended Robert's political career and "indeed I consider it as the seal of the influence of the Smiths."

Many people in the Republican Party had said worse things about Madison but not in public. It simply wasn't done. As for Sam, he had not approved his brother's pamphlet and had in fact argued against publication, but he was tarnished by his brother's ignominy. Robert was more than Samuel's brother; he was his political protégé. Two presidents had appointed the undistinguished brother to high office at least in part because they wanted to please Sam. In any event, both brothers were besmirched and the administration took steps to curtail the general's power and influence.

The summer and fall of 1811 were tough for the Smiths. In Washington they found themselves "under a cloud" socially as Republican hostesses, including First Lady Dolley Madison, crossed them off their guest lists. In November, without informing Sam, the administration peremptorily recalled Sam's son, John Spear Smith, as acting U.S. chargé d'affaires in London. This dismissal of his son saddened Smith not only because of the crude way it was handled, which offered further proof of his disgraced position, but also because he had long hoped that John would become a career diplomat. His own downfall made that seem highly unlikely.

Even back in Baltimore Smith realized the administration was doing all it could to wreck his career. He learned that William Pinkney, whose nomination as minister to England he had opposed in 1806 because of Pinkney's federalism, had replaced him as the Republican Party's chief agent in the city. With control over the distribution of federal patronage, Pinkney began to build a political machine to rival Smith's. In the spring of 1812, Joseph Hopper Nicholson, an old Smith antagonist, joyfully reported with some exaggeration that the senator was almost isolated politically in Baltimore.

Sometimes the darkest days are not nearly as dark as they seem. Samuel Smith would remain in Congress for another 20-plus years, and he still had many friends in high places. But in a sense, the political odyssey he had begun 20 years before had ended. Never again would he influence presidents or sway Congress as he had in the years since Jefferson took office. Madison and Gallatin would take part of the credit, but only part, for Smith's decline. Vast demographic, economic and social changes were leading the United States toward a new era in which the old leaders and the old issues were of less and less importance. Although 59 years old, the general still had many productive years before him. He belonged, however, by age and temperament, to an era of America that was passing, the era of Washington and Jefferson, of the Revolution and the creation of national institutions, of an America oriented toward Europe rather than the limitless reaches of the west. That era was destined to expire not quietly but amidst the din of war.

Gathering Clouds

The social stigma attached to the Smiths in the wake of Robert's disastrous pamphlet was in the overall context of things a minor affair. Of far greater concern were the unremitting attacks of the British on American shipping and growing Indian unrest in the Northwest at least partly due to British provocations—that kept adding up. In May 1811 the American frigate *President* commanded by Captain John Rodgers, having been ordered to protect American commerce off the American coast, engaged the much smaller British sloop *Little Belt*. Rodgers easily overcame his adversary and even though it was an uneven fight, the American people took it as just revenge over the *Chesapeake* affair. There was a new militancy among the public that extended to the western frontier where the Indians were wreaking havoc on settlements. There were growing calls for the U.S. government to expel the British from Canada in order to eliminate the source of arms for the Native Americans.

The British government steadfastly refused to take the U.S. government seriously, and after a while the resentment was reaching a boiling point. In his annual speech to Congress in November 1811, Madison acknowledged that diplomacy was getting nowhere and asked for a larger army, reorganization of the militia and expansion of the navy. In the Senate, Samuel Smith supported the president's requests despite his previous unpleasantness with the administration. Congress approved most of the president's requests, but Madison seemed incapable of translating the legislation into action. In March, only five months before Madison declared war, the president had yet to add one man to the army, not a single one of the 25,000 that had been authorized.

As for Smith, he had been sounding his war bugle for years. He had been repeatedly overruled by the president and the majority of Republicans in Congress who believed war was impractical. Even his efforts to get the government to arm merchant vessels and organize defensive convoys had been rebuffed. But now it seemed as if the political pressure was moving in his direction and he was doing all he could to keep it going.

Smith was absent during the vote to expand the army because he strongly believed the war with Britain would be mainly fought on the water. Thus, he gave his wholehearted support to measures that would increase the navy and coastal defenses. Since the French also were engaging in anti–American activities, he suggested a declaration of war on both Great Britain and France, instead of England alone as Madison preferred. Other voices argued against declaring war on both Britain and France, but Smith contended that the British had already destroyed the French fleet at the Battle of Trafalgar and thus the United States had nothing to fear from the French.

The concept of a dual war got some discussion, but most legislators believed taking on one world superpower at a time was challenge enough. The president sent his war message to Congress on June 1, 1812, and four days later the House voted its approval. The Senate formally gave its consent on June 18, and the following day Madison declared war on Great Britain.

Smith may have been stricken from the White House guest list, but he was still a colossus in Baltimore. The federal government had little money available to conduct a war. Uncle Sam in those days depended mostly on duties collected at the ports on incoming merchandise for its revenues. The government did not in those days tax citizens directly. Much of Smith's influence stemmed from his ability to tap the reservoirs of money in his home city. Baltimore was a wealthy enclave in its own right and knew it could not depend on outside help. Bankers and businessmen in Baltimore listened closely when Smith talked because he was one of them. They knew his stake in the city was even greater than theirs, and they understood that he knew what he was talking about. He had been to war and knew what was involved. He was also held in esteem by the working people and seamen. Part of this was due to Smith's constant campaigning for office, when he invariably rolled out the booze barrels, but mainly they all knew he had been a comrade in arms of George Washington. Everybody who was anybody in Baltimore knew and respected Sam Smith.

Smith had been organizing Baltimore's defenses for two years. He knew the British were coming and had no patience with the whining voices who believed the British would move on, even after they burned Washington. A major motivation for the British military, Smith knew only too well, was the lure of booty. Line officers and admirals of the fleet could establish their family fortunes by bringing home valuable goods and Baltimore's warehouses were stuffed with valuable goods they could not sell because of the British blockade. Burning Washington did not line their pockets, but burning Baltimore would offer a tremendous payoff. The British were coming, of that he had no doubt.

The year 1813 had seen much inconclusive fighting along the northern border with Canada. But 1814 would not be inconclusive. The British had already defeated an American army at Bladensburg and went on to burn Washington. They had not found much booty in Washington but the stolen ships full of valuable cargo they picked up in Alexandria had whetted their appetite for more. So here they came up the bay toward Baltimore.

Baltimore, a raw, brawling seaport, ranked high on the British military's target list. It was generally considered a "nest of pirates." In was, said Admiral Cochrane, "the most democratic town and I believe the richest in the union."[2] When Cochrane said Baltimore was democratic, it was not praise. The British leaders spent some time contemplating Baltimore's fate. There may have been some excuse for protecting private property in Washington but not in Baltimore. "Baltimore may be destroyed or laid under a severe contribution," Cochrane wrote Earl Bathurst back in London on August 28. Six days later in another letter to another British lord, Cochrane no longer spoke of ransom. Instead, he was worried about a delicate problem that might spoil his plans for total destruction. "As this town ought to be laid in ashes, if the same opinion holds with H. Maj. Ministers, some hint ought to be given to Gen'l Ross, as he does not seem inclined to visit the sins committed upon H. Maj.'s Canadian subjects upon the inhabitants of this state."

It was not that Ross lacked zeal, Cochrane hastened to add. It was just that he was soft. "When he is better acquainted with the American character," Cochrane said, trotting out his favorite simile, "he will possibly see as I do that like Spaniels they must be treated with great severity before you even make them tractable."[3]

Admiral Cockburn may have really thought Ross, one of the toughest general officers in the British army, was "soft," but with that alleged softness came pliability. Many times on the road to Washington Cockburn had won disagreements with Ross about how to handle the Americans, so now he went back to work on the diffident general. Cockburn wanted to get at Baltimore and he wanted to do it right away while the British forces were still on hand. He thought the Americans were demoralized after the burning of Washington—they had to be—and the moment was right to squash them before they had time to regroup, bring in fresh troops and extend their defensive fortifications.

Ross on the other hand was chary about the Baltimore adventure. The British had had a cakewalk into Washington but now the enemy was fully aroused. Ross took counsel with his deputy Adjutant Captain Harry Smith. Here he heard another voice of caution. Smith was all against another attack so soon. The British action had already drawn fresh troops into Baltimore. A brilliant stroke like the capture of Washington could rarely be repeated, he said. The approach up the Patapsco River could be easily blocked and there was no other way to get at those waterfront warehouses filled to overflowing with expensive commodities. Also many of the British troops suffered from dysentery. In sum, Harry Smith said, there was little to gain and much to lose. Washington was a tour de force. Baltimore would be at best an anticlimax and at worst a disaster.

"I agree with you," Ross said. "Such is my decided opinion."[4]

Smith was about to carry Ross' dispatches back to England and with this in mind asked if he could tell Lord Bathurst that there would be no similar attack on Baltimore. Yes, said Ross, he certainly could convey that message.

On September 3, Smith left. As he headed up the gangway to catch the launch to the frigate *Iphigeniai* General Ross walked alongside of him. Reaching the rail, they shook hands and on an impulse Smith repeated his question. "May I assure Lord Bathurst you will not attempt Baltimore?"

"You may," said Ross without a hint of doubt in his voice.[5]

So it looked like the fighting was over, at least for a while. On September 4–5, a flurry of orders went out to the various commanders, dispersing the fleet to new assignments. Admiral Malcolm was to take most of the warships and all the transports to a point south of Block Island (just off New Hampshire), Captain Sir Thomas Hardy was to take 13 ships and relieve Admiral Cockburn on the Chesapeake, Cockburn was to take the *Albion* now loaded with prize tobacco, dispose of it in Bermuda and rejoin Cochrane at a secret rendezvous, apparently south of Block Island. As the ships started on their separate ways, Admiral Cochrane sent a hearty "well done" to all hands. "The Commander-in-Chief cannot permit the fleet to separate without congratulating the Flag Officers, Captains, Commanders, officers, seamen, and marines, upon the brilliant success which has attended the combined exertions of the Army and Navy employed within the Chesapeake."[6]

And so amid grateful felicitations of their chief the arsonists of Washington moved down the bay convinced that their mission, for the time being, anyway, was completed in these waters and that further adventures lay ahead, who knew where. The people of Baltimore would have been greatly relieved had they known of these exchanges.

But the only voice they heard was that of Sam Smith, and he said the British were coming their way.

11

Three Distinct Cannon Shots

It is well that war is so terrible otherwise we would grow too
fond of it.—Robert E. Lee (at the Battle of Fredericksburg)

Sunday, September 11, dawned quietly in Baltimore. Rumors
abounded but there was nothing specific to arouse anxiety. While Sam
Smith and Commodore Rodgers huddled over their scheme to sink hulks
in the Northwest Branch, the better sort of people in Baltimore went to
church as usual. At the Wilkes Street Methodist Church, some soldiers
stacked their arms outside the church door before going inside to join the
congregation. In these troubled times the sermons tended to drag a bit
long, but no one seemed to mind. It was a good time for God-fearing folk
to renew their supplications to the almighty to help them through the trial
they knew was coming. Suddenly, about 1:00 p.m. the quiet of the holy day
was shattered by three shots fired from cannon on the courthouse green.
As the Wilkes Street Methodists buzzed with anticipation and the troops
scrambled for the door to retrieve their weapons, the minister closed his
Bible. "My brethren and friends," he said, "the alarm guns have just fired.
The British are approaching and commending you to God and the word of
his grace, I pronounce the benediction, and may the God of battles accompany you."[1]

It was a similar reaction at the Light Street Methodist Church; the
Rev. John Gruber was even more to the point: "May the Lord bless King
George, convert him, and take him to heaven, as we want no more of him."[2]

A number of senior citizens had volunteered for service in this
emergency—among them David Poe, grandfather of Edgar Allan Poe.
Ulster-born Poe had been a quartermaster during the Revolution when he
served with Lafayette, earning himself the affectionate nickname "General" Poe. At age 71, the spinning wheel–maker offered his services as a
private in the Maryland 5th Regiment Company of "Baltimore Patriots"
under Captain Lawson. Another elderly volunteer was Uriah Prosser, a
shoemaker and Revolutionary War veteran who served alongside his son,

Private Samuel Prosser, a grocer. Father and son were privates in the Captain Benson Edes Company of the Maryland 75th Regiment.

In the streets it was bedlam. Troops were rushing to their positions, wagons laden with women, children and furniture were headed north on Charles Street, headed out of town. Families of the "poorer sort" (to borrow a phrase from yet another Methodist minister—didn't Baltimore have any Baptists?) fled on foot, some carrying children on their backs. Breasting the stream of refugees, Private Mendes I. Cohen, an 18-year-old recruit in Judge Nicholson's Fencibles, hurried to get back to his post at Fort McHenry. Like the rest of his unit, Cohen had come into town the previous evening but somehow missed the midnight summons to report for duty at once. Now he was trying to make up for lost time, but late as he was, he couldn't help pausing at the observation station on Federal Hill. In the shimmering haze 12 miles down the Patapsco, he could make out the whole British fleet standing into North Point.

Yes, the British really were coming. General Ross may have had his sights set on a vacation in Rhode Island or some other placid shore, but it

Typical soldiers of the War of 1812 (drawing by Gerry Embleton, in *In Full Glory Reflected: Discovering the War of 1812 in the Chesapeake* by Ralph E. Eshelman and Burton K. Kummerow, published by the Maryland Center for History and Culture, July 15, 2012).

was not to be. In a sudden change of strategy, Admiral Cochrane, who had opposed the assault on Washington, and also dismissed the plan to take Baltimore, had a change of heart. He suddenly dropped his plan to go to Rhode Island and decided to hit Baltimore instead. It was never clear what changed his mind. He did get a report the day before from intelligence gathered by the *Menelaus* on a foray up the Chesapeake that the Baltimore defenses looked weak. Someone took that report to Ross who no doubt went to work on Cochrane. The admiral knuckled under. The decision was reached on September 7 at which point the British squadron anchored off Tangier Island suddenly weighed anchor and headed north. Orders were sent to other ships to cancel their plans and join the fleet for a party in Baltimore.

For a while that party was put in abeyance as the British command had heard that its squadron under Captain Gordon was having trouble making its way down the Potomac with its booty from Alexandria—on the 22 sloops it had captured. The Americans were reportedly building batteries along the bluffs overlooking the river. So the fleet headed north to rescue Gordon who suddenly hove into sight, unthreatened. So once again it was back up the bay toward Baltimore.

Of course, every time the British fleet changed its direction it caused a frantic reaction among the Americans on the shore. The people in Annapolis were sure they were next on the British hit list and responded accordingly. They were ill-prepared for defense and even less inclined to defense. They were terribly afraid that someone in their midst might take a shot at the British, as was the case with Alexandria. There were actually American troops on their way to rescue Alexandria, but there the city fathers were already giving the British everything that wasn't nailed down, plus a few things that were.

But the British spared no time for Annapolis—they had bigger fish to fry. They skimmed right by Annapolis and made a beeline for Baltimore. All afternoon one of Smith's reliable sources counted them from his perch atop the state house dome, oblivious to the panic in the streets below. From time to time he sent express messages—via fast horses—to Baltimore, filling in Sam Smith on his latest calculations. By nine o'clock it was too dark to count but as of 8 o'clock he had counted 50 ships altogether, all heading north under full press of canvas.

Baltimore was preparing a welcome party. By September 10, Sam Smith, whose mythical authority was all he needed, had more than 16,000 men packed into a network of land and water defenses covering the eastern and southern approaches to the city. Smith was betting the ranch that the British would not come from the north or west. He did not have enough trench diggers to counter that possibility. But he figured the British would come from the east and he was right. On some things Sam Smith was always right, probably because he could not afford to be wrong. His defenses on the western side of the city were minimal, but his defensive works on the eastern side by now stretched from Bel Air Road in the north south to Harris Creek in the harbor, a full mile in length. The earthworks were designed by Robert Cary Long and William Stuart, men who knew what they were doing. The key strong point was the redoubt in the center of the defensive line which quickly became known as "Rodgers Bastion" for its commander, the favorite son of Havre de Grace commodore John Rodgers. When the British burned Havre de Grace they made a lifelong enemy of Rodgers and now they would pay for it.

Smith was most fortunate in having qualified officers under his command like John Rodgers. "He came with 1,200 seamen, many of them combat veterans," wrote John Pancake, author of *Samuel Smith and the Politics of Business*. Rodgers, who had served in four highly successful cruises against the British in the Atlantic, "was muscular and vigorous, capable of strenuous energy, his tanned and burned face surmounted by a shock of coal black hair. His seamen were probably not as home on land as on water but an 18 pound cannon was an 18 pound cannon whether on the deck of a rolling ship or on Hampstead Hill. Rodgers was everywhere—helping at the fort, building earthworks, planting batteries, drilling seamen."[3]

The commodore had fortified the redoubt located on Hampstead Hill (present-day Patterson Park) with 16 guns that included a mix of naval and field artillery. Among the cannons were 12-pounders that Rodgers had borrowed from the U.S. sloop of war *Erie*. Rodgers battery adjoined redoubts armed with four- and six-pound field pieces manned by seven companies of the 1st Regiment of Maryland Artillery. Captain George Stiles' Marine Artillery manned by seamen and officers of blockaded Baltimore privateers with letters of marque were positioned on the Philadelphia Road. Stiles' sailors stood at five 18-pound field guns, waiting for Ross and his Redcoats to come up the road from North Point. From Philadelphia Road south to the harbor, four batteries that made up the rest of the defensive line, ending west of Harris Creek, were similarly crewed by experienced naval gunners.

Fort McHenry was the keystone of Baltimore defenses and Smith had greatly strengthened it. Among other things, he had improved the "water batteries" close to the waterfront, built a furnace for heating shot (to set fires), and installed 15 36-pounders from the *L'Eole*, a French warship stranded in the port. Now he extended the harbor boom around the top of Whetstone Point and beefed up Major Armistead's 250-man garrison with hundreds of regulars, flotilla men, Sea Fencibles, militiamen and Judge Nicholson's Artillery Fencibles. These last were a company of gentleman volunteers who had their own hot coffee specially brought out of the city every morning. By September 10, at least 57 guns and about 1,000 men were crammed into the little fort.

From the debacle at Bladensburg came Tobias Stansbury, a brigadier general who was a Revolutionary War veteran. "He took some criticism for Bladensburg, but the vacillations of Winder and erratic activity of Monroe, were the real cause of that blunder. His fifth regiment had stood up to Wellington's Invincibles."[4]

There was Brigadier General John Stricker, a neighbor and friend of Smith, whose father had fought with Smith on Long Island during the Revolution. "Young Stricker had been an artilleryman. It was he who spoke up before the Committee of Public Safety suggesting they give Smith the supreme command."[5]

Even with all that Smith could not help fretting about longshot possibilities. It was just possible the British might break into the Ferry Branch west of Fort McHenry and enter the city from Ridgely's Cove. To forestall this possibility, Smith was counting on two small works that backed up the main fort and lay a mile or so to the west. At the first, an earthwork ambitiously called Fort Babcock, he put six guns with Sailing Master Webster and 52 flotilla men. The second, a somewhat stronger position called Fort Covington, was entrusted to a company of Sea Fencibles. If there was time, a boom would be laid across the Ferry Branch too, but this was a matter of low priority, for Sam Smith really saw little danger from the west.

None of which was lost on General Winder who was put in charge of the "defense on the Ferry Branch." As it happened, forts McHenry, Babcock and Covington were under his command—but not the garrisons that defended them. He commanded the 905 regulars, but 600 of them were out of his reach at Fort McHenry. His Virginia Military were mostly military leftovers that no one else could use. He had only enough cartridges for 20 rounds per man. He had no artillery, no engineers and no work force. It is interesting to wonder what he thought each morning as thousands of Baltimoreans trooped out to dig the earthworks—but none of them came his way.

Winder's complaints to Smith went unanswered. His letter to Monroe protesting the command setup got a rebuke. Slowly, painfully, relentlessly Winder gradually learned that a routed commander rarely gets a second chance. It seems unlikely Sam Smith spared much thought for Winder's dilemma. Of further concern was a wave of complacency that swept his command—a sense that the British would never challenge the defenses that Smith and his people had organized. A company of volunteers from Frederick asked to go home. Not just yet, Sam said. General Forman expected his brigade to be discharged by September 13 or 14—"then home with all speed to see my darling wife." But not just yet.[6]

Even Commodore Rodgers was not immune to the homesickness bug. Writing to a friend in Philadelphia on the 9th, he observed that Baltimore "now has nothing to fear even should the enemy making his appearance tomorrow. It is understood, however, that he has descended the bay, and whatever might have been his intentions, that he will not now attempt an attack on this place…. I hope to leave here in two or three days for Philadelphia, as I begin to feel tired of playing the soldier." Again, not just yet.[7]

All of those sentiments faded quickly when the cannon fired three shots. What ensued was all just as Sam Smith said it would be. He knew the greatest danger lay to the east in a British landing on the jagged peninsula that jutted into the bay between the Patapsco and Back rivers, ending at North Point. That is why he had put nobody on the north and only Winder to the west. Now he could see he was clearly right and made his next move. Determined to avoid anything like the four-day game of peek-a-boo that preceded the Battle of Bladensburg, he ordered General John Stricker to take his 3rd Brigade totaling some 3,200 men and head for North Point immediately.

Stricker was close to Smith. He was also a Revolutionary War veteran and had served under Smith in militia operations. Stricker's troops came from Baltimore, were highly motivated to defend their town and included most of the 5th Regiment and Pinkney's riflemen who had served at Bladensburg. On the surface this may not have been the highest qualification, but on the other hand, they had been under fire and they had at least made a brief stand at the Bladensburg races. In the current company, that made them seasoned veterans.

Mixed in with the Baltimore veterans were three companies of volunteers from Pennsylvania and a group from Hagerstown, strutting along with a few small bore cannon. At 3 p.m. the troops headed east on Baltimore Street. Led by a fife and drum corps, they displayed the usual array of dashing uniforms and street clothes. "They ranged from military dandies like Captain Aaron Levering's Independent Blues, with their stylish red cuffs and white cross-belts," wrote Lord, "to rank amateurs like Private John Smith of the Union Volunteers." Tramping down Baltimore Street, they presented less a picture of martial splendor than one of earnest endeavor. "Yet there was something poignant about them too," Lord wrote, "and as they passed the house of the Reverend John Glendy, he blessed them and prayed for their safety and success."[8]

They moved on to the Philadelphia Road and continued east past the earthworks on Hampstead Hill, past the seamen already manning the guns at Rodgers' Bastion and finally turned right onto Long Log Lane, a rambling country road that led to North Point. Three more miles and at 8 p.m. they reached a one-room Methodist (of course) meeting house at the edge of the road. To their left was a branch of the Back River the locals called Bread and Cheese Creek; to their right, a major inlet of the Patapsco called Bear Creek. At that point the peninsula was less than a mile wide—ideal for defense. In fact, Smith had foreseen that and had already stocked it with rations enough for 3,000 men and 200 horses.

At that point Stricker called a halt for the night, putting his riflemen at a blacksmith shop two miles farther down the road, and his cavalry still another mile ahead of them at Robert Gorsuch's farm house. The men made their beds on the ground with maybe a rolled blanket under their heads, but it seems doubtful they slept well. There were largely young men untouched by war, and the British were only a few miles away.

Everywhere along Smith's carefully crafted

Brigadier John Stricker was a lifelong friend and colleague of Smith. He fought in the Revolution and knew what he was doing. At the critical Battle of North Point, he moved troops around to counter moves by the British. He was one of Smith's reliable assets and a key factor in the American victory (c. 1817–1818 painting by Rembrandt Peale, Baltimore City Life Museum Collection, image ID BCLM-CA.683, courtesy Maryland Historical Society).

lines thousands of men spent an anxious night. By the time the sun went down, lookouts on Federal Hill had counted 47 to 50 British sails, including 10 transports. On Calvert Street, the postmaster once again got ready to move the mails to Ellicott Mills some 10 miles west of town. At his new museum on Holiday Street, Rembrandt Peale was abed with his wife and eight children nearby. Others could flee, and many were doing so, but he had staked his modest fortune on this place, and he hoped if the British came they might accord it residential status as they sacked the city.

On Hampstead Hill, 10,000 men were behind the recently completed earthworks. At Fort Covington, such as it was, some 80 sailors took over from the Sea Fencibles that were mostly down with a fever of some kind. In the Northwest Branch, Lieutenant Charles Ridgely, acting skipper of the sloop of war *Erie*, lined her up with the gun barges blocking the channel, cleared her decks and loaded her guns on the side facing downstream. At the Lazaretto, Lieutenant Solomon Rutter went over the night signals he had just worked out with Major Armistead at Fort McHenry. "Enemy in sight or approaching—one gun, one false fire, one blue light, repeated until answered."[9]

Armistead himself was worn down by too much work and anxiety and not enough sleep. His was the usual loneliness of command. But in his case the anxiety was compounded by the knowledge—that he had not shared with anyone else—that his powder magazine was not bombproof. He had sent his wife Louisa off to safety with family in Gettysburg, but she was expecting a baby any day and he was worried. Friday night he had dreamed she had presented him with a son. This night he could not sleep.

The British boys were also sleeping poorly, or at least some of them were. About eight miles down the river from Fort McHenry, Lieutenant Gleig of His Majesty's 85th Foot was spending a restless night aboard the transport *Golden Fleece*. He listened to his more battle-worn comrades snoring alongside of him. He tried counting sheep and gave up after 10,000. In the end, he gave up and paced the deck, studying the dim outline of the Maryland shore. He listened to the tide washing against the side of the ship and at midnight the clanging of a dozen ship bells echoing across the water.

Nearby on the sloop *Fairy*, General Ross and Admiral Cockburn were discussing their landing plan. They had transferred to the sloop from the *Albion* so they could get as far as possible up the Patapsco and closer to shore. Their plans were set but not exactly to Ross' liking. He had wanted to lead the barges and cutters up the Patapsco and to storm Fort McHenry, but he had been overruled in favor of a two-pronged attack instead. Now the British troops would go ashore at North Point and advance up the peninsula to assail Baltimore by land, while the bomb vessels and frigates would advance up the river to strike the city by water. It seemed perfectly logical, as military plans invariably do before the guns start shooting.

The British commanders without doubt had dark intentions for Baltimore. A recent letter from Governor Prevost in Canada related recent atrocities committed by Americans, and Admiral Cochrane was determined to retaliate in Baltimore. As he always said, one had to treat "these people" like spaniels. The British troops were equipped for serious business. The ammunition allotment was increased from 60 to 80 rounds per man, and all the frills were to be left behind.

At 2 a.m. on September 11 the silent ships suddenly sprang to life. A gun brig moved closer inshore, prepared to rake the beach if any Americans appeared. Barges and cutters swarmed around the transports, taking off the troops and moving them toward shore. In half an hour a thousand troops were landed. The general order was much the same as on the march to Washington, but with a few variations. This time around the British had eight big guns drawn by teams of horses. Also there was an extra brigade of some 600 seamen and marines to make up for the losses of casualties and desertions during the Bladensburg unpleasantness. But the command remained the same—General Ross and his gutsy sidekick Admiral Cockburn. At 7 a.m. the bugles sounded and the British force—some 4,700 strong—started toward Baltimore.

American general Stricker was looking south wondering where the British were. At 7 a.m. his cavalry had reported seeing the enemy landing in force, and by 7:30 they were already approaching Robert Gorsuch's farm only three miles away. As his scouts retired Stricker sent his baggage back and ordered his troops up to the positions he had carefully picked out. Here he protected the junction of the only two roads leading into Baltimore. On his right was Bear Creek, on his left a marsh bordering on Bread and Cheese Creek. Behind him was a copse of woods offering cover in case of emergency. He posted the 5th Regiment on the right, the 27th on his left and six cannon in the middle, across the single road that continued on to North Point. Then he established two lines of reserves in his rear and settled down to wait.

One hour—two hours ticked by and still no British. The soldiers marked time as best they could, with the usual grumbling. In a rare oversight, Sam Smith had provided plenty of food but nothing to cook it in. Stricker wrote a quick note to headquarters—send cooking utensils as quickly as possible.

Then another irritation. Along with his cavalry Stricker had sent his riflemen forward to harass the British when they appeared. But it was a nervous moment for all. At some point a rumor spread that they had been flanked. They came rumbling back to the main line, and now it was too late to reorganize and send them back out again. Stricker knew to expect this sort of thing from militia. He put them on his right wing and continued waiting.

Then another report—the British had stopped at the Gorsuch farm and were "feasting and frying." Stricker interpreted this as a calculated insult to his troops, but when one of his officers offered to go forward and disrupt their picnic, he thought better of it. Back to waiting.

By noon, he was having second thoughts. He thought maybe the British were deliberately holding off in favor of a nighttime bayonet attack. The militia were notoriously squeamish about night fighting and always chary about those bayonets. He decided to go ahead and provoke a fight right then and there. He pulled together a force of about 250 men which moved out about 1 p.m. headed for North Point.

For about half a mile nothing happened and then a shot rang out. Stricker's little group got careful quickly. They inched along to a rise overlooking open ground. Across the way they could see three men, one with a spyglass, watching them. The American muskets and rifles exploded in a volley of fire. When the smoke cleared, the British were gone.

For Admiral Cockburn, the sudden blast of American gunfire proved the point he had been trying to make to General Ross—that their advance guard of 50 to 60 men was way too far ahead of the main force. Now there was nothing to do but put up a brave front and stave off the enemy until more of their troops came up. Up until then the British had encountered little difficulty. Pushing ahead from North Point, the British advance force burned the Todd house and carved a Union Jack over the mantel of the Lodge family's living room. All in good fun, apparently. When they got to the Gorsuch farm, they had Mrs. Gorsuch cook them breakfast. It seemed they had all the time in the world at their disposal.

While Ross and Cockburn were enjoying Mrs. Gorsuch's eggs and country butter, possibly a little bacon too, three captured American dragoons (cavalry) were brought in and briefly questioned. How many troops were defending Baltimore? Ross asked. About 20,000, the prisoners said, an apparent exaggeration but not far off. "But, they are mainly militia, I presume," Ross said. The prisoners said that was true. Ross was relieved. "I don't care if it rains militia," he said.[10]

As Ross and Cockburn rose and prepared to leave, Mrs. Gorsuch asked if they would be back for dinner. "No," smiled Ross. "I will eat in Baltimore tonight, or in hell."[11]

Ross and Cockburn started back down the road and the advance guard once again drew ahead of the light companies. At this juncture, Cockburn advised Ross that they were much too far ahead of the main force. He said this wasn't the way it was supposed to be done. Ross knew that was right, but the officers now leading the advance guard were inexperienced. But he also knew Cockburn was right and he was just about to call a halt when once again they heard the fire of American guns.

The British soldiers responded in kind and the Americans faded back into the woods. The action simmered down to occasional shooting. Seeing a lull in the shooting, Ross told Cockburn he would go back and hurry up the light companies. Starting back along the road they had just come up, Ross was riding alone when a shot rang out. One of those accursed militia for whom Ross had an endless well of contempt had spotted the well-adorned senior officer on his horse—a prime target—and taken careful aim. A bullet pierced Ross' right arm and buried deep in his chest. Staggered by the blow, he fell off his horse.

Eventually the following troops caught up to where Ross lay on the ground. When the first man reached him, Ross was still conscious. He managed to gasp: "Send immediately for Colonel Brooke." Colonel Arthur Brooke, commanding the 44th Foot and second ranking officer in Ross' army, was soon at Ross' side.

Soon others were there including Cockburn, Captain Duncan Mac-Dougall and other staff officers. A mile or so to the rear Lieutenant Gleig was marching along with the 85th Foot when MacDougall came riding up shouting for a doctor. Gleig sensed something dreadful had happened, and his worst fears were confirmed when his company reached the spot a few minutes later. The troops marched silently by, pretending not to notice.

Ross sensed the effect his wound was having on his men and asked to be covered with a blanket. He was gently dissuaded—it was by now too late to hide the reality of the disaster. A surgeon appeared and began binding Ross' wounds, but Ross said it was hopeless. Pulling a locket from his tunic, he handed it to Cockburn. "Give this to my dear wife and tell her I commend her to my King and country."[12]

Someone commandeered a passing rocket wagon to carry Ross back to the fleet, but Ross declined to use it. Faintly he said he wouldn't deprive his men of a weapon so important to their success. Then a regular cart from a local farm was found and Ross was carefully placed in that. At last the

Major General Robert Ross of the British army was a heroic figure who led the Redcoats against Napoleon, always from the front. He was a tough disciplinarian but his men were loyal to him because they knew at the end of the day he would bring most of them home. His contempt for American militiamen came back to haunt him when they shot him out of his saddle at the Battle of Baltimore (Wikipedia).

cart started off with Ross' aide, Lieutenant Haymes, in attendance. As it bumped and jolted along the road, the general suffered terribly and finally lapsed into a coma. Seeing the end was near, Haymes stopped and they rested beside a tree. Ross came to long enough to murmur, "My dear wife." When they reached the beach, he was gone. They wrapped him in the Union Jack. On ship they would stuff him into a barrel of whatever booze they had handy and preserve his body on his long ride back to his home.

The men who shot Ross—making an irrevocable dent in the British battle plan—were from the 1st Rifle Battalion. "Private Daniel Wells and Private Henry McComas considered the fine British officer with many large feathers in his hat to be a good target," wrote Marc De Simone and Robert Dudley in *Sam Smith, Star Spangled Hero*. They are believed to be the ones who took aim and fired what were possibly the most important shots of the War of 1812.[13] Those two gentlemen were later killed in combat.

There was no cheering on the American side largely because they did not realize what had happened. When the news was eventually received, it was unclear who deserved the credit but for sure they had accomplished their mission. They had been sent to pick a fight with the British and they did as instructed. Now the troops along the main line rested their muskets along a fence and waited. They didn't have to wait long. Around 2:30 the rockets began whizzing by. The militia crouched low but this time they didn't run. By now they had heard all about the noisy rockets that never seemed to hit anyone. Even so, they were relieved when their own cannon began to return the fire.

Stricker noticed that most of the British firing was on his left. Anticipating an attack there, he began strengthening that part of his position. Calling up his second line, he put the 39th Regiment to the left of the 27th, then two of his guns still farther to the left, then the 51st all the way to the flank but at right angles to the rest of the line. Presumably this was to cover a turning movement, but some thought it a waste of firepower to put these men at right angles to the enemy. All in all, it caused a good bit of confusion among the green troops of the 51st.

Lieutenant Gleig—whose memoirs elucidate this account of the fighting—watched the Americans marching back and forth perhaps 600 yards away. It struck him as a massive waste of effort and he was amused to see the militiamen avoid any spot where a British cannonball had landed. They seemed to believe if one hit there, another would soon follow. In contrast, the British professionals were smoothly moving into position without fuss or undue commotion. The 85th Foot and the other light infantry spread out along the entire front backed by the 44th Foot and the brigade of seamen. The 21st stood in column on the main road. The 4th tramped through a hollow on the extreme right. The army's new commander,

Colonel Arthur Brooke, planned a surprise blow on the American left—just as Stricker expected. As the 4th picked its way slowly to the flank, the rest of the troops marked time—the 21st dodging occasional cannonballs on the road, the 85th lying in the grass, and the seamen munching biscuits from their haversacks.

By 2:45 all was ready. Colonel Brooke and Admiral Cockburn rode the full length of the line on a last-minute inspection. The admiral was a conspicuous target in his gold-laced hat and the American gunners were watching him closely. "Look out, lads," said one sailor. "Here's the admiral coming—you'll have it directly."

About 3:00 Brooke gave the signal. The orderly bugler sounded the charge and the other buglers took it up all along the line. The troops moved silently forward and for a moment it was all quiet on the American side as well. Then a crash of artillery and the Yankee version of grapeshot came screaming across the meadow—old locks, horseshoes, nails, bits of broken muskets, anything that could be crammed into a cannon.

The British troops began falling but still they came on—crouching low, sometimes crawling on their hands and knees. To the Americans, raised on tales of Redcoats impervious to any kind of fire—this seemed a good omen, but they held their musket fire and not a voice was raised on either side. When the British reached perhaps 200 yards from the American line, one impulsive militiaman jumped over the fence, ran forward a few yards, knelt and fired his musket. That seemed to break the trance. The troops behind him began firing too, and in seconds the whole line was ablaze with musket fire.

The British answered with one of their organized huzzahs and began shooting as they charged—totally contrary to the best European practice. Cochrane later wrote Lord Melville somewhat apologetically that this breach of decorum happened because the Americans just wouldn't stand up to an honest bayonet charge.

Oddly, the 4th Foot, whose flanking movement was the key to the whole attack, played little part in these dramatics. As often happens in war, they took longer than expected to complete their assignment. Now they were just emerging from some thickets on the American left when the rest of the line charged.

It made no difference to Captain Lewis Weaver's frightened militiamen that as yet they had no real opposition. Stationed with the rest of the 51st Regiment on the far left, they felt very much alone. Then came all that firing that seemed to be coming from behind them because of the way they were facing. And then an ominous crackling in the bushes on their flank....

They broke and ran. Then the rest of the 51st collapsed too, and as the men ran across the rear of the American position, they carried part of the 39th Regiment along with them. Long before that clever British flanking movement could even develop, the American left was gone.

The British charge did the rest. For 20 minutes there was a frantic firefight along Stricker's center and right, with the militia grimly hanging on. Above the chaos, Captain Lowrie Donaldson could be heard shouting to his men to shoot low; then some Redcoat aimed low and Donaldson was down. Private Uriah Prosser, an old shoemaker and Revolutionary War veteran, was killed fighting alongside his son. Scores more fell as the entire line gave way.

The British troops swarmed over the timber fence and into the woods where a dangerous game of hide and seek began. "One shrewd Yankee, finally cornered, started arguing for his right to keep a silver dagger which he claimed as 'private property.' Another American hiding behind a tree, took a shot at Lieutenant Scott which only grazed him but brought down William Edmondson, clerk of the frigate *Melpomene*," wrote Lord. "Then to everyone's horror, Edmondson was finished off by a saber blow from another British officer who mistook him for a skulker."[14]

As the Americans streamed back through the woods, General Stricker fought to keep some semblance of order. The last thing he wanted was another Bladensburg with the troops dispersing and heading for home. He led his men down Long Log Lane to some high ground designated by Smith at Worthington's Mill near the east end of Smith's earthworks. Somehow he managed to herd them together behind the 6th Regiment which lay in reserve nearly a mile to the rear. Here he rallied and reformed his charges back into a fighting unit. But they were still dead tired. Now at last they could be rested and reorganized.

And that was all right with the men, exhausted and discouraged. They had been badly mauled with some 163 killed and wounded and another 50 taken captive. But those who remained felt a certain sense of satisfaction. They had met "Wellington's Invincibles," fought them at long range for two hours and then face to face for about 10 minutes. They brought all but two of their big guns, and here they were, still intact, ready to try again the next day. For their part, the British under their new commander Brooke also paid a price. They lost the popular Ross along with 38 others killed, 251 wounded and 50 missing. The loss of Ross was critical. He was the kind of hands-on senior officer that fighting men have long admired and willingly followed. He was ever and always near the front lines because he understood the vital importance of intelligence on a battlefield and knew he could not rely on scouts. Now he was gone and Brooke, though a competent officer, could not replace Ross' leadership.

During the night, rain began to fall. The soldiers on both sides took shelter wherever they could find it, but there wasn't much to be had. The men in the trenches were intimidated by the roaring of the thunder and the tremendous flashing of the lightning at the same time being within musket shot of the enemy.

Meanwhile…

Admiral Cockburn's aide Lieutenant James Scott was satisfied with the outcome of the battle, if not the death of Ross. He labelled it "a second edition of the Bladensburg races." But of course there was one great difference between this fight and Bladensburg—Lieutenant Colonel Arthur Brooke was now commanding the British army. He was unsure of himself and tentative in his decisions. His casualties already totaled more than 300. The day was nearly over. It was enough to give a man pause and pause is what he did. Late afternoon bugles sounded "halt" and the army prepared to camp for the night by the Methodist meeting house, less than half a mile further along the road to Baltimore.

On the Patapsco River, Admiral Cochrane was making progress on his part of the two-pronged advance. After landing the last of the troops and supplies at North Point, he shifted his flag to the *Surprise* and at 1:30 p.m. ordered the frigates and bomb vessels to head upstream for Baltimore. As they got underway, Cochrane was unaware of Ross' death or the change of command, but he could plainly hear the gunfire ashore and knew the army was advancing. He had his role to play.

It was tough going. The Patapsco was both shallow and full of unexpected shoals that played havoc with deep draft ocean going sailing vessels. Cochrane had only two pilots who knew the water. The *Seahorse* went ahead to feel the way but ran aground almost immediately. For nearly four hours she was either stuck or warping slowly through the mud. On the *Severn*, Captain Nourse sent his small boats ahead to take soundings. In the ship's launch, Midshipman Robert Barrett worked with the stream and kedge anchor until he was literally covered with mud.

At 3:30 or thereabouts *Surprise* anchored at a point about five miles below Fort McHenry where she was soon joined by the *Severn* flying Cockburn's flag and other frigates and brigs. The five bomb vessels and the rocket ship *Erebus* continued creeping closer until they anchored only two and a half miles from the fort. The bomb vessels were a curious creation that the British were relying on to reduce Fort McHenry. Their big vessels could not get near the fort because the river was too shallow and, in any event, Smith and company had sunk hulks to prevent large ships from getting near the fort.

But the bomb vessels were small and light enough to get close, or at least close enough. Each one carried two huge mortars—a 10-inch and a 13-inch—that could fire heavy bombs for miles. A single British bomb, a cast-iron sphere of 13-inch diameter and 1.5-inch thick walls, weighed 190 pounds with a bursting powder charge of nine pounds. Ignited through a wood fuse packed with finely-mealed powder, this bomb left the ship from a muzzle-loading mortar that weighed more than 8,000 pounds. Elevated to 45 degrees, the mortar could hurl the bomb 2.38 miles. When it landed, according to the British schematic, it "destroys the most substantial buildings by its weight and, bursting asunder, creates the greatest disorder and mischief by its splinters."[15]

No one knew how the Americans might react, but Cochrane was taking no chances. He ordered every ship to have grapnels ready in case the enemy tried fire vessels as they had on the Potomac near Alexandria. Torpedoes were always a menace (in those days torpedoes were floating mines), although the admiral considered them outlawed by the rules of war. He issued careful instructions on towing them clear of endangered craft. Sets of passwords and countersigns were distributed for use in the night.

Sweeping his glass along the shoreline, Cochrane discovered one defense measure he did not know how to counter. The Americans were busily sinking block ships across the mouth of the Northwest Branch. These would effectively keep him from storming the inner harbor, either to bombard the town or to carry off prize goods which tickled his fancy. He decided there was no alternative but to take Fort McHenry.

Examining the earthworks on Hampstead Hill, Cochrane felt more encouraged. The defensive line swarmed with people and ran right to the water's edge, but it did not seem to extend very far back into the country. "I think it may be completely turned without the necessity of taking it in the front," he wrote that afternoon in a letter addressed to General Ross. He also took the opportunity to outline his own plans. "At daylight we shall place the Bombs and barges to bombard the fort. You will find them over upon the eastern shore, as the enemy have forts upon the western side which it is not necessary to encounter."[16]

At 7:30 the letter was returned unopened with the shattering news that Ross was dead.

12

The Rockets' Red Glare

Hard pounding, this, gentlemen. Let us see who will pound
the longest.—Wellington at Waterloo

Francis Scott Key was a quintessential Georgetown lawyer and
in fact may have been the first of the breed in his capacity for offering
advice where none was requested and sticking his nose into other people's business. He was a slave holder—brother-in-law to Roger B. Taney
(pronounced Tawney) who would, years later, as chief justice of the U.S.
Supreme Court, rule in *Dred Scott* that no black man had any rights that a
white man was obliged to respect. But Key was also ready, willing and able
to donate his legal services to freedmen in peril of being returned to slavery—which he did often. Go figure.

On the eve of the Battle of Bladensburg, Key was seen riding his horse
around the battlefield (before the battle was joined) giving advice to General Winder and other officers on how to arrange the troops. Key had never
served in the military and knew nothing about the topic but the mere lack
of knowledge did not impede his astounding self-confidence. He left the
field before things got really ugly.

The day after the British had done their damage and left Washington, Taney came and took Key's wife Polly and their children to the Key
farmhouse near Frederick. Meanwhile, Key was asked to perform a delicate mission by President Madison. It involved a longtime Key family friend, Dr. William Beanes, a prominent landowner and physician in
Upper Marlboro who had served in the American Revolution and who, as
previously noted, had rolled out the red carpet for General Ross. Beanes
was "the leading physician in Upper Marlboro," Taney later wrote. "He
was highly respected by all who knew him ... and the intimate friend of
Mr. Key. He occupied one of the handsomest houses in Upper Marlboro,
and lived very handsomely."[1]

However, on August 27, before all the British troops had made their
way aboard ships at Benedict (Maryland) bound for Baltimore, a group

of them broke off from the main force and raided several farms in Maryland, including one owned by Dr. Beanes. Beanes organized a group of local men to go after the renegade British troops. The makeshift posse captured several British soldiers and locked them up in a local jail. However, one of the British prisoners escaped and the next night, August 28, he returned with a company of soldiers and took prisoner Dr. Beanes and two other locals—Dr. William Hill and Philip Weems. The British rousted the three men from their beds at midnight and forced them to ride old, wobbly horses 35 miles to Benedict. The British, Taney said, scarcely allowed Dr. Beanes time to dress. The good doctor was treated harshly and closely guarded.

Prisoner releases, or paroles, were common practice during the War of 1812 since neither side was equipped to take care of large numbers of prisoners. General Ross, for example, had paroled Commodore Joshua Barney at Bladensburg on the spot, after he had his own surgeon tend Barney's leg wound. At Benedict the British released Hill and Weems but not Beanes. Ross had it in for Beanes, apparently because he had been so ingratiating to Ross and then arrested British soldiers. Beanes was put aboard the British man-of-war *Tonnant*, Vice Admiral Cochrane's flagship, in a tiny cubicle with minimal creature comforts.

Friends of the Beanes family tried to intervene with Ross and Cochrane but to no avail. One of them appealed to Key for help, who for unknown reasons agreed to go see Ross and Cochrane. On September 1, Key secured permission from General John Mason, the commissioner general of prisons in matters relating to military prisoners. Mason spelled out in a letter the next day what he wanted Key to do. He addressed it to both Key and John Stuart Skinner who was on Mason's staff and had been appointed by the State Department to deal with prisoner exchanges. Skinner, an Annapolis attorney, had already arranged several exchanges with British naval officers.

Mason was also in contact with the senior British prisoner held after the Battle of Bladensburg in Washington, Colonel William Thornton. Mason told Thornton he would arrange to have letters from his fellow British prisoners—many of whom had been wounded and were being treated humanely—delivered to Ross and Cochrane. Thornton eagerly accepted the offer.

Many letters were written, and Key collected them before he left. These letters would come in handy.

Mason also gave Key a strongly-worded missive to be delivered to General Ross demanding Beanes' release. In this letter, he referred to his emissary Key as "a citizen of the highest respectability." On September 2, Key wrote to his mother from Georgetown: "I am going in the morning to

Balt to proceed in a flag vessel to Genl Ross. Old Dr. Beanes of Marlboro is taken prisoner by the enemy who threatens to carry him off. Some of his friends have urged me to apply for a flag of truce and go & try to procure his release."

He was cautiously optimistic about his mission. "I hope," Key wrote, "to return in about 8 or 10 days, though it is uncertain, as I do not know where to find the fleet."[2]

Key met Skinner on September 4 and the following day the two hitched a ride on an American 60-foot sloop, a cartel ship sailing under a safe-conduct flag—most likely the *President*, under the command of John Ferguson. The sloop sailed out of Baltimore harbor down the Northwest Branch of the Patapsco toward the Chesapeake Bay in search of the British fleet. For those who haven't sailed it, the Chesapeake Bay is a formidable body of water many miles long and wide but amazingly shallow in many places. They found the *Tonnant* three days later in the early afternoon on September 7, near the mouth of the Potomac River below the Northern Neck of Virginia. General Ross and Admiral Cockburn were well rested after their adventures in Bladensburg and Washington and spoiling for adventures to come. They were hospitable and invited Key and Skinner to discuss the prisoner-exchange matter over an early dinner later that afternoon.

Ross and Cockburn, "particularly the latter," Taney wrote years later, "spoke of Dr. Beanes in very harsh terms and seemed at first not disposed to release him." They were holding Dr. Beanes below deck under conditions Taney described as "harsh and humiliating."[3] He had not had a change of clothes since he was taken and was treated with indignity.

Key did not take kindly toward his hosts. "Never was a man more disappointed in his expectations than I have been as to the character of the British officers," he wrote in a letter to a friend. "With some exceptions, they appeared to be illiberal, ignorant and vulgar, and seem filled with a spirit of malignity against everything American."[4]

Key and Skinner told the officers that Beanes should have never been arrested, though it is unclear if Ross explained his grievance against the doctor. But then they conveyed the letters from the prisoners to Ross and Cockburn. Key and Skinner later differed in their accounts of what happened next, each insisting he was the one who persuaded the British officers to relent and set Dr. Beanes free, but it was clear the letters from the British prisoners made a profound impression on Ross. In his official dispatch to General Mason, Ross said that the "friendly treatment" given to "the wounded officers and men of the British army" after Bladensburg enabled him "to meet your wishes regarding Dr. Beanes."[5]

The British did have one condition—their guests including Dr.

Beanes could not depart until after the British attack on Baltimore. Skinner quoted one British officer saying why: "After discussing so freely as we have done in your presence our purposes and plans, you could hardly expect us to let you go on shore now in advance of us. You will have to remain with us until all is over, when I promise you there will be no further delay."

One might have argued that by then the cat was out of the bag regarding British intentions toward Baltimore, but probably Key and Skinner were the only ones who weren't in on it. In any case the three of them were set up for a dramatic view of the assault on Fort McHenry which would soon be getting underway.

While the ground troops were exchanging volleys, the British fleet could be seen crawling up the Patapsco toward Baltimore. Smith had his people sinking ships to tighten the barrier across the Northwest Branch. Up until now the merchants of Baltimore had taken a dim view of the plan to sink their ships, but with the British on their doorstep their attitude had come full circle. Down went John Donnell's handsome ship *Chesapeake*, John Craig's brig *Father and Son* … Elie Claggett's schooner *Scudder* … 24 vessels altogether.

Ultimately the barrier was extended across the Ferry Branch too, although there was no time for that just now. As always, Sam Smith looked to the east; the west could take care of itself.

General Winder knew this all too well. For a whole week he had seen his western command neglected or nibbled away. Now a new order came from Smith to send his cavalry to Colonel Nicholas Ruxton Moore operating east of town. Winder of course complied, but at the same time sent a last, despairing note to headquarters. "This has finally robbed my command of its only means of availing itself of favorable opportunities at annoying the enemy. In fine, I am now fairly destitute of every means by which I can render command honorable to them or myself as essentially useful to the country, unless by mere accident."

Sam Smith did not have time to answer—there was too much going on to take time to soothe the ruffled feelings of a forgotten general on this particular day. Around 4 p.m. word spread that Stricker was beaten—that his army was falling back—and the whole city plunged into a frantic, last-second rush of preparation. Commodore Rodgers pulled Commander de la Roche off the block ships and hurried him to Hampstead Hill where his skills in naval gunnery would be put to better use. The Committee on Vigilance and Safety ordered all lights out tonight—no point in giving the British gunners lights to shoot at. Nervous citizens reread the morning *Telegraph*'s instructions on handing incendiaries. "Should Congreve rockets be thrown into the city," the paper advised, "we should recommend to every house keeper to have a servant ready with buckets filled with water to extinguish the flames."[6]

Everyone could hear the roar of cannon and muskets off to the east that seemed to be drawing closer and closer. Meanwhile, the number of British warships hovering off Fort McHenry grew to 16, plus numerous cutters, gigs and barges. Not yet evident but soon to be were the gun boats built around heavy duty mortars. The British ships of the line drew too deep to come up close to Fort McHenry but in any event they did not have the explosive power of the gun boats. There were about a thousand men in Fort McHenry ready to rumble with whatever the British sent against them, including 250 of Commodore Barney's flotilla men. These guys liked to fight and did not run away when the action got hot. (There is little in the record to distinguish flotilla men from Sea Fencibles, but they all were definitely forerunners of the Marines.)

Convinced that the final assault was in the offing, General Forman ordered the great ropewalk of Mssrs. Calief and Shinnick set afire to keep it from falling into British hands. Ropewalks were hard to build and expensive to equip, but there was no question this one would be scooped up by the British if they got a shot at it. Nobody needed ropes more than the British with their massive fleet. Shortly after 4 p.m. flames and smoke rolled skyward consuming the hemp and cordage for the new frigate *Java* and throwing the city into even greater consternation.

Inside Fort McHenry Major Armistead studied the ominous line of British ships lying just out of range. Their gun ports were open and small craft were clustered along the sides. "From the number of barges and the known situation of the enemy," he wrote Sam Smith at 4:30 p.m., "I have not a doubt but that an assault will be made this night upon the Fort."[7]

At the Lazaretto across the channel Lieutenant Rutter was worried about British trickery. To guard against an unhappy surprise, he and Armistead quickly worked out a set of challenges for the night. The password would be "William," the answer would be "Eutaw."

The precautions were wise and necessary, but at such times men require inspiration. The defenders of Fort McHenry got theirs in Mrs. Pickersgill's monster flag. Armistead had worked with Smith and the committee to get this awesome sign created for just this moment. It would be shimmering when the wind rose, and the wind was rising as the rain clouds drowned out the sunshine. It was going to be a long night.

But nights do not last forever. At 5 a.m. on September 13, 1814, the *Volcano* weighed anchor and began moving toward Fort McHenry. Close behind came another bomb ship, the *Meteor* and the rocket ship *Erebus*. Behind them came the *Cockehafer*, a small schooner and then three more bomb ships—the *Terror*, the *Devastation* and the *Aetna*. These were not ships in the proper sense, more like big boats, but they actually had as much or more firepower than the British ships of the line. A few frigates were there to join in the fun.

At about 7 a.m., the *Meteor* opened up. Then one by one the other bomb boats and the Erebus began firing on the fort. The guns of the fort replied in kind, firing erratically and not scoring many hits. "The enemy shot falling short and over us,"[8] noted the keeper of the *Meteor*'s log. At 8:40 a.m. a cannonball ripped through the mainsail of the *Cockehafer* leading Admiral Cochrane to dial his offensive back a bit, moving off to a point about two miles from the fort. This meant sacrificing the firepower of the frigates and the *Erebus* but then that is why he brought the smaller gun boats along. They were harder to hit and were more disposable.

"Compared to the stately frigates and ships of the line, these ungainly vessels weren't much to look at," Lord wrote. "The *Aetna*, for example, was a stubby 102 feet long. Nor was service in them fashionable. They fired shells that burst—a bit unsporting that—and their operation was left largely to the Royal Marine Artillery, who didn't seem to mind. Nevertheless, they were useful and in many ways remarkable ships. Armed principally with two guns—a 10- and a 13-inch mortar—they fired huge bombshells that weighed over 200 pounds and carried up to 4,200 yards."

The mortars were set in circular beds that could be turned on pivots. The beds were made of ponderous timbers solidly bolted together. The trunnions of the mortars lay in semicircular notches in the timbers, and their bellies rested on another great beam called the bolster. Beneath them, in the ship's hold, upright timbers stood like the thick pilings of a wharf, supporting the enormous weight of the beds and mortars.

It took enormous force to shoot 200-pound bombs out to more than 4,000 yards, and this put enormous strain on the ships every time the mortars were fired. A complicated system of beams and springs tried to cushion the blow, but even so, the jar was terrific. They rattled the crews' teeth, shook everything loose that wasn't made fast, and sent the entire vessel bucking and plunging like a frightened horse.

The shells matched the weapons. They were iron spheres filled with powder and equipped with two iron handles, one on each side of the fuse hole. Handling them was extremely difficult and dangerous. Booms had to be rigged, hooks thrust into the handles, and the shell raised with block and tackle to the muzzle of the mortar. To fire them safely took elaborate precautions. So great was the risk of premature explosion from a flying spark that in recent years the mortar ships had not carried their own ammunition. The shells were brought up in tenders and especially trained details of marine artillery men "fixed" them in the small boats lying alongside. "Fixing" was the process of driving the fuse—a conical tube of beech or willow wood—into the fuse hole. The large end, protruding, was kept sealed with tallow until the last moment.

Loading one of these mortars was a lot like filling a trash barrel. Five to 20 pounds of powder went in first. Then came a layer of hay and then a wooden plug and then a layer of sod. The squealing tackle lowered the shell into the barrel. Over it and around the mortar men packed hay or straw or chunks of turf. The tallow cap, made stiff with pitch or bees wax, was cut off or broken open. One man touched a slow match to the fuse, and another laid his slow match to the priming powder.

Fire spouted from the vents at each discharge; sparks shot up toward the rigging and rained on the deck; the touch-hole blast was like a fiery trail of a small rocket. Plank screens, five feet square, were hung above the vents to take the flame; even then, the booms had to be kept drenched; details of seamen manned the fire pumps and long rows of leather buckets were kept filled with water; and the smallest bolt hole had to be plugged to keep out flying sparks.

The shock of firing, in those small ships, was terrific. The mortars had no recoil mechanism, the hull took the full blow. Bulkhead doors had to be kept shut to prevent the cabin from being injured by the explosions. Every discharge wracked the ship and drove her down two feet into the water. She could stand it and in fact she was built to stand it. And the shells she threw were six times as heavy as the solid shot thrown by a British line of battle ship.

Erebus also was a special engine of destruction in her own right. She had been a 20-gun sloop of war—a stout, hard-hitting cruiser. On the day she moved into attack Fort McHenry, she still had her 20 cannon. From the outside she still looked like another cruiser. But Sir William Congreve, the inventor of the rocket, had converted her into a new and unique weapon for attacking land defenses. Along both sides, just below her gun deck, he had cut a row of small square holes. He called them "scuttles" and the name was fitting. They looked a good deal like the square hole cut into the side of a frame dwelling for the convenience of the coal man (in a time when many housekeepers heated their homes with coal). Inside each scuttle was a boxed-in frame—a kind of coal chute carefully enclosed to keep the dust from spreading through the cellar. In *Erebus*, the long-boxed frames that slanted down into the hold had been designed to serve a similar purpose: they kept the burning fuses of the rockets from spreading flame and sparks throughout the ship.

Inside each coffin-shaped box, the metal tube of a discharger thrust its round nose up to the square hole in the ship's side. The tubes of the rocket battery on *Erebus* were larger than the dischargers with which rocket troops had been equipped for land campaigning; they fired

32-pound missiles—five times the weight if the land rockets normally employed. The tubes were equipped with gunlocks and could be discharged by lanyards. They could be loaded, aimed and fired more easily and quickly than a cannon; the frames that enclosed them could be raised or lowered or traversed. *Erebus* could throw a rocket broadside horizontally against a hostile ship or almost straight up—at an 85-degree angle—to come hurtling down on buildings, forts or batteries onshore. Iron shotters, built into the frames, confined the sparks and flame. The rockets' flight carried their fiery tails beyond the rigging and eliminated the danger of sails catching fire. The sailors on the deck above could work the ship and man the guns "without the least risk" to the crew or vessel. They could carry a 24-pound solid iron shot, or an explosive shell, or an incendiary carcass—a fire bomb—filled with a furiously inflammable mixture of pitch, powder, tallow and saltpeter.

When a mortar was fired, that also lit a fuse in the bombshell itself. With luck, it exploded about the same time it landed, scattering fragments far and wide. But the luck was seldom coming. While every effort was made to cut the fuse to fit he distance, the shells were wildly erratic and quite likely to burst in mid-air. They were bursting like crazy when Francis Scott Key saw it from a distance of several miles and hoped against hope the following morning to see that precious flag stitched by Mrs. Pickersgill still flying above the fort. Anyway, that's where the phrase "the rockets' red glare, the bombs bursting in air" came from.

Time seemed to be on Admiral Cochrane's side. A well-handled bomb vessel could hurl 45 to 50 shells an hour, and he had five of them at his disposal. With all that fire power—and safe from any annoyance from return fire—the fall of Fort McHenry seemed only a matter of time.

Return fire was very much on Major George Armistead's mind. He tried to coax just a little more out of his guns. He had already increased the elevation as much as he could, but it wasn't enough. Now he loaded them with extra charges of powder—a dangerous experiment since the barrels could only stand so much. Happily, they didn't burst, but three of his guns gave a mighty kick that threw them off their carriages. They could be fixed but the problem remained. Armistead had tried everything but his guns simply could not reach the British fleet. The best the fort could do was 1,800 yards with the 24-pounders and 2,800 with the big French 36-pounders. But since the British ships were more than two miles out, Armistead was just wasting his ammunition. At 10:00 a.m. Armistead grimly ordered his guns to cease fire, and the garrison settled down for a long, hard wait.

The gunners crouched by their parapets, and the infantry huddled in a dry moat that ran around the fort. Trying to make himself small, Judge

Nicholson felt that he and his Artillery Fencibles were all "like pigeons tied by the legs to be shot at."

By a half hour before that Cochrane was also feeling discouraged. He was supposed to be helping the army but this flashy bombardment had been going on for more than two hours and nothing visible had been accomplished. The firing was too slow, the shells were too erratic and the fort was too strong. He sent a note to Admiral Cockburn who he assumed was attacking by land with the troops. "My Dear Admiral—It is impossible for the ships to render you any assistance—the town is so far retired within the forts. It is for Colonel Brooke to consider under such circumstances whether he has force sufficient to defeat so large a number as it is said the enemy has collected, say 20,000 strong, or even a lesser number and to take the town. Without this can be done, it will be only throwing the men's lives away and prevent us from going upon other services. At any rate a very considerable loss must ensue and as the enemy is daily gaining strength, his loss let it be ever so great cannot be equally felt."

Thus by mid-morning caution was once again creeping up on Admiral Cochrane. He had given up all idea of supporting Colonel Brooke. He wasn't even sure the army should go through with its attack. But assuming the troops did take the city, the navy must continue battering at the fort, hoping ultimately to open a passage through which he could join Brooke and share the glory and remove the riches of Baltimore. The five bomb boats continued their bombardment…

It was about 2:00 p.m. when a British shell landed squarely on the southwest bastion of the fort, exploding with a blinding flash. For a moment all was lost in a ball of fire and smoke, then it cleared away, revealing a 24-pounder dismounted and its crew sprawled at odd angles in the dirt. Several of Judge Nicholson's Fencibles rushed over but they were too late to help Lieutenant Levi Claggett or Sergeant John Clemm, two of Baltimore's prominent merchants who served in the company. As the dead and wounded were carried off, Private Philip Cohen must have felt unusually fortunate. He had been standing next to Claggett when he was killed, but Cohen escaped without a scratch.

Many of the fort's garrison seemed to live charmed lives. Captain Henry Thompson dashed through a hail of shrapnel carrying messages to and from Hampstead Hill. Master's Mate Robert Stockton constantly exposed himself as Commodore Rodgers' courier. "And every man in the garrison had a horseshoe in his pocket that terrifying moment when a shell finally did crash through the roof of the magazine," wrote Lord. "It didn't go off … just lay there sputtering as some quick-witted hero doused the fuse in time."[9]

That was too close a call to suit Major Armistead. He ordered the powder barrels cleared out and scattered under the rear walls of the fort. Better risk one or two than see the whole place go up in smoke. Private Mendes Cohen of the Fencibles joined the crew rolling out the kegs. It was dangerous work with the shells flying about, and he finally took a moment to rest—but sitting on the end of a full powder barrel.

Actually there was little to do but trust in luck and that is why some of the men took it as a good omen when a rooster appeared from nowhere, mounted a parapet and began to crow. The exhausted troops laughed and cheered, and one man called out that if he lived to see Baltimore again, he's treat that bird to a pound cake.

Toward 3:00 p.m. Major Armistead noticed that three of the British bomb vessels had weighed anchor and together with the rocket ship were moving toward the fort again. Apparently, Admiral Cochrane thought he had softened the fort up enough—and that it could no longer hurt his ships even if they closed within range. So they were closing in for the kill.

That suited Armistead just fine. For six hours he had sat there taking his punishment, firing only occasionally to reassure Baltimore that he and his guys were still on the job. But most of his guns were still in working order, and Armistead's troops—like him—were thirsting for a chance to work off their frustrations. Now they stood eagerly at the embrasures waiting for a signal. At the Lazaretto across the Northwest Branch, Lieutenant

Fort McHenry bombardment. The cannons of the early 19th century generated a lot of smoke and noise. This artist's depiction of Fort McHenry shows the smoke from the fort's guns as they fired at the British ships which were mostly out of range. The larger British battleships could not get near enough to the fort to fire on it. The British relied on smaller "bomb" boats that fired mortars from miles away and did some damage, whence the phrase "the bombs bursting in air." But mostly their munitions missed the mark. Fort McHenry never fell (c. 1826–1830, painting by Alfred Jacob Miller, item ID 1901.2.3, courtesy Maryland Historical Society).

Rutter stood ready too, as did Lieutenant Solomon Frazier's flotilla men on the gunboats in the channel. The British ships glided closer—two miles—a mile and a half. Then with a roar that shook the entire harbor, Armistead let go with everything he had.

At last the British were close enough. The *Devastation* shuddered as a cannonball plowed into her port bow, springing timbers and starting a leak. Another ripped through her topsail. The *Volcano* took five straight hits—miraculously none serious. A gunboat observing fire 300 yards ahead caught a freak shot that cut a royal colonial marine in half.

Admiral Cochrane quickly did a U turn. Apparently the fort was not done for, not by a long shot. In fact, after all those bombardments the fort seemed barely damaged. Signal flags fluttered from the *Surprise*, ordering the squadron to disengage and pull back again out of range.

By now the admiral felt more frustrated than ever. The long-range shelling was getting him nowhere fast, but what's an admiral to do? His frigate captains had an answer. They wanted to run the *Hebrus*, *Severn* and *Havannah* right alongside the fort and blow the place out of the water. Cochrane said no. It would cost too many men. Cochrane was 3,000 miles from home and beginning to feel lonely.

Cochrane had painted himself into a corner. There was little point in taking Baltimore unless he could lay his hands on the immense wealth of the city, but there was no way to do that without taking Fort McHenry. And there was no way to do that without risking high losses. That might compromise his plan to score even more bounty in New Orleans.

He felt the same about Colonel Brooke's attack. Even if the army succeeded breaking into Baltimore, what good would it do if the navy couldn't take Fort McHenry and clear the way for ships to come in and pillage the city? Of course, if Brooke could break into the city he could simply burn it, which would be a welcome event for the British, but if Brooke's losses were excessive, it would diminish the victory.

And right at that time, it did seem like Brooke was having problems. A long-delayed letter from Brooke arrived. Written the previous midnight, it was full of optimism. He planned to advance in the morning and hoped to be in Baltimore by noon or 1 p.m. But it was late afternoon already and still no sound of Brooke's guns, no sign of commotion among the Americans on Hampstead Hill. It seemed something was holding Brooke up.

Indeed, several things were holding Brooke up. His day has begun on a high note. After a wet night his troops had fallen into line at dawn in exceptionally good spirits and they were all looking forward to plundering Baltimore. Tramping west, they were for the first time bothered by trees cut down to impede their progress, but the biggest problem was the rain. It was coming down hard like a cow pissing on a flat rock, and the men held their muskets close to their sides, using their elbows to cover the firelocks and keep them dry. It was a reasonable precaution but it made marching difficult.

They reached the Philadelphia Road about 10:00 a.m. and swung left heading straight for Baltimore now only four miles away. Another three quarters of a mile and they found themselves on the crest of a hill overlooking the city. Their view was blocked however by an even higher rise two miles away. This was Hampstead Hill which Smith had seriously fortified. Along its crest they could see hordes of American soldiers, mostly militia, waiting to receive them. It was raining militia though General Ross was no longer there to disregard the danger. To the living British soldiers, it must have looked like the gates of hell.

From the second-floor window of Judge Thomas Kell's house just off the road, Colonel Brooke and Admiral Cockburn surveyed the American line. Smith's engineers knew their business. There were not only intricate earthworks but ditches, palisades and in front of the whole position a perfect field of fire. Brooke estimated there were 15,000 men altogether, and a staff officer nearby counted 120 cannon. Those estimates were pretty close to the actual numbers.

But could the position be overrun? Cockrane's letter of the night before suggested the American left was weak, and now Brooke decided to test that possibility. Toward noon he led the army on reconnaissance working his way north and west beyond the end of the earthworks. To his dismay, Brooke discovered the Americans had enough troops to not only man their extended line but to protect their flank as well. A large enemy force moved into position just where Brooke had hoped to go. Colonel Brooke had no way of knowing it but these were Stricker's troops—the very same force the British had beaten the day before—ready to take him on again. And along with them at last released from his western "exile" was General Winder at the head of the Virginia brigade.

At about one p.m. Brooke was back by the Philadelphia Road. The left end of the American line was in fact weak, but he had nowhere near enough troops to overcome the Americans who seemed to shadow every move he made. Instead, he and Cochrane decided to wait for nightfall. Then the Americans would lose the advantage of their artillery, and the panic-prone militia would be nervous and uncertain. At 2 a.m., all four British brigades would hurl themselves at Hampstead Hill and those scary British bayonets would do the rest.

But to make his grand scheme work Brooke needed the royal navy's help. If only Admiral Cochrane could stage a diversionary attack on the Ferry Branch of the Patapsco, on the other side of Baltimore, it should confuse the Americans enough to draw off some of their troops. Cockburn, of course, was all for it. He sent Lieutenant Scott to the fleet with a message outlining the plan and asking Cochrane for the diversion.

Admiral Cochrane was not in the mood for grandiose schemes. At this point he had pretty well written off the whole Baltimore business. His only aim was to get all his people back on the ships and ready to go to New Orleans where the pickings should be better. But the admiral figured he could not simply order Brooke not to carry out his project. Lord Baltimore's instructions were very clear that the army commander should have the final say about the troops ashore. Of course, no one had contemplated at that time that the army would be commanded by a mere colonel, but London was strict about keeping the lines straight between the two services. The most Cochrane could think to do was to throw his reputation against what struck him as a hare-brained scheme cooked up by an overly ambitious junior officer.

Addressing his response to Cockburn—not Brooke who as an army officer was not in Cochrane's chain of command—Cochrane said again that the navy could lend no direct support: the block ships kept the fleet out of Baltimore harbor, and the town was too far beyond the fort to be bombarded directly. All things considered he urged Brooke (through Cockburn) to return to the troop ships. And by the way if Brooke went ahead and suffered high casualties, he would be responsible for the effect on "ulterior operations," meaning the attack on New Orleans.

By 8:00 p.m., as the September sun was setting, Scott was back with the army and the message was in Cockburn's hands. Cockburn had been through all this before. Cochrane had tried to stop the operation against Washington. But with a little prodding from Cockburn, Ross had gone ahead anyway and won a glorious victory. Now he urged Brooke to follow in Ross' footsteps and win his own glorious victory.

But Brooke was not Ross. Brooke had simply fallen into his job and he wasn't going to ignore the senior commander's advice. He told Cockburn he saw no alternative but to retire from the field. When Cockburn protested, Brooke decided to assemble his staff and have a council of war. He invited Cockburn to attend but Cockburn could not bring himself to attend a meeting hosted by a mere colonel, so he declined. The staff wrestled with the pros and cons until midnight. But it is an axiom of military lore that councils of war invariably opt for timidity. Brooke sent another note to Cochrane: "From your letter to Admiral Cockburn this evening, I called a council of war. Though I had made all my arrangements for attacking the enemy at three in the morning, the result was that from the situation I was placed in, they advised I should retire. I have therefore ordered the retreat to take place tomorrow morning and hope to be at my destination the day after tomorrow—that is the place we disembarked them."[10]

But back on the *Surprise*, Cochrane had no idea whether the expedition commanders would take his advice or not. He only knew that the last time he tried to stop an operation—the march on Washington—the army had gone ahead anyhow and won big. Moreover, given the primitive state of communications, there was no way to get an answer from Brooke and Cockburn before the time set for his attack. So to be on the safe side, he had to go ahead and stage the diversion as requested.

13

Once More
into the Breach

The first virtue in a soldier is endurance of fatigue; courage
is only the second virtue.—Napoleon Bonaparte

For a man who had never commanded large groups of men in battle before, Smith was displaying remarkable poise and imagination. Not
waiting for the British to strike, Smith ordered Stricker and Winder to
arrange their troops in a line at right angles to the left end of the American entrenchments. Now if Brooke attacked his troops would be exposed
to fire not only from Hampstead Hill but also from their right flank. In
that deadly crossfire, the English would be surely cut to pieces and Brooke
could plainly see that. He had orders not to attack Baltimore if the price
was too high in casualties. Heading an army smaller than its adversary
and dispirited by the loss of its celebrated leader General Ross, and confronted by an unknown but obviously capable American general, Brooke
decided to retreat.

That decision did not come a moment too soon because at the moment
Smith was contemplating an attack of his own next morning. Thus, at 1:30
a.m. on September 14, the British army slipped quietly away covered by
that severe rainstorm. At daylight, when the British withdrawal became
obvious, Smith sent General Winder with his brigade to harass the British rear guard. He could not do more than that because his men had been
drenched all night and had enjoyed little rest. Ergo, the British returned to
North Point and boarded their transports with minimal hassle.

Communications were slow and irregular between Colonel Brooke
and Admiral Cochrane who was still operating as if in conjunction with
Brooke's ground troops. Cochrane hoped to smash through the American defenses into the inner harbor from where the city could easily be
shelled. Should this prove impossible he still hoped to get close enough
to the land operations so he could support Brooke's forces with his big

naval guns. If the cannon at Fort McHenry and on the Lazaretto could be silenced, it would be an easy matter to wipe out the whole right flank of the Hampstead Hill line anchored at Fell's Point. But none of this was possible until—and if—that star-shaped bastion at Whetstone Point was destroyed.

Cochrane had opened his attack from two miles below Fort McHenry on the morning of September 13. From couriers who dashed between the fort and Smith's Hampstead Hill command post, Smith learned that hundreds of bombs and rockets had hit the fort and that Major Armistead, along with his thousand-man garrison, could do little but huddle around their shelters because their cannon fire could not reach the British ships. Around 2:00 in the afternoon, about the time Colonel Brooke's men prepared to attack, Cochrane sent his frigates in toward the fort to test its resilience. This represented the high point of the British campaign to conquer Baltimore.

Armistead's gunners quickly swung into action and the British ships veered away. But Cochrane had one more ace up his sleeve. On the 13th, he was still operating under the assumption that he had to provide naval support for Brooke's land operation. The navy of course was not averse to fighting on land when necessary, any more than Smith's flotilla men were averse to fighting without their flotilla. Enter Captain Charles Napier, the flamboyant skipper of the frigate *Euryalus* and second-in-command in the highly successful raid on Alexandria. Unfortunately, the *Euryalus* herself was not on hand—coming back down the Potomac she had run aground so hard that her guns had to be removed to get her off. But that did not discourage Napier in the least. He loaded the ship's cutter and two barges with royal marines and chased after the fleet toward Baltimore. This man thrived on challenges.

Now Cochrane gave him a challenge worthy of his creative spirit. Around midnight Napier was to take a picked force of seamen and marines in small boats and lead them quietly—with muffled oars—into the Ferry Branch west of Fort McHenry. Continuing about a mile and a half they were then to anchor and wait. At 1:00 a.m. the bombs would open up again on Fort McHenry, and when signaled by skyrockets, Napier was to open fire too. To make as much uproar as possible, he would use guns, rockets and mix in blank cartridges. It was vital for him to put on a good show. "An attack is to be made upon their lines directly at two o'clock," Cochrane ordered.[1]

At 9 p.m. the fire of the bomb vessels slackened, then ceased altogether. Cochrane hoped the Americans would take this as the end of the day's work. At 10:00 the small boats of the squadron loaded with men came alongside the *Surprise* for final instructions. Morale was sky-high, but to add that extra ounce of fortitude, a half-ration of rum was passed out to the men.

Midnight and they were on their way—20 boats altogether, carrying perhaps 300 men. It was raining hard now—a pitch-black night—and with the guns of the fort and the fleet all silent, there was nothing to guide them in the pitch black sky. The last 11 boats lost the others in the darkness, missed the turn into the Ferry Branch, and continued rowing straight for Baltimore harbor. A less weary group of defenders might have seen them and perhaps caught them squarely between the guns of Fort McHenry and the Lazaretto. As it was the lost boats managed to turn around and splash back to safety. Leaderless and confused, they returned to the *Surprise.*

Reduced to nine boats and 128 men, Captain Napier led the remainder of his little flotilla into the Ferry Branch, unaware of the fiasco behind them. Sticking close to the far shore—the oars still muffled as directed—he slipped safely by Fort McHenry. Now he was passing Fort Babcock and soon would be opposite Fort Covington—about where he was supposed to drop his hook and wait.

At Fort Babcock, Sailing Master John A. Webster was listening closely to the roar of the British bomb boats as they opened up at 1:00 a.m.. It struck him that they were firing harder than before and that this just might mean more trouble for him and his men. He had his people change the charges in all six of his guns, this time double-shotting them with 18 pound cannonballs and grapeshot. Finally satisfied he wrapped himself in a blanket and, despite the rain, lay down on the breastwork for a nap.

He was dreaming of his home when he suddenly jerked awake. He could hear the unmistakable sound of oars and sweeps. Ordering his men to their posts, Webster peered into the darkness. He noticed an occasional dim light moving up the Ferry Branch about 200 yards offshore. He quickly checked the priming and personally trained each of the big guns, then gave the signal to open fire by shooting his pistol in the air. Just before 2:00 a.m. the battery thundered into action.

Five hundred yards upstream at Fort Covington, Lieutenant H.L. Newcomb also saw the lights and opened fire—perhaps even quicker than Webster. Then Captain Napier—realizing there was no longer any point in hiding—opened up too. Fort McHenry joined in and the British ships fired their hardest yet. The fuses of their great 200-pound bombshells traced fiery arcs across the sky, while flights of Congreve and signal rockets gave a weirdly festive glamour to a deadly earnest night.

At Fort Babcock, Sailing Master Webster hammered away at the silhouettes of the British boats and felt sure he was getting some hits. But it was hard work handling the big 18-pounders, and he dislocated his shoulder in the process. Needing more hands, he sent a young midshipman named Andrews to get back 30 men he had previously lent Lieutenant George Budd a half mile to the rear.

Budd refused to release them. He said he needed every man to cover Webster's retreat when the British drove him from the shore. This gloomy appraisal was too much for young Andrews who, instead of reporting back to Webster, galloped off to Baltimore spreading news that Fort Babcock was lost.

Baltimore was almost ready to believe him. Every building in town was shaking from all the explosions, compounded by lightning flashes across the darkened sky that was lit by the flash of bursting bombshells. To the spectators who crowded the city's rooftops, it was hard to see how anyone could live through the "most awful spectacle." And of course it might be only the beginning of more serious trouble because the British army was still out there lurking in the silent blackness beyond Hampstead Hill.

It was shortly after 3:00 a.m. when orders went out in the British camp to get everyone up. Lieutenant George Laval Chesterton, royal artillery, tried to uncurl from his square foot of floor (or so it seemed) in a crowded barn. His friend Captain Mitchell of the royal marines had an easier adjustment to make—he was quartered all alone in a pigsty.

Several hundred yards to the north, three other officers were called in from the best billet of all—Surrey, the fine country estate of Colonel Joseph Sterett currently with his regiment on Hampstead Hill. As they left, one of them paused long enough to leave a waggish thank-you note on a dining room sideboard: "Captains Brown, Wilcox and McNamara of the 53rd Regiment, Royal Marines, have received everything they could desire in this house, notwithstanding it was received at the hands of the butler, and in the absence of the colonel."[2]

Spirits were high as the men fell in. Off toward the harbor they could hear the guns of the naval bombardment, they could see the flashes and trails of fire. They assumed the fleet was doing its part and soon it would be their turn. They were greatly outnumbered—one look at the American campfires on Hampstead Hill told them that—but they had handled militia before; they would do it again tonight.

Shortly after 3:00 a.m. the columns began moving but not toward Hampstead Hill. To the general (but perhaps not universal) dismay of the troops, they were headed in the opposite direction. Away from Hampstead Hill, away from Baltimore away from the sound of the fight. As decided at the midnight council of war that the fighting men had not been party to, Colonel Brooke had them returning to North Point where the troops ships awaited.

As the men gradually figured all this out, they ranted at Colonel Brooke, at cautious staff officers, at military planners in general. Of course, they could have taken that hill. Maybe they would have suffered a few casualties, maybe a lot of casualties, but anything was better than this business of retreating, as one officer put it, "before the parcel of fellows who had scarcely even seen a gun fired in their lives … a parcel of tailors and shoemakers."[3]

In the Ferry Branch, Captain Napier was beginning to wonder what was going on. Admiral Cochrane's orders said to keep firing until he saw the army was "seriously engaged, and then return to the *Surprise*. But it was now after 3:00 a.m. and still no gun flashes—no rumble of cannon— from the hills to the east. Something must have gone wrong, he thought. In any case, he had done his part: surely by now he had diverted all the Americans who could be diverted. So far he had miraculously escaped getting hit, but to stay any longer was courting disaster for no conceivable purpose. Signal lights flickered; Napier's boats swung around and began rowing back to the ship.

Passing Fort McHenry they again hugged the far shore and almost slipped by unnoticed. But one of the officers chose this moment to fire a signal rocket to let the fleet know they were returning. The fort instantly responded with cannonballs and grape shot. Later, the British claimed only one boat was "slightly struck" and one man mortally wounded. The Americans, however, found the remains of at least two boats and the bodies of three seamen.

At 4:00 a.m. the boats were again alongside the *Surprise* and the bombardment came to an end. Two or three of the vessels continued to take an occasional shot, but to all intents and purposes the fireworks were over, and the whole blazing, tumultuous night gave way to a black, predawn quiet.

Francis Scott Key was torn with anxiety. He was standing with John S. Skinner and Dr. Beanes on their flag-of-truce ship anchored amid troop ships in Old Roads Bay, about eight miles down the Patapsco. They were a long way from the fighting but could see the fort clearly with Key's spyglass. Key could see the flag clearly and hear the bombardment, so he knew the fort had not fallen—at least not yet. But toward dawn the shooting petered out, interrupted by an occasional shot. He loathed "this abominable war" yet somehow found himself in the middle of it. He thought of himself as gentleman who would be at ease among polished British officers, but had found them—at least the ones he met with—to be vulgar.[4] He detested the rough and tumble people of Baltimore, sometimes felt the city was getting what it deserved, but now that the city was fighting for survival he knew where his heart really lay. He was first, last and always an American. He awaited the dawn with a fervent prayer that the flag was still there.

All night long he and his companions paced the deck looking toward the eastern horizon awaiting daybreak. They kept looking at their watches wondering when the sun would appear, but the clouds obstructed the view.

At 5:00 a.m. they detected the first rays of light, but still could see nothing of Fort McHenry. Half an hour later they still could not make out anything through the rain clouds. At last an easterly breeze sprang up and again Key raised his glass and this time he saw it—standing out against the gray sky was the flag. The one Armistead said he needed, the one Mary Pickersgill and her daughter Caroline had so lovingly sewn. The one that today—tattered and worn—is on display at the Smithsonian in Washington.

Francis Scott Key composed the lyrics to the "Star-Spangled Banner" but not the music which he "borrowed" from an old British drinking song. According to some of Key's friends, he was tone deaf. But he was on a boat watching Fort McHenry as the sun came up and was inspired to see the flag still flying. So we all have to sing that song though few of us can actually hit the notes (Rembrandt Peale, oil on canvas, c. 1796, National Portrait Gallery, Smithsonian Institution; funded with support from the Secretary and the Smithsonian National Board and Chapter I–Baltimore, Maryland, the Colonial Dames of America, the Elizabeth Welsh Young Legacy Fund).

(It is possible that the one flapping in the breeze that day was a smaller version—also stitched by Mary Pickersgill and submitted on the same day—that measured only 17 by 25 feet. Either way, that woman was one busy seamstress. This is the kind of detail that drives high-falutin' historians like yours truly to distraction. This was more than 200 years ago. I'm not worried about it. You shouldn't be either.)

To put the icing on the cake for the three watchful Americans, at 7:00 a.m. the *Surprise* signaled the bombarding squadron to retire down the river. At 8:00 a.m. the *Erebus* and the five bomb boats were under way and soon the supporting frigates were moving too. The siege of Fort McHenry was over. Meanwhile Key and his chums begin to see signs that the land offensive had likewise stalled. A steady procession of boats streamed out of Bear Creek carrying scores of wounded British soldiers in various transports. To Key it all meant that the enemy had been "roughly handled."

He pulled out his spyglass again and took another look at the fort and the flag. Suddenly a poetic muse whispered in his ear. Using a pencil he carried and writing on the back of a letter that happened to be in his pocket, he began to scribble some likely phrases. It is doubtful that he hummed the tune he was thinking of, assuming he was thinking of a tune.

Baltimore was already celebrating when the small sloop bearing Key, Skinner and Dr. Beanes finally docked in Baltimore at Hughes Wharf about 9 p.m. Bystanders pumped them eagerly for news. What would the British do next? Key said, based on conversations with British officers, that they would probably go to Poplar Island for repairs and then on to Halifax. Was Ross really killed? Yes, said Skinner, no doubt about it. But the main focus of attention was Skinner's list of 91 prisoners held in the British fleet. Assured they would have their freedom, a great surge of relief ran through the city.

The three arrivals retired to the Indian Queen Hotel, but there would be no rest for Francis Scott Key, at least not yet. He had a strong mental picture of what he had witnessed at Fort McHenry. He had tried to capture his feelings in a few random lines—like the thrill of seeing the flag still flying at dawn—in a few random lines scribbled right after the attack. Later he added more during the long wait and sail back to Baltimore. His lines had gradually jelled into a song and he had to get it down before he forgot it.

Key was notoriously unmusical. He played no instrument and did not sing. Someone who knew him insisted he was tone deaf, and so he may have been. Some critics referred to him as Francis "Off" Key. But Key wrote his lyrics to fit a song popular at the time, "To Anacron in Heaven," composed by someone named John Stafford for a men's club in London. Within days people all over Baltimore were singing it. They are still singing it at sporting events, as are all of us. It is arguably the most well-known song in the English-speaking world, at least in terms of the total number of people who have heard it and can sing at least part of it. Without doubt Steven Foster would have come up with a better tune but he wasn't born until 1836 by which time "The Star-Spangled Banner" had spread to other cities too, as the entire nation savored news of the victory at Baltimore.

The victory was unexpected. As late as 7:15 a.m. on September 14 (15 minutes after Cochrane began his withdrawal) the common consensus throughout the region was that Baltimore was destined to fall. In Philadelphia crowds filled the streets all day despite the rain waiting for the news that never came. The stage was not running, the outlook was bleak.

Coming so soon after the debacle in Washington, the situation had all the earmarks of another disaster in the making.

And now the impossible had happened. Joy and relief swept the country. In Norfolk, Virginia, the *Constellation* fired rousing salutes: at Salem, Massachusetts, the town cannon boomed in celebration. "Never have we witnessed greater elevation of public spirits," exclaimed the *Salem Register*. The triumph of Baltimore had erased all past impressions of the enemy's irresistible strength. "Ten thousand victories cannot give them their former hopes, and the spell is broken forever."

But in that pre-electronic era it took a while for the news to spread. "The enemy has been severely drubbed—as well his Army and Navy—and is retiring down the river after expending many tons of shot, from 1800 to 2000 shells, and at least 700–800 rockets," wrote Commodore Rodgers to Navy Secretary Jones on the 14th, while the British were falling back to North Point.

True to form, Sam Smith was not convinced. "The enemy has retired, not departed—this retiring may be a stratagem to throw us off our guard," he warned in a general order issued during the day. Some British deserters appeared to confirm that suspicion. Several said Brooke was pulling back merely to pick up replacements.

Sam Smith was ever and always a careful man. Even by the 15th, when the enemy were clearly re-embarking, Smith was concerned it was merely a ruse so they could hit Baltimore from another angle, one of several angles Smith had not prepared for. That evening General Douglass had his brigade prepare to counter an assault on the south side of the city, and Smith warned those at Fort McHenry that he believed an attack would be made in the course of the night on this post and on the city by way of the Ferry Branch.

"It was a bad moment for Fort McHenry to face such a prospect," wrote Lord. "Exhausted by five days of superhuman effort, Major Armistead was delirious with fever, and his subordinates were fighting over seniority. A new British attack would catch the place torn with dissension. Sam Smith hurriedly put Commodore Rodgers in charge. A little unorthodox, perhaps, to have a naval officer run an army fort, but as with most of Sam Smith's solutions, it worked."[5]

On September 16, Cochrane's ships still hovered off North Point, but they were now anchored well out in the bay. Slowly, almost imperceptibly, it dawned on Baltimore's defenders that they had actually accomplished what they had scarcely dared hope—they had actually turned back the British. At Fort McHenry, the men found it hard to believe that only three days before they were crouching behind ramparts, praying for their lives and relying on such a dubious talisman as a homeless rooster crowing on the ramparts. But one man remembered and kept his word—bringing the rooster that pound cake he had promised.

On Hampstead Hill, the troops were released from the earthworks and marched back to their regular quarters. Free from tension at last, the men exploded with ribald joy that appalled Private John A. Dagg, a sometime clergyman from Virginia. "During the last few days everyone had spoken softly and seriously, and no oaths had been heard, but this night our barracks were in an uproar with noise and profanity, giving painful proof of human depravity," he wrote.[6]

"The noise and foolishness soon gave way to a deeper, quieter gratitude," Lord wrote. "For Baltimore it had been a very near thing, and everyone sensed it. Gifts poured in for the comfort of the wounded—not just money and medical supplies, but small things too from people who had little else to give except their thanks: two large pots of preserves from Mrs. Samuel Harris ... one jar of crab apples from Mrs. William Lorman."[7]

For the heroes there were dress swords and testimonial dinners, and for a convalescent Major Armistead, a fine silver punch bowl of the exact dimensions of a 13-inch British bombshell. But he won more than that. His wife Louisa presented him with a baby girl that made him forget the son he wanted. Professionally, Madison

The Fort McHenry rooster actually did receive his pound cake (drawing by Gerry Embleton, in *In Full Glory Reflected: Discovering the War of 1812 in the Chesapeake* by Ralph E. Eshelman and Burton K. Kummerow, published by the Maryland Center for History and Culture, July 15, 2012).

sent him a spot promotion, and even better, he had that dream of every soldier—a little military fame. "So you see, my dear wife," he wrote Mrs. Armistead, "all is well and at least your husband has got a name and standing that nothing but divine providence could have given him, and I pray to my Heavenly Father that we may long live to enjoy."[8] He apparently was one of those devout Methodists who seem to have been ubiquitous in Baltimore in those days. (Smith, of course, was a Presbyterian which at the time was considered "high church" in some circles.)

At almost the same time of the Baltimore upheaval word came of an equally glorious victory on the Canadian front where victories were in short supply—unless you were Canadian or British. But on September 11, just as things were getting interesting in Baltimore, word came that a large British invasion force was thrown back at Plattsburg, New York. The naval arm of this expedition was annihilated on Lake Champlain by the brilliant tactics of Captain Thomas Macdonough commanding a hastily assembled U.S. squadron while the British army of 11,000 peninsular veterans retired in confusion before the far smaller numbers of Brigadier General Alexander Macomb. It was yet another miracle and the defenders of Baltimore responded appropriately. Promptly at noon on September 18, the guns of Fort McHenry sounded loud and long. But this time it was not an act of defiance; it was rather a "federal salute" in honor of the victory on Lake Champlain.

It was probably just as well that Admiral Cochrane knew nothing about the results at Plattsburgh. His debacle on the Chesapeake Bay was sufficiently discouraging. There were no rousing cheers on the boats as he collected his troops at North Point on September 15. There was mostly silence disturbed by the groans of the wounded on deck of the *Seahorse* where 25 shattered forms awaited the surgeon's knife. Drenched with blood, the sail used to carry the wounded was thrown overboard. General Ross' remains were carefully preserved in 120 gallons of good Jamaican rum.

That evening Cochrane transferred back to his flagship *Tonnant*. He clearly preferred being on the *Surprise* with his son Sir Thomas; on the other hand the evidence suggests that the boy left much to be desired as a frigate captain. The log was a mess and mishaps seemed to plague the ship: an upset gig, a drowned sailor, desertions, groundings—no one could predict what would happen next. This very day two of her signal flags blew away.

All day on September 16 the fleet lay at anchor taking stock. "Carpenters went over the damage to the *Devastation* and *Volcano*, the wounded were transferred to the *Diomede*, which was refitted as a hospital ship; and the troops were generally sorted out. In the process it became painfully clear that desertions were again a problem, altogether some 237 men were listed as prisoners or missing." Something had to be done "to encourage the rest" and before the week was out two recaptured deserters were hanged from the yardarm of the *Weser*. Boats from every ship in the fleet were ordered to be present so the men could be properly encouraged.[9]

Admiral Cochrane did all he could to put on a brave face. On the 16th he issued a ringing proclamation to all hands praising their exertions in the "demonstration and reconnaissance which it was deemed advisable to make upon the city of Baltimore." On the 17th he sent off the official dispatch to the admiralty in which he again described the action as a "demonstration" and Brooke's modest success was hailed as a "decisive victory" and "a brilliant affair." The final withdrawal was explained thusly: "The primary object of our movement had already been fully accomplished."[10]

That of course was for public consumption and anticipated the advances in public relations that have occurred in modern times. The same day he privately wrote Lord Melville that the entire project was "contrary to my opinion, but extremely urged by the General, to which I reluctantly consented but to preserve unanimity between the two services." Cochrane added that he now "extremely regretted" the whole operation. "Even the tactics were bad; the army should have landed on the other side of Baltimore and attacked from the west."[11] That would have certainly challenged Smith's plans but he did have Stricker and Winder there just in case.

Of course, Ross was no longer around to explain or defend his decisions, which was dreadfully inconsiderate of him. Otherwise he might have felt obliged to point out that it was Cockburn and Cochrane who insisted on the Baltimore campaign. As for Cochrane, he was moving on to bigger things. "The ball is at our feet," he wrote to Melville, "and give me but 6,000 men including a rifle and cavalry regiment, and I will engage to master every town south of Philadelphia and keep the whole coast in such a state of alarm as soon to bring the most obstinate upon their marrow bones."

That very afternoon the frigate *Vesta* arrived with a dispatch from London that gave Cochrane everything he wanted except the cavalry regiment. The government was sending out to America Lord Hill with 7,000 men. They would rendezvous with the fleet at Jamaica on November 20, and the united front would then proceed to the Gulf Coast. Brimming with optimism and confidence Cochrane quickly wrote to Lord Melville promising to be in New Orleans in December. But even as he wrote, forces far beyond his control were at work in London which would not only affect his plans for Louisiana but alter the entire course of the war itself.

Of course, while the British in America were reeling from the setback in Baltimore the good people of Great Britain were still savoring the destruction of Washington and looking forward to reports of more from Baltimore. The first news to hit London, the report of what happened in Washington, appeared on September 27, which was remarkably fast for a sailing ship in those days. "War America would have and war she has got…. Washington is no more," proclaimed the *Courier* (a newspaper) that very afternoon. "The reign of Madison, like that of Bonaparte, may be considered at an end." A few days later, the *National Register* reported that in the hour of disaster, President Madison shot himself. That never happened.

All in all, it was almost a morality play and, as the *Sun* observed, "a lesson for the past and an example for the future of how dangerous and fatal it is to rouse the sleeping lion of the British isles." The victory seemed to continue a summer of almost continual joy. Napoleon had been gone for six months already, but the party kept on going. The burning of Washington was an indisputable, glorious reality and it silenced the war's critics—a small minority who continued to harp on the unsustainable cost and the almost invisible gains produced. Instead of cutting the military budget, the impetus was for more spending on guns and ships. Having no knowledge of Ross's demise, the government authorized Cochrane and Ross to go wherever they liked—Rhode Island, the Delaware, the Chesapeake, the Carolinas and of course New Orleans. And if they went to Baltimore, so much the better—they would "make its inhabitants feel a little more the effects of your visit than what has been experienced in Washington."[12]

London was quick to pass the word across the channel to its negotiators in Ghent who were trying to put the squeeze on American delegates. The British tone became distinctly tougher and any inclination to compromise receded. In August, they had presented a shopping list that included creation of Indian "buffer states" in the Northwest Territory and exclusive British control of the Great Lakes. The future president John Quincy Adams, son of former president John Adams, made it clear these demands were unacceptable. The British leadership also wanted peace because the spending entailed by sending armies to battlefields 3,000 miles away was grinding the government down, but they didn't share that at the negotiations. For the time being they wanted to let the American negotiators ponder the weakness of their position.

In Parliament the cry was for further chastisement—a term that had come to dominate British policy toward the United States. And what could be a more legitimate target than the public buildings of the would-be democracy? "Such as the fruits which America has derived from this unnatural war," opined the *Courier*, adding, "But the vial of our wrath is not yet exhausted; a few days, perhaps hours, will bring us evidence of further successes."[13] The *Public Ledger* took the cause a few degrees higher.

The editors said they would not be surprised to see Boston, Philadelphia, New York, and Baltimore all turned into "heaps of smoldering rubbish" by the end of the year.[14]

And in fact rumors swept London in the first week of October that Baltimore had already fallen. The details were persuasively specific: 100 sailing ships taken along with a prodigious amount of flour "ready packed in barrels." The *Morning Chronicle* reported that "Baltimore had not only fallen, but was under the protection of the British forces it had seceded from the Union and proclaimed itself neutral."

On October 17, real reports came in poking a pin in the journalistic balloons. The government hustled to select a reputable general to replace Ross. They picked Major General Sir Edward Pakenham—Wellington's brother-in-law and one of his most trusted staff officers. Meanwhile, the British papers struggled to correct the earlier reports. They said it was all because the cowardly American militias refused to stand up to British bayonets like honorable men. No one was really fooled.

The "corrected" report from Baltimore was soon followed by news of the British disaster of Lake Champlain and Plattsburgh. The British ruling class was on its heels. In a letter to the Marquis of Tweeddale (a priceless title), Colonel Torrens wrote: "Good God! Is it to be borne that an officer in command of 9,000 British troops shall retreat before a handful of Banditti because he forsooth thinks that the objects to be gain by an attack after the loss of the fleet would not justify the loss—as if there were no such thing as national honor and professional credit to fight for."[15]

The negotiators in Ghent had to choose between doubling down or asking for less. They were instructed by London to ask for less. Out the window went the pompous demands cooked up in August. Instead Britain would settle for the doctrine of *uti possidetis*—each side to keep what it held. The Americans would have no part of it. Instead, each side would keep what it had at the outset of hostilities.

National pride aside, the British were suffering from ruinous taxes and business was poor and getting worse every day the war dragged on. The end of the French war did not bring prosperity. The American privateers—many operating out of Baltimore—were costing Great Britain dearly. Some 1,400 British ships had been lost to privateers. Marine insurance rates were higher than before Napoleon fell. Some 10,000 cases of goods lay on the docks at Liverpool awaiting shipment to America.

Perhaps even worse for the government was growing moral revulsion at what Britain had been doing in America—in particular the burning of Washington. A growing number of citizens spoke of the "unmanly vengeance" exhibited in the burning of the Library of Congress. There were others demanding an even harsher approach to the United States, but the voices of moderation were more persuasive. On November 1, Cochrane was ordered to dial back his policy of retaliation.

As for the States, the forlorn British hope of dissension was dissolving. American newspapers that reached London on November 18 suggested Americans were closing ranks. The harsh peace terms the British had offered in August had evoked widespread anger. Thousands of Americans were flocking to join local militias. Parliament too was in an uproar. In the House of Lords, the Marquis of Lansdowne declared it was one thing to fight for a great principle like Britain's maritime rights but a totally different matter to conquer territory, impose boundaries and generally hem in America. He wanted no part of it. In the House of Commons, Alexander Baring declared that the whole business was like asking England to surrender Cornwall.

So the British negotiators caved. The United States gave way on free trade and sailors' rights; Great Britain dropped its strong stand on the American Indians and any thought of gaining territory. About all that remained was whether Massachusetts fishermen could dry and cure their catch on the shores of Newfoundland and whether English vessels had freedom of navigation on the Mississippi River. The negotiators dealt with these issues by simply omitting any mention of them in the treaty.

But there was still one little hurdle remaining. Normally treaties took effect when they were signed, but not this one. It would become operative only when unconditionally ratified by both parties, with the ratifications to be exchanged in Washington. To the end, the British wrote off President Madison as a sly, malevolent gnome quite likely to reject the treaty altogether in some dark political maneuver or equally likely to change a line here or there to snatch an undeserved advantage. "So the war would go on," Lord wrote, "His Majesty's forces would press as hard as ever, until the treaty was actually ratified and this slippery man was nailed down to its terms."[16]

14

War Without End, Amen

Peace has its victories no less than war but it doesn't have
as many monuments to unveil.—Ken Hubbard

The great patriotic victory at Baltimore did not end the War of 1812
any more than the victory at Yorktown ended the American Revolution.
Most of the time, wars are eventually settled by peace treaties that are
invariably complicated and long in the making. The American Civil War
was an exception—it came to an end at Appomattox when General Robert
E. Lee surrendered to General Ulysses S. Grant. By that time there was no
Confederate government to negotiate a treaty with. But there were negotiators meeting in Ghent in 1814 when the Battle of Baltimore was fought,
and it informed the terms of the peace treaty.

However, it took a while. Meanwhile the war went on. While the negotiators negotiated, the soldiers and sailors continued to fight. In the Chesapeake, British naval forces under Admiral Malcolm resumed raiding the
local creeks and estuaries. Along the Maine coast British frigates dipped
into and out of steeply wooded bays, cowing the inhabitants into submis-
sion. At Halifax and later Jamaica, Admiral Cochrane planned his next
venture for a prize possibly even richer than Baltimore—New Orleans.
From the Chesapeake Bay, Malcolm sailed to join him with Ross' old force,
or what was left of it, and three batches of reinforcements from England
went to join him. Sir Edward Pakenham, whose repute had not been tarnished by the unfortunate setback in Baltimore, sailed from England to
assume command.

But once again, nothing went quite the way it was planned. The expedition was supposed to rendezvous at Jamaica by November 20 and then
sail to the Louisiana coast where light-draft boats would ferry the troops
through the lakes and bayous to some spot near New Orleans. But the rein-
forcement left England piecemeal and only the first group reached Jamaica
on schedule. The rest would have to catch up later.

And there were not enough flatboats assembled in Jamaica as

planned. The central command in London had promised more but did not follow through. And perhaps typical of the time and place, there was zero security. As early as August before the fracas at Baltimore, Albert Gallatin with the peace negotiators in Ghent warned that a big expedition was being organized and Louisiana was the objective. James Monroe sent a warning to the district military commander, Major General Andrew Jackson, who, in anticipation of some gambit by the British, was already assembling an army. The notorious pirate Jean Laffite reported to Jackson that he had been visited by a British naval captain seeking his cooperation. The British were also trying to recruit Indians, blacks and other dissidents to assist in "liberating" their soil in the coming campaign. And in Jamaica, British captain William Fathergill was trying to collect flatboats which he made clear were for an attack on New Orleans. If they had had airplanes at their disposal, they would have no doubt sent several flying over New Orleans with streaming banners reading "The British Are Coming, the British Are Coming."

Oblivious to these blunders, the expedition left Jamaica pretty much intact on November 26–27 bearing four regiments from the Chesapeake plus the new arrivals from Great Britain—mainly the 93rd and 95th Foot. On the way more ships joined the parade including the 5th West India, perhaps the best of the black colonial regiments. By then the British invading army totaled 5,700 men under Major General John Keane. He was young and untried but the best they could do until someone more senior and experienced became available. Meanwhile, Admiral Cochrane would be pleased to give him guidance just as he did for Colonel Brooke at Baltimore. What could go wrong?

By December 2 the leading ships were just off the Apalachicola River where Cochrane hoped to make contact with thousands of Creek warriors supposedly coming to help with the fighting. But only a handful appeared dressed in red Guardsmen jackets, huge, cocked hats and no pants. He had about the same response from his efforts to recruit slaves to the Union Jack. But as in Baltimore, few blacks wanted a piece of this fight. By the time Cochrane's whole fleet was assembled off Lake Borgne the prospects must have seemed dicey at best—at least to someone equipped with a modicum of skepticism or perhaps someone who had seen how the British operated against Baltimore.

Despite such considerations, Cochrane almost pulled it off. For his part, Jackson inadvertently did all he could to assist Cochrane. He just couldn't believe that a "real military man" like Cochrane would attack through Lake Borgne which entailed a row of more than 60 miles to some as-yet unidentified landing point near the city. So he left a small flotilla of gunboats to cover that approach which Cochrane quickly captured on

December 14. This deprived Jackson of critical intelligence and also added five desperately needed shallow draft vessels to the small British fleet.

Even with these boats, Cochrane had only enough room to haul 2,200 men at one time. But that was a start and on December 16 he began moving his troops from the ships to a base on Pea Island about halfway across the lake. Then Cochrane got even luckier. While searching for a place to land, his scouts came upon a village of Spanish fishermen who were most cooperative. For a mere $100 plus $2 per diem as "head pilot," their leader showed the polite English visitors around the Bayou Bienvenu—the only waterway to New Orleans that Jackson had not blocked. Disguised as fishermen, the scouts tried it out. Through a lacework of connecting branches and canals, they ultimately found themselves on the left bank of the Mississippi, less than eight miles below New Orleans.

Actually Jackson knew all about the Bayou Bienvenu and had specifically given orders that it be blocked, but the junior officer he put in charge, Major Gabriel Villeré, apparently felt there was little chance of the British coming his way. His family owned one of the plantations lying between the bayou and the river, and rather than obstruct such a useful means of communication, he decided a picket guard would be enough. On the morning of December 23, a British advance force of 1,600 men snapped up the pickets, including Major Villeré, and moved in. Thus at a single stroke all of Cochrane's complex plans had been redeemed. His majesty's troops were at the Mississippi astride a good, hard road just two hours' march from the city itself.

Colonel Thornton wanted to push on—to strike while the iron was hot. That was the way they did it at Bladensburg and it worked just fine. But General Keane said no. The men were tired, and he had only 1,600 on hand. They had only two small cannon. Plus one of the captured pickets said Jackson had 15,000 men well-armed. Far better, said Keane, to rest until more troops, guns and ammunition were in hand. So the campfires were lit and the men relaxed on the firm ground beside the levee. Firm ground is always a highly desirable quality in that part of the world where the mighty Mississippi changes its direction from time to time.

The overwhelming fact was that the enemy was almost within sight of the city and as yet not one gun had been fired. "By the eternal, they shall not sleep on our soil,"[1] Jackson said when he learned where they were. At 1:55 p.m. the alarm gun sounded and by 5:00 the available troops were marching: Colonel Thomas Hind's Mississippi dragoons, the regulars in their tight blue jackets, the city battalion with their peacock finery, Brigadier General John Coffee's hard, lean Tennessee volunteers, 200 free men of color, and a handful of painted Choctaws—2,100 men altogether.

At the same time the schooner *Carolina* slipped her moorings and drifted downstream. Her crew were idle sailors drafted from the New Orleans waterfront; her gunners were Baratarian freebooters happy to be in any sort of action. Jackson's plan was simple: when the *Carolina* opened up on the British left, his troops would attack the enemy right.

It all began at about 7:30 p.m. with a withering broadside on Keane's unsuspecting men gathered by their campfires eating supper. As planned, Coffee's troops then charged the British right, and a wild melee ensued which lasted until nearly midnight. Keane's regulars fought hard and well, finally forcing a standoff.

The morning of December 24 found the British army still occupying a strip of firm ground that lay between the Mississippi on the left and a maze of swamps and bayous on the right. The narrow plain ran all the way to New Orleans, but two miles ahead the American army was waiting. Pulling back after the battle, Jackson was now digging in behind the Rodriguez Canal where the plain was less than 900 yards wide. For his part, Keane was in no hurry to find Jackson. Thoroughly jolted by the unexpected scrap, he decided to await the remainder of his troops before resuming his advance. Christmas Eve was allowed to pass without massive bloodshed. Just a few Christmas carols, but no visit from Santa who actually didn't exist yet.

On Christmas Day Sir Edward Pakenham arrived at long last catching up with his army after an eight-week voyage across the Atlantic and a final row of almost 20 hours. The British gunners were so happy to see him they fired a loud salute that led the Americans to think a major attack was in the offing. That notion passed but Pakenham did inject new life into the British force, bringing up men and guns as fast as possible. On December 27, the British gunners tested their skills by blowing up the *Carolina* which had become a pest to His Majesty's finest. That seemed such a good omen that Admiral Malcolm, who had caught up with the troops, to write a note to Admiral Cochrane who was back with the ships. "The general proposes to move tomorrow at daylight…. I think he will be in possession of New Orleans tomorrow night—he appears determined on a bold push."[2] It may have reminded Cochrane of Ross' boasts of dining in Baltimore.

In any case, the push wasn't bold enough. As the army advanced in the early morning of December 28, the American line erupted in gunfire. Then from the river the armed ship *Louisiana*—her guns served by Baratarian volunteers—began raking the British left. The British wavered and stopped; seeing the left in trouble, the right also came to a halt. With his troops pinned down, Pakenham called off the attack.

General Keane now decided he could never break the American line without some heavy guns of his own, so he spent the next three days bringing up 10 18-pounders and four 24-pound carronades all taken from royal navy ships. The seamen performed prodigies, floating the guns in on canoes, then dragging them through the swamp to hard ground. Once again the British spirits soared and on the night of the 29th, Cochrane wrote to his son Tom who was presumably still with his command saying he hoped to be in New Orleans in about eight days.

On New Year's Day 1815 Pakenham was ready to try again. During the previous night, under cover of darkness, his men had scooped out four batteries only 800 yards from Jackson's line. With too little time to do the work properly, sugar casks were used to build up the parapets. By dawn the guns were planted and army waited for the morning fog to burn off.

Across the Rodriguez Canal, the unsuspecting Americans were preparing for a New Year's Day review. Then at 9:00 a.m., the fog suddenly lifted and the British guns crashed into action. Jackson's men scrambled to their posts and the general rushed from his headquarters at the nearby McCarty plantation house. By the time he reached the embankment, flights of Congreve rockets added to the noise. "Don't mind those rockets," Jackson said to his troops, "they are mere toys to amuse children."[3]

It was 10 minutes before the American guns returned fire, but when they did the effect was devastating. Sugar and splinters flew in all directions as Jackson's big 24- and 32-pounders pulverized the British batteries. In contrast, Pakenham's gunners did little damage. They were short on ammunition, their aim was bad and most of their good shots plowed harmlessly into the American earthworks. By 3:00 p.m. the guns were silent, Jackson's band was playing "Yankee Doodle," and for the second time Pakenham conceded failure.

So Sir Edward decided once again to wait for more men before trying again. The 7th and 43rd Foot, two of Wellington's best regiments, were expected any day. Those additional forces would enable him to try new tactics. Next time it would not be just another frontal assault. He would send troops across the river to attack on the other side, to create a diversion and outflank Jackson's line. It made sense on paper.

But to do that, boats were needed, and they would have to come from Cochrane's collection. For the next five days the British soldiers dug dirt trying to deepen the bayou, extend the canal and cut a breach in the levee to accommodate the boats. By January 6, the work was done and the reinforcements had arrived under Major General John Lambert. To ease the shortage of ammunition, each man carried a cannonball in his haversack. Sergeant Jack Cooper of the 7th Foot had only one complaint: he really needed another cannonball for the other side of his haversack to keep them in balance.

Behind the Rodriguez Canal, Andrew Jackson was also making plans. He built up his embankment. He started two more defense lines nearer

New Orleans. He transferred guns from the *Louisiana* to a new position he was digging across the river. He strengthened his front by shifting men from other points that no longer seemed threatened. On January 3, he got some welcome reinforcements when the long-awaiting Kentucky Militia arrived. Only there was one hitch. Someone told him only a few of the Kentuckians had guns. "I don't believe it," snorted Old Hickory. "I have never seen a Kentuckian without a gun and a pack of cards and a bottle of whiskey in my life."[4]

As his preparations progressed, from time to time Jackson studied the British camp with his telescope. He noticed the British working on the canal and rightly guessed they were planning an attack across the river. He also noticed they were making scaling ladders and thus decided the main blow would fall on his own position. On January 7, when he saw them cutting the levee and repairing the batteries in front of his line, he felt sure the attack would be coming on the following day.

Like Sam Smith, Andrew Jackson had a knack for guessing right. During the afternoon of the 7th, Pakenham called his commanders together and announced they would strike at dawn. As a preliminary, Colonel Thornton would cross the river during the night with 1,400 men, capture the American guns on the other side, and turn them on Jackson's line. These were to open fire when the general attack began, which would be signaled by a rocket.

The assaulting British force was to advance in two columns, with the main blow to be delivered by the column on the right under Major General Samuel Gibbs who had come with Pakenham as his second-in-command. The other column, under General Keane, would advance in two parts. On the far left a picked force under Lieutenant Colonel Robert Rennie would assault a redoubt that anchored the right end of the American line. The rest of the column was to stick more toward the center, ready to support either Rennie or Gibbs, depending on the ebb and flow of the battle. Waiting in reserve would be General Lambert and his two fresh regiments.

In advance of them all would go Lieutenant Colonel Thomas Mullins's 44th Regiment which had the job of picking up the 16 ladders and 300 fascines needed to scale the American parapet. The Brits had come to wage serious war, but Mullins did not appreciate his assignment. "The 44th will have the forlorn hope tomorrow," he grumbled to his officers. "I think they will catch it."

Pakenham's best-laid plans quickly went astray. It proved incredibly difficult getting the boats from the canal into the Mississippi. The levee wasn't cut deeply enough. There was too little water in the canal. The boats had to be dragged 250 yards through mud and slime. Instead of getting off early in the evening, it was 1:00 a.m. on the 8th before the first barge was finally afloat on the river.

About the same time Jackson was awakened by a messenger from Commander Daniel Patterson across the river who reported a "very uncommon stir" in the British camp and requested reinforcements. The main attack, Jackson responded, would be on his own side of the river, and he had no men to spare. Then, turning to his aides, Jackson said, "Gentlemen, we have slept enough."[5]

At 3:30 a.m. the first British troops began moving to the front. Colonel Mullins led his 44th Regiment forward to pick up the scaling ladders and fascines but apparently misunderstood his orders. He went to the "advanced battery" about 500 yards beyond the "advanced redoubt," where all of the implements were stored. When he finally realized his mistake, he sent 300 men back on the double, but by then it was almost dawn—time for the attack to begin.

Both Gibbs and Pakenham learned what was going on and fumed about blundering junior officers but were reassured by staff that the 44th would get its equipment and be back in position in time. Pakenham was more worried about the failure of his scheme for a night attack across the river. It was now after 5:00 a.m. and Thornton had not started yet. At long last it was decided to send the boats that were ready with as many men as they could hold. Mullins finally shoved off toward 5:30 with only a third of his force.

"Thornton's people will be of no use whatever to the general attack," Pakenham said to an aide, Captain Harry Smith. There was still time before daylight to call off the assault, Smith diplomatically suggested. "This may be," Pakenham said, "but I have twice deferred the attack." As they talked streaks of light began to appear, and the Captain urged more strongly that the advance be postponed. Pakenham was beyond that. "Smith, order the rocket to be fired," he said.[6]

The rockets soared into the sky signaling to friend and foe alike that the assault had begun. Thornton's troops at last began to cross the river. Mullins' men struggled to bring up the ladders and fascines. And the remainder of the troops started toward Jackson's earthen wall, behind which crouched Jackson's men who were eager to get on with it. At 500 yards a long brass 12-pounder opened the artillery action up and down the line. At 200 yards General Billy Carroll's Tennessee riflemen opened up and the whole line blazed with fire. Presumably by this time the Kentuckians had apparently found some of those celebrated Kentucky long rifles. "Give it to them boys," Jackson called out. "Let's finish this business today."[7]

The British troops wavered on the right. The men of the 44th, returning with the ladders and fascines, failed to get back in time. When they did arrive, they floundered about the rear of the column where the ladders were of no use, confusing the other companies as well as themselves. They began dropping their ladders and firing blindly at the American line. The leading troops, being fired at from their front and rear, panicked and broke ranks—just like the American militia so scorned by General Ross.

General Gibbs rushed up shouting encouragement, but it was too late. His men streamed toward the rear and Gibbs himself was cut down, taking four bullets that left him dead on the field. Now Pakenham rushed over waving his hat and shouting, "For shame, remember you are British soldiers! This is the road you ought to take."[8] American gunners hit him in the knee and brought down his horse. Borrowing Duncan MacDougall's mount, he was soon back in the saddle and just as soon hit with bullets in his groin and spine. Collapsing into MacDougall's arms he mumbled, "Tell General..." but was unable to finish his message and was soon gone.

"Bayonet the rascals," called out General Keane as the fleeing troops cut across his column to the left. Then he also went down hit in the torso and thigh. The Kentucky long rifles were remarkably accurate in the right hands.

Now leaderless, the remaining troops struggled on to the slaughter. Blinded by grape shot, Lieutenant Duncan Campbell of the 43rd was carried dying from the field, still clutching the hilt of his shattered sword. Colonel Rennie and a few others reached the American line before falling. Captain Thomas Wilkinson of Gibbs' staff died at the foot of the parapet, gasping, "Now why don't the troops come on? The day is our own."[9]

Back with the reserves General Lambert learned that he had inherited the command. Clearly there was only one thing to do. Around 8:00 he cancelled the assault and pulled back what was left of Pakenham's army. Ironically, Thornton's attack on the other side of the river was a big success. But that was a sideshow and the battle was lost by then. Lambert pulled him back too. Admiral Codrington protested—they had to keep on or the army would starve. "Kill plenty more, Admiral," said Harry Smith bitterly. "Fewer rations will be required."[10]

On the evening of February 4, candles were burning in windows along Pennsylvania Avenue, if not the White House, where extensive repairs were underway. Washington had just received word of Jackson's victory at New Orleans. When word reached Baltimore, the guns of Fort McHenry boomed out a grand salute which no doubt worried many citizens who were unaware of the news.

And then even better news—the British sloop of war *Favourite*, still flying a flag of truce, slipped into New York harbor bringing the negotiators and the peace treaty they had recently negotiated. Within 20 minutes lamps blazed along lower Broadway and cheering men were parading through the streets.

The cheering crowd ignored the fact that the treaty had not yet been ratified and no one seemed to notice that the Battle of New Orleans had been fought after the treaty was agreed to and the war was over. Of course, technically the war wasn't over—at least not just yet. But there was a hunger for peace. While newspapers were blasting out the good news, the peace delegates made their way to Washington and hurried to President Madison's temporary home at the Octagon House. Soon the cabinet assembled and they all went over the treaty paragraph by paragraph and they were soon joined by hordes of legislators eager to get the news. Political differences disappeared, at least temporarily. First Lady Dolley Madison stood in the center of the room happily receiving congratulations. "No one could doubt," a guest recalled later, "who behind that smile lighted up her countenance and diffused its beams all around that all uncertainty was now at an end."[11]

The president soon appeared and pronounced the terms satisfactory. "Peace," Dolley cried. Soon others took up the call, "Peace, peace." The war had gone on so long and fostered so much dissension that it would have taken a brave politician to quibble at the terms. On the 17th, the Senate unanimously ratified the treaty, blinding speed for that crowd. The deed was done. At long last the guns were silent, or at least soon would be after word reached the scattered military forces.

Off the New England coast, the British sailors—weary of long months of blockade duty—staged their own celebration. Rear Admiral Sir Henry Hotham gave his squadron double rations of rum, and the sailors of the *Superb* threw their caps into the sea.

There was a sharply different reaction among the top command. Admiral Cockburn was operating off Georgia when the news reached him, and writing his friend Captain Palmer of the *Hebrus*, he couldn't conceal his disappointment. "That Jonathan [his term for Americans] should have been so easily let out of the cloven stick in which I thought we so securely had him, I sincerely lament," he said.[12]

Likewise, Admiral Cochrane was deeply depressed. He had withdrawn his shattered force from Louisiana, seized Fort Bowyer at Mobile as a rather limp consolation, and was getting ready for fresh adventures on the Chesapeake—but suddenly there was this obnoxious peace. To Admiral Codrington, he seemed "most amazingly cast down," and Codrington decided it must be at the thought of missing out on so much prize money. No doubt Cochrane had been counting on vast amounts of booty from Baltimore and having lost that, even more from New Orleans. And even worse yet, possibly because of the situation, the two admirals—Cochrane and Cockburn—were now barely on speaking terms.

Curiously, Lord reports that Cochrane's son Sir Thomas had a different reaction to the peace. "Despite all his father's protection—all that parental pampering—the young man had a set of values that were quite his own. He would take the prize money with the rest of them, but the wanton destruction of farms and villages appalled him."[13] Sir Thomas confided his thoughts to a private journal and now, as word of the treaty arrived, he again picked up his pen:

> I confess this intelligence gives me the most immense joy both of my own, and my country's account, and I devoutly hope the President will not hesitate as to whether he will approve the treaty.
> Already the war between Great Britain and some power or other has lasted longer than I can recollect…. Our country groans under the weight of its expense—and the dreadful annual expense necessary to maintain the war scarcely leaves wherewithal to support life in the middling class of society. Relatives are torn asunder to supply men for our Army and Navy, and there's scarcely a family in England that does not mourn the loss of a father, husband or brother.[14]

But there was no peace, at least not yet. On March 10—three days before news of the American ratification of the treaty reached London—devastating news arrived from the Continent. Napoleon had escaped his island exile in Elba, landing on the southern coast of France and moving toward Paris. The people of France, or at least many of them, rallied to his banner. Soon Wellington was running around trying to reassemble his army—including elements in the United States.

But political fortunes wax and wane.

His progress was reported in subsequent headlines of French newspapers: the Anthropophagus has quitted his den; the Corsican Ogre has landed at Cape Juan; the Tiger has arrived at Gap; the Monster slept at Grenoble; the Tyrant has passed through Lyons; the usurper is directing his steps toward Dijon; Bonaparte is only 60 leagues from the capital; Bonaparte is advancing with rapid steps but he will never enter Paris; Napoleon will, tomorrow, be under our ramparts; the Emperor is at Fontainebleau; His Imperial and Royal Majesty arrived at the Tuileries amidst the joyful acclamations of his devoted and faithful subjects.

After the desperate battle at Waterloo—which Wellington called "a near run thing, the nearest run thing you ever saw"[15]—Napoleon was once again under lock and key, this time on the island of St. Helena way, way down south in the Atlantic. Elba was a rowboat ride from France. St. Helena might as well have been on the other side of the moon. Napoleon would die there.

The British could defeat Napoleon, but not the Americans.

15

Parade? What Parade?

No good deed goes unpunished.—Anonymous

Tradition teaches us that in the days of ancient Rome, when a conquering general returned from the battlefield with wagonloads of booty and throngs of prisoners, he was permitted what they called a "triumph," a great parade through town riding a chariot among cheering crowds. According to legend, the slave driving the chariot as it went along would whisper in the hero's ear that all glory is fleeting.

Sam Smith was greatly loved and respected in Baltimore, but such popularity invariably engenders jealousy and resentment among political rivals. One such rival was Joseph Hopper Nicholson, a member of the House from North Carolina who was present at Fort McHenry during the shelling. Nicholson had hated Smith for years and tried to defeat Smith's bid for reelection to the Senate in 1809. To his friend North Carolina congressman Nathaniel Macon, a former speaker of the House, Nicholson wrote long, vitriolic letters condemning Smith and urging an investigation into the way he handled the Baltimore battle. Macon expressed sympathy but said Nicholson's scheme was impractical because "the affair near Baltimore is highly spoken of" in Washington. A few days later, Macon added a note that no doubt upset Nicholson even more. The reputation of the commanding general has unquestionably, he said, gained much, taking the whole affair into view.

Even so, in August 1814, as the Battle of Baltimore reached its climax, Smith was informed that the Federalist majority in the Maryland State Senate would not reappoint him Senator. Since his friend Nicholas Moore occupied Smith's old seat in the House, it appeared he would be without employment when Congress adjourned the following spring. As if to rub salt in the wound, Smith learned that General Winfield Scott, a successful leader in the fight against Indians on the norther frontier, had been appointed General Winder's successor as commander of the 10th military district, which specifically included command of Baltimore in case of another attack. Smith suspected, and friends in Washington confirmed, that this was an attempt by the Madison Administration to embarrass him. Smith decided he would not serve under an officer of lesser rank and submitted his resignation.

Smith had held his rank with the militia for more than 35 years and this news came as a kick in the teeth and seemed to knock the wind out of him. He was already 62 years old, an advanced age for that place and time. "I think that Genl. Smith has rather a melancholy and mortified appearance," said Nathaniel Macon soon after Smith's announcement. "I am sorry to see it. I cannot see such appearance without feeling sorrow."[1] Losing his military position also took away one of Smith's greatest political assets. No longer would he be able to mobilize the city brigade to support his political campaigns. His ability to harangue his troops while feeding them liquor on the eve of elections was gone. For two decades, Smith had been a major force in Baltimore politics. An era had ended. The city had entered a new phase as younger men rose to prominence.

But somehow Smith's destiny was about to take a new turn ceding him perhaps even more influence than in previous years. The war was over and Smith's ships were again free to plow the seas in search of profit. Nicholas Moore had opportunely resigned his seat—perhaps deliberately—and the city had voted overwhelmingly to return Smith to Congress. But before Smith left the Senate, he had a good shot at doing something he thought long overdue. Ever since the Jay treaty, Smith had expressed strong disapproval of the system of discriminating duties that gave American vessels a near monopoly on the import trade. These duties had been useful during the American Revolution, but Smith had been arguing since 1795 that they would inevitably produce results inimical to American commerce. He had argued that eventually all maritime nations would retaliate against American ships by imposing duties of their own. Smith continued to believe that American ships could successfully compete in a free trade environment and that a reciprocal lowering of discriminating duties was the most effective means of expanding this nation's commercial opportunities.

In a powerful speech before the Senate in late February 1815, when his term was almost expired, Smith focused attention on the growing threat to this nation's commercial success. He showed that new British countervailing duties had gained for English ship owners complete control over the transport of many vital American products. Because of the duties, it was simply cheaper to use British vessels than the more highly taxed American ships. Fish oil, tobacco, cotton, rice, pearlashes and many other exports formerly carried in American ships were now moving on British vessels. Smith said he had found that Spain, France, Sweden, Denmark and Holland had recently imposed discriminating duties on American ships.

"If we continue our discriminating duties," Smith's long and somewhat tedious speech concluded, "the result must be that our ships will be rendered useless."[2]

Ship owners, already beginning to feel the pinch, and Americans generally, were more receptive to a freer trade than they had been a decade before when Smith began promoting his views. Smith's reciprocity bill easily passed through Congress and lay the groundwork for a commercial convention negotiated with the British a few months later. Within three years all of Smith's confidence in the efficacy of his measure was rewarded as American vessels rapidly achieved preeminence in the carrying trade both ways across the Atlantic. "The reciprocity act of 1815 stands as Samuel Smith's most significant legislative accomplishment," wrote Cassell in *Merchant Congressman in the Young Republic.*[3] In subsequent years Smith continued to work for complete reciprocity.

But not in the Senate. After an absence of 13 years, Smith took his seat in the House of Representatives on December 4, 1815, in the Fourteenth Congress. One of the first items on Smith's agenda was the new national bank proposed by President Madison. Smith had opposed that initial proposal arguing that state banks were all the country needed. The war with Britain had popped that balloon. When a new national bank came before the House in 1816, Smith was all for it. The bank bill was enacted. A tougher call was the protective tariff intended to protect domestic industries from foreign competition. The majority of Americans favored somewhat higher duties to protect American manufacturers and help pay off the national debt. (Today it seems somewhat quaint to remember that Americans in past years were concerned about the national debt.) The result was a proposal that put an average duty of 25 percent on imports that competed with American made goods but which domestic industry did not produce in sufficient quantity to satisfy demand. When the chairman of the House Ways and Means Committee William Lowndes of South Carolina took ill, it fell to Smith to manage the bill. In March and April 1816 he was constantly on his feet beating back efforts to gut the proposal. Smith believed that a moderate yet permanent tariff was the best policy and helped make it happen. He was proud of the result and had reason to be.

The third prong of President Madison's agenda was internal improvements and on that Smith definitely saw eye to eye with the president. Maryland had long been in the forefront of the quest for better roads and waterways to move commerce, and in Smith the state had a champion who would make that cause his own. Smith had been supporting federally directed internal improvements long before Madison came along and even before Smith's nemesis Albert Gallatin took up the cause. He was a driving force behind the plan to build a national road linking Baltimore with the

Cumberland, to be paid for with proceeds from land sales. The National Road was begun in 1811 and reached Wheeling, now in West Virginia, in 1818 and Columbus, Ohio, in 1833. It helped give Baltimore a jumpstart on taking advantages of the riches in the west of the growing nation and anticipated development of the Chesapeake and Ohio Canal that would come along a few years later.

On March 4, 1817, James Monroe assumed the presidency. Smith had neither supported nor opposed him, but Monroe's election removed a major barrier—Madison—impeding his relations with the administration. Now Madison was retired and Smith's other antagonist, Albert Gallatin, was out of the country on diplomatic duty. President Monroe and his administration were eager to embrace Smith. Nearly 65 years old, Smith enjoyed the status of an elder statesman and most people regarded him as a venerable figure who had given much to his party and his country. Also, the new administration needed his unmatched knowledge of commercial and financial affairs. When Smith in 1818 became chairman of the Ways and Means Committee, his friendship was all the more desirable.

The years 1818–1824 were generally satisfying ones for Smith, at least from the political point of view. He once again had access to the treasure chest of patronage as he began securing influential government jobs for his friends. He also began receiving letters requesting his advice from rising political stars who clearly valued his opinion. He grew ever closer to Monroe over the years. Unknown to Smith, he was actively considered for a couple of diplomatic posts, but that was squelched by John Quincy Adams who bore some grievances against Smith from earlier years. Or maybe Adams, like many others, simply considered Smith temperamentally unsuited for diplomatic posts.

Smith was active in the House up until 1822 when Maryland sent him back to the Senate. He kept voting for internal improvements and several tariff measures that were in keeping with his advocacy of mild protection of the domestic market. He was engaged in the explosive question of Missouri's admission to the union which John Quincy Adams described as a title page to a great tragic volume. As a representative of a slave state and an owner of domestic slaves himself, it is not surprising that he voted to admit Missouri without banning slavery. Nor was it surprising that he supported the great compromise of 1820 which admitted Maine as a free state and Missouri as a slave state and prohibited slavery anywhere else in the old Louisiana purchase territory, nor that he voted for the lesser compromise of 1821 permitting the entrance of Missouri into the union with the understanding that the state would never pass laws contrary to the rights of American citizens.

But positions he took on two subordinate votes drew attention. The first occurred in 1819 when he deserted other southerners and voted in favor of the second part of an amendment that called for freeing all slave children born in Missouri when they reached the age of 25. In a second vote in January 1821 Smith joined with only five other representatives in supporting a resolution demanding that before Missouri became a state it should expunge from its constitution that section preventing free blacks from entering its boundaries. To further confound future historians trying to pin him down, in his only lengthy speech given during the Missouri debates he unequivocally asserted the power of Congress over the territories in all matters, presumably including whether or not to allow slaves in them. But he quickly added that once a territory became a state, federal authority ended and that state could admit slaves if it decided to do so.

There is nothing in Smith's papers to explain these apparent inconsistencies nor any evidence to suggest he ever gave systematic thought to the great issues involved in the Missouri Compromise. His attitude toward slavery was, in a word, ambivalent. If there is a connecting string among his votes and statements it is his patriotic loyalty to the country and determination to uphold the power of the central government. In a period of history when sectional interests were beginning to rise to the forefront, Smith rejected the strong states' rights position of other southerners in preference to the strong central government he had done so much to create. Overall he remained focused mainly on national defense, internal development and commerce.

Predictably he was always looking out for the interests of the army. As chairman of the House Ways and Means Committee, he had ample opportunity to assist the military. Indeed, from the army's point of view, it is most important that Smith had his hand on the budget spigot during these difficult years. The great economic collapse of 1819 made retrenchment of government necessary—and the army was front and center on the chopping block. In fact, feeling was so strong that the administration's plan to slash the army budget by half was rejected by some congressmen as not radical enough. For four years it became Smith's self-appointed duty to mediate between the budget-conscious Congress and the leadership of the army. He no doubt would have preferred no cuts at all, but he bowed to the inevitable and usually reported military budgets less than the war department requested. When the budget was debated, he vigorously defended the army spending against efforts to reduce it further. Overall he was significantly successful and even was able to save the military academy at West Point, much of the coastal fortifications program and pensions for veterans. However, despite his best efforts he was unable to prevent Congress from slashing the standing army from 12,000 to 6,000 men.

All seemed to be going along splendidly for the hero of Baltimore, but such interludes never last for long. All along through the years Smith's financial status was built upon the success of his company which he had turned over to his business partner, James A. Buchanan, a lifetime friend who had years before moved his family along with Smith's to Baltimore from Carlisle, Pennsylvania. It was the largest and most profitable company in Baltimore where there were many large, profitable companies. But when the second Bank of the United States had been chartered in 1816, Buchanan had been appointed president of the Baltimore branch and a member of the central board of directors based in Philadelphia. Buchanan got caught up in the post-war speculative fever sweeping the country. Unchecked by the bank's incompetent president William Jones, Buchanan had participated in gross mismanagement, speculating wildly in the stock of the Bank of the United States. Buchanan and two conspirators lent themselves large sums from the Baltimore branch without collateral and purchased the stock on margin hoping it would go up in price so they could sell the shares and make a good profit on a small investment. Buchanan had conducted much of this business in the name of S. Smith & Buchanan, thus implicating the company in his fraud, all the while telling Smith nothing about what he was doing. Eventually Buchanan and his cronies had squandered about $3,000,000 of the company's money—money the company did not have.

The financial panic of 1818 shone a light on this mischief. To save the Bank of the United States, the directors began to curtail credit and exert strict supervision over the bank's affairs. Sam Smith may have got his first inkling of trouble afoot when a congressional committee investigating the bank reported in January 1819 that there were "irregularities" in the activities of the Baltimore branch. At about the same time, Jones resigned from the bank and was succeeded by Langdon Cheves of South Carolina. By the end of April the conspirators had been exposed. Buchanan resigned from office, and within a few weeks the company of S. Smith & Buchanan failed. "The House of Smith and Buchanan, which has been these thirty years one of the greatest commercial establishments in the United States," John Quincy Adams confided in his diary, "broke last week with a crash which staggered the whole city of Baltimore and will extend no one knows how far."[4]

With that, Sam Smith was bankrupt after a lifetime of extraordinary financial success. Most of his landholdings were swept up by the Bank of the United States to help cover the huge deficit. Buchanan, however, having known in advance what was coming, had transferred ownership of much of his property to relatives. He even managed to hold on to his house in Baltimore.

But Smith did not see it coming, had no idea it was coming, and was devastated financially and emotionally. Throughout May and June 1819, Smith reportedly bordered on insanity and considered suicide. To add insult to injury, his brother Robert, whose career Sam had nourished over the years, refused to add his name to the list of those agreeing to secure Sam's personal obligation of $300,000. By the end of May, Smith was a shattered old man who declined to get out of bed. "It is impossible for him to continue to feel as he does and live or retain his senses," wrote his daughter-in-law Cary Anne Smith. In the same letter she noted that Smith had ceased eating, sleeping or behaving rationally. "The dread of disgrace, the stings of ingratitude, the loss of fortune, altogether is too much for his sensibility and pride," she wrote.

A week later Cary Anne saw no improvement in Smith's health. Although others in the family were coping with the tragedy relatively well, she noted that Smith's "mind and body appear to be sinking under it." Much of his grief, she believed, was caused by a concern that he would be blamed for what Buchanan had done.

But aside from his brother Robert, other friends of Smith were clearly supportive, offering sympathy and help. Several merchants, among them Smith's brother-in-law William Patterson, joined John Spear Smith, Samuel's son, in securing the debt. Secretary of the Treasury William H. Crawford, a close friend of many years, expressed his deep concern and that of many others in Washington for Smith's situation. Crawford assured the general that no one had "even whispered a doubt of your being in any degree a participant in the highly improper acts of some of the officers of the branch bank" and offered his friend whatever help he could give. Much later, General Lafayette, with whom Smith had kept up a sporadic correspondence since the Revolution, wrote that the Marylander's misfortune had deeply affected "your old Companion in arms and constant friend."

By the end of summer Smith was regaining his poise and good humor. After prolonged legal wrangling (is there any other kind?) he was able to retain in his wife's name some property and a handful of stock in the Bank of the United States. With some help from his son, he was able to rebuy his house in Baltimore. But he was forced to sell all but three of his slaves along with his well-stocked wine cellar. John Spear Smith pleased the family in 1822 when he purchased Montebello, but to keep up the payments he had to convert it into a working farm which he managed full-time.

The Smiths had once upon a time—not so long ago—been the richest family in Baltimore, but now they went to extraordinary lengths to save money. For several years Smith and Margaret lived with their son and daughter-in-law, alternating between Montebello and the city house in order to cut living expenses. This arrangement did not always please their daughter-in-law Cary Anne who did not enjoy being cooped up with the "old folks." The general's meager per diem that he received as a member of Congress became an important source of their income. In 1823, Smith wrote to his daughter living in England that he and Margaret lived so frugally in Washington that they returned to Baltimore with a surplus of $300.

The years between 1819 and 1826 were tough ones for the old warrior until he was finally released by the bank for the balance of the debt. In 1822, for example, he was not able to travel to England to visit his daughter and her family (one can only wonder what kind of reception he would have received there) because of the danger that one of his creditors would have him arrested for debt on the expectation that his daughter's husband would pay. He also resented the appearance of his name as a defaulter in the annual financial statement of the bank that was widely published in newspapers. By the arrangements made in 1819 he was not technically in debt to the bank and he greatly resented the embarrassment these reports caused him. Finally in 1824 the bank agreed to correct this error. Smith wrote back that this gesture would greatly relieve his feelings.

He remained a member of Congress in good standing, where he was respected for his knowledge and experience. "I have lost nothing in the opinion of the people and the nation," he told his family after being reelected to the House in 1822. "I have more consideration paid to me in Congress than I ever had and have as admitted rendered special service since I have been at the head of the Ways and Means."[5]

But age and misfortune were taking a toll on the general from Baltimore. His letters to friends, family and colleagues show an increasing bent toward introspection. He took increasing interest in his children and grandchildren, a not-uncommon predilection in people his age. He was not only an old man, but he was also beginning to feel like one. While his own position in Congress was secure, he could not use it to influence the election of others. He was little more than an interested bystander in the election of 1824 in which there were five presidential candidates. Since they were all Republicans, the choice came down to personalities. The choices were Henry Clay of Kentucky; John C. Calhoun of South Carolina; John Quincy Adams, son of the second president, Andrew Jackson of Tennessee, the hero of the Battle of New Orleans; and William H. Crawford of Georgia—who was Smith's favorite. But Smith was not active in the election which saw a closely-run contest between Adams and Jackson. None of the candidates had the required majority of electoral votes, so the election was decided in the House.

By that time, Smith had given up his House seat to return to a seat in the Senate created by the death of William Pinkney.

When Adams became president in March 1824, Smith switched his

political allegiance to Jackson. But he retained his stubborn determination
to vote for what was right for the country, not for party loyalty or personal
aggrandizement. He believed public policy should be carried on rationally
and independent of political motives. "I never did, I never will, and I never
can oppose measures because of the man," he said to his friend Crawford,
"you know my disposition on that point." Until the day he retired from
Congress, he adhered to that creed.[6]

As in earlier years, much of Smith's work in Congress during these
years revolved around trade issues—trying to preserve a level playing field
for American merchants like himself. He was committed to low tariffs and
reciprocal treatment of commerce among nations. He continued his dedi-
cation of internal development which he saw not only as vital to economic
growth but also as a deterrent to sectionalism. Already the rifts between
Northern and Southern states were beginning to grow ominously.

Jackson's election to the presidency in 1828 pleased Smith, and he led
the roll-out of the red carpet in Washington for Jackson's inauguration.
Jackson reciprocated Smith's outreach and made patronage available to
him. Jackson told Smith that he was seriously considered as next minister to England but concluded he was more valuable in the Senate. Smith
realized that Jackson was just buttering him up, that no such appointment
was actually considered, but he was still pleased that Jackson thought him
worthy of being buttered. He had differences with Jackson, in particular
with regard to the National Bank which Smith supported and Jackson was
determined to eliminate, but overall no president had given him so much
attention since Jefferson many years before.

Approaching his 80th birthday, Smith had arthritis but did not
allow it to slow him down. It was a rare issue before the Senate that he
did not take the floor to discuss and he remained focused on tariff policy
and the future of the National Bank. The tariff bill that eventually came
before Congress in the spring of 1832 was not to Smith's liking. Though it
removed many of the worse features of existing law, he did not believe the
reductions were sufficient to halt the nullification movement in South Carolina. But it became law. Four months later a special convention met in
South Carolina and passed an ordinance decreeing that federal officials
would not be permitted to collect the duties in that state. Here were the
first rumblings of the secession that would tear the country apart in years
ahead. For now Smith and his colleagues were able to head off the nullification movement.

As for the bank, it was a typical Smith imbroglio. He supported the
bank because he had seen firsthand in earlier years that state and regional
banks could not supply the nation's financial base during a conflict. But
Jackson was an outspoken foe of the bank and determined to get rid of it.

The bank's charter was up for renewal. On June 11, 1832, the Senate passed the re-charter measure by a vote of 28 to 20. As he had promised, Jackson vetoed the legislation in spite of a half-hearted appeal from Smith that he not do so. When the Senate voted on a measure to override the veto, Smith—seeing the writing on the wall—was absent from the chamber.

The national bank and the tariff were the last chapters in Sam Smith's long career in national government. After 40 continuous years in Congress, 18 in the House and 22 in the Senate, he retired to Baltimore in the spring of 1833 at the age of 83. Few men have served so long in Congress, and fewer still have combined longevity with such a distinguished record.. At some time during the presidencies of George Washington, John Adams, Thomas Jefferson, James Madison, James Monroe, John Quincy Adams, and Andrew Jackson, he had held every important position in Congress save Speaker of the House. His list of legislative accomplishments was lengthy and impressive. He had sponsored innumerable bills dealing with commerce, defense, banking and internal improvements, many of which found their way into law.

After the War of 1812, in which he played a critical role, Smith's horizons widened considerably. As he grew older he came to see that the welfare of one part of the Union was organically related to the conditions existing in all of the other parts. Although he never forgot his loyalty to Baltimore and American commerce, Smith had evolved into an advocate of genuine national interests by the end of his congressional career. "Smith's congressional experience was also characterized by a rugged individualism, and, with one or two exceptions, an admirable integrity," Cassell wrote. "No matter whether or not he approved of the administration currently in office, he had made his own judgements on the issues. Nor had he ever been afraid to tell presidents when he thought they were wrong."

He had earned a peaceful and honored retirement, but it was not to be. Honored, to be sure, but peaceful—no such luck. That simply was not in Samuel Smith's DNA. During his last few months in the Senate, he had lobbied for an appointment to ease his financial plight—say, as minister to Great Britain. Instead he was offered the job of collector at the Port of Baltimore. He declined that job because he thought it would be too taxing for a man his age. So he and Margaret settled back in their home near Exchange Place in Baltimore where they could enjoy each other's company and that of their children and grandchildren. Nearby were John Spear Smith and his family who still lived at stately Montebello. John had risen to prominence in Baltimore, having been appointed a brigadier general in the Maryland militia. Along with a cousin, John had started a sugar plantation in Louisiana which had proven lucrative. (It would have been heavily reliant on slave labor.) Together with that income and that of Montebello, his fortune had reached modest proportions.

Much less happy for Sam and Margaret were their relations with Christopher Hughes who had married their daughter Laura. Sam had done all he could for Hughes, securing for him a series of minor diplomatic posts, but Hughes had a poor reputation. John Quincy Adams had once described him as a man who believed that the "whole science of diplomacy consists of giving dinners." He ended up with the post of chargé in Stockholm, a job given to him out of deference to Smith, but Hughes considered it beneath his dignity. He became alienated from Smith who he blamed for his failure to progress in the Foreign Service. When Laura died in 1832, it broke his last remaining tie to the general. Hughes wrote a blistering letter to Smith accusing him of an "uninterrupted series of wrongs, of injustice and cruel persecutions that I have suffered at your hands and those of your family."[7] Hughes later apologized but it was too little, too late.

Even more wearisome for General Smith was the lingering distress related to the collapse of the Bank of Maryland. Many small depositors had been ruined by the bank's failure, but months went by without an accounting of what happened. Only the former president of the bank had surrendered his mansion and personal possessions to pay off the debt he had incurred as part of the speculations. The directors—Reverdy Johnson, John Glenn, Evan Ellicott, David Perine and Hugh McElderry—continued to live in splendor. Tensions grew and as a result one of the worst riots in American history began on August 6, 1834, when a small group of men began breaking the windows in Reverdy Johnson's home on Monument Square. Roaming mobs burned and sacked the homes of several of the directors. The result was pitched battles between police and the mob in which rioters were killed. After a few days the mayor dismissed the deputies he had sworn in out of concern for their safety. The mob controlled the city.

The emergency demanded strong action. In a time of civil unrest, who do you call? Why, Sam Smith, of course. Soon the 83-year-old retired general appeared on the scene walking ramrod straight and clutching an American flag. He began marching through the streets. By the time he reached Howard Park, several thousand people had rallied behind him, ready to follow his instructions. At the park Smith was joined by the president of the first branch of the Baltimore City Council, General Anthony Miltenberger, who had legally assumed the duties of mayor, and Smith's own son, General John Spear Smith, commander of the militia. The three men addressed those present, telling them to arm themselves and then report to the mayor's office for orders. Within an hour Smith and his son had dispatched armed parties to key points within the city, and large patrols were sent to march through the riot areas. The rioters had fled and no resistance was encountered. "The moment the citizens marched from the Exchange, under the veteran General Smith," the *Baltimore Patriot* reported, "and the American standard was seen moving in the air, riot and rebellion ceased."

So once again Smith had come forward to save his city in a time of crisis and so it was that he was elected mayor, one of the few titles that had to date eluded him. On September 7 the voters turned out in unprecedented numbers to vote for Smith. When Smith had first arrived in Baltimore in 1759, it was little more than a village. By the 1830s it was the third largest city in the country after New York and Philadelphia. It was also one of the most beautiful cities. Visitors acclaimed its white-marbled buildings, the splendid fountains and monuments, and the tasteful brick mansions which abounded within the city limits.

Some may have thought that at the age of 83 being mayor of a large, bustling city might have proven too much for Smith, but as always he was energetic and competent. There were no more riots, but the city was plagued with gangs, white and black, which fought with each other and broke the peace. Smith ordered the police to patrol the streets, break up the gangs, arresting those carrying weapons. Reflecting the deep-seated racial bias of the time, the city was especially vigorous in punishing blacks who misbehaved. They received twice as many lashes as white miscreants for committing the same crimes. It isn't clear that Smith ordained this discrimination but it occurred on his watch and he did not challenge it. Order was what he wanted and order was what he got. "Never was a city of 100,000 more quiet or more peaceable than Baltimore,"[8] Smith confided to one of his daughters. Tapping his years of political experience, he secured substantial investments in Baltimore from Washington and the state. Also he took the lead in persuading the city and state to invest in the Baltimore and Ohio Railroad and the Chesapeake and Ohio Canal. Smith's annual messages to the city council resembled the president's messages to Congress and the council usually followed his lead.

In November 1838 Smith relinquished his post as mayor and six months later, on April 22, 1839, he died apparently of a heart attack. "Another patriot gone," mourned Niles' *Weekly Register*, commenting that the general had died "full of years and honors."[9] Most of the Baltimore papers printed the editions announcing Smith's death with heavy black lines around the borders of the pages. All of them included editorials praising him and recounting the major events of his life, usually stressing his military service in the Revolution and the War of 1812. Relatively little was said of his political career. But his business career got high marks, with one editor styling him as the "founder of commerce in our city."[10]

Smith's funeral was the grandest display Baltimore had seen up to that time and probably for all time. With great care the Baltimore city council supervised the spectacle which took place on April 25. Hours before the funeral procession began, crowds had already assembled. Along every avenue through which the hearse would pass, thousands of citizens jostled each other for a better view. Every window that overlooked the route contained eager spectators anxiously straining for a first glimpse of the cortege. Finally, at half past four in the afternoon, the long, somber parade began.

Leading the mourners were units of the Baltimore militia followed by carriages containing the general's family and innumerable dignitaries. Of particular interest was the presence of almost every important official in the city, state and federal government. The mayor of Baltimore, the governor of Maryland, and the president of the United States, Martin Van Buren, all shared the same coach. Van Buren's participation in the ceremonies undoubtedly stemmed not only from the respect for a deceased elder statesman but also from genuine grief at the loss of a friend he had known for many years. Next in line were the carriages containing members of the president's cabinet, including Secretary of State John Forsyth, Secretary of War Joel Poinsett, Secretary of the Navy James K. Paulding, and Attorney General Felix Grundy. The line of notables stretched back for many blocks.

The very last group in the cortege proved the most interesting—thousands of plain citizens spontaneously joined the procession. Unlike the others, these people had no official reason to be there; only genuine sorrow and respect compelled them to come. The hearse, drawn by four white horses, and flanked by mounted dragoons, passed through Baltimore's streets amid signs that the city attached great significance to the general's funeral. Bells tolled, stores were closed, and in the crowded harbor, activity ceased as every ship, regardless of nationality, lowered its flag to half-mast. Each minute a cannon at Fort McHenry boomed a salute to the man who had saved the city from invasion a quarter century before. But it was the crowds that most impressed observers, both because of the numbers and the intensity of feeling that many individuals manifested. It was not an uncommon sight to see both adults and children crying as the cortege passed. The procession ended at the cemetery of the First Presbyterian Church of which Smith had been a lifelong member. After prayers and the eulogies, the casket was placed in the Smith family vault and the mourners slowly dispersed.

Epilogue

Silence on the Patapsco

Only the dead have seen the end of war.—Albert Einstein

As far as the war was concerned, there were intangible results beyond anything that could be written down in a treaty. "For one thing, America gained new respect abroad," wrote Lord.[1] "For 20 years she had been regarded as a sort of semi-nation—almost a freak—by the great powers of Europe. Considered too weak to stand on her own, she had seen her rights ignored by both sides during the Napoleonic Wars. Now all that was over. America had fought, and this fact alone gave her prestige."[2]

"The war has raised our reputation in Europe," James Bayard wrote his son on Christmas Day in 1814 right after signing the treaty, "and it excites astonishment that we should have been able for one campaign to have fought Great Britain single handed…. I think it will be a long time before we are disturbed again by any of the powers of Europe."[3]

Reviewing the brief British assault on Baltimore it is possible to surmise that the relatively easy "cakewalk" they had in Bladensburg had given them a false confidence in their superiority. "I don't care if it rains militia," Ross said, a couple of hours before one of those maligned militia put a fatal hole in him. Ross was a seasoned infantry officer who enjoyed the confidence of his troops. It is a conceit of highly organized military organizations that any cog in their machines can be replaced. But inspired leaders like Ross are few and far between. The death of Ross was a crucial factor in the failure of the British to subdue Baltimore.

And the British had no way of knowing the resourcefulness and mettle of Sam Smith. After burning Washington, they dallied a few days. That was all Smith needed to put the final touches on his grand scheme to defy and deny the British on land and sea. When Brooke got to the Philadelphia Road, three miles east of Baltimore, he saw legions of Smith's troops moving into position in well-designed fortifications. Here was a height crowned by strong defenses and, said the British lieutenant George Robert Gleig, manned by "the great army consisting of 20,000 men." Smith had already won the propaganda war; he had no more than 15,000 men.

Brooke was no patsy. He had risen in rank under Ross who recognized his talent and character. Brooke decided to test the American left along the Bel Air Road. Smith sat tight and ordered Stricker and Winder to swing their brigades around so that the left flank was refused and all three of the northern roads were covered. The whole operation could have been blown had Winder been dilatory, but he and Stricker executed the movement promptly "with great skill and judgement," according to Pancake in *Samuel Smith and the Politics of Business.*[4]

Therefore, when Brooke formed his order of battle along the Bel Air Road, he found two brigades facing him and a third, Stansbury's, held in reserve behind entrenched works. Brooke tried again with no more luck than before. About 2:00 in the afternoon he withdrew to his original position along the Philadelphia Road and began a demonstration to test the strength of the middle of the American line. He concentrated his largest force on the right where the Philadelphia Road emerged from the angle and the northern end of the earthworks.

This was the closest the British came to a concerted land and sea attack for it was at this time that the naval vessels in the harbor began their assault on Fort McHenry. Of course, neither Smith nor Brooke could have known that. Once again Smith matched the British maneuver. He swung Stricker and Winder back in toward the Philadelphia Road so that as Brooke advanced, he found his heaviest concentration of troops moving into a deadly obtuse angle formed by Stricker and Winder to his right and the face of the fortified ridge in front of him. "Winder may have been above his level of competence commanding an army," wrote Pancake, "but with a capable officer in the lead, he could execute orders."[5] The American commander refused to leave his entrenched position. The British advance halted and then retired. At this point Brooke decided that his only hope of success was a night attack in cooperation with an attack, or at least a diversion, by the fleet. This was when he called his war council which voted to withdraw from the field. That was the end of the fighting on land.

For his part, Cochrane was stymied. He did not know Brooke had decided to withdraw and assumed he was still obliged to provide the naval part of the fighting. God knows he was trying. He had sent against Fort McHenry's defenses the most powerful naval siege artillery in existence. He had been given two-thirds of the British navy's whole supply of special fortress battering equipment. He had with him five of Britain's eight bomb vessels and the only rocket cruiser on the high seas anywhere in the world. He had been using them for nine hours under ideal conditions in smooth water, at medium range, and without the slightest danger of retaliation. The bombardment basically had been target practice, not a battle. But after nine hours of incessant pounding, the American defenses had been able to pour forth such a storm of fire upon the ships when they advanced that Cochrane almost immediately recalled them. He did not dare to risk, within range of that cannonade, the only weapons with which he could hope to crush the fort's batteries. He could have sent his smaller warships directly into the fire to duke it out with the fort's defenders, but he knew that would lead to a massive bloodletting with scant prospect of success. When he received word that Brooke was abandoning the fight, he did the same. The Battle of Baltimore was over.

Smith could take satisfaction in the fact that he had maneuvered so skillfully that the veteran British army had not even risked a full frontal attack either on land or on the fort. "He had repulsed the best fighting machine in the world," Pancake wrote, "without even being compelled to beat off a direct assault. It was the only time in the nation's history that an American city has been defended by its citizens."[6]

Some of Smith's officers advised him to undertake a night attack on the British, but he quickly put an end to such talk. "Yes, but when you fight our citizens against British regulars you are staking dollars against cents," he said, adding that their job was to defend Baltimore, not destroy the British army.

The Battle of Baltimore was over. Baltimore won. Smith was still wary that the British were pulling some kind of stunt to lull his people into complacency before resuming their assault. So it took a couple of days to confirm that the British were actually leaving the bay before it began to sink in—Smith and his loyal city had actually defeated the British.

So what did it all mean? What was all that fighting and dying about?

Historian Michael Page Andrews, writing in the ever-popular *Tercentenary History of Maryland* in 1925, said it had far-reaching ramifications.

Had the British been successful in Capturing Baltimore, the most prolific source of American sea offensive would have been destroyed; and the Federal Government, already confronted with disaffection, nullification and threats of secession in the northeastern states, would have received a stunning blow.

Again, had Baltimore fallen, Washington would scarcely have been tenable for reoccupation by the Federal Government, and the Hartford conventionists might not have had any permanent headquarters to which to carry their complaints; so that the proposed secession of New England might easily and naturally have become an accomplished fact, with but little discussion of the processes for carrying it out. The Federal Government would have been, for the time at least, helpless, even had it been within the purview of the administration to use compulsion. Certainly, any Jacksonian recourse to force in New

England would assuredly have set that section on fire with an ardor of resistance second only to that offered King and Parliament in 1775.

As for Maryland—the war had reduced the domestic and foreign exports to $248,434 in 1814. In the first year after peace was declared, these exports leaped to more than $5,000.000.[7]

It is an interesting historical exercise to play "what if" this or that happened, but it does appear rather obvious that if Sam Smith had not

Many years had passed when George Henry Preble took a photograph of Old Glory in 1873. She was already a bit the worse for wear. People stroll through that quiet room all day long in a sense of reverence. Despite everything the old girl—both the country and its flag—are holding up pretty well. The original Old Glory was owned by a 19th-century sea captain named William Driver, whose credibility persuaded the Smithsonian that his flag was the original from Fort McHenry. It is the flag now housed in the American History Museum of the Smithsonian (Wikipedia).

performed his magic, the British would have stormed Baltimore and looted all those bulging warehouses. There would have been much bloodshed because there were at least 10,000 angry, armed men in Baltimore who would have resisted British pillaging. But a disorganized rabble could not hope to defeat the disciplined British ranks. The subjugation of Baltimore would have given the British the upper hand in peace negotiations at Ghent. In any event, the British would have been too engaged in looting Baltimore to move on to New Orleans. It seems unlike there would have been a Battle of New Orleans—but then the game of "what if" never actually comes to an end. Thanks to Sam Smith, the Battle of Baltimore did come to an end and with it the War of 1812.

"The war has raised our reputation in Europe," wrote James Bayard, one of the American negotiators at Ghent, in a letter to his son on Christmas Day 1814, right after signing the treaty, "and it excites astonishment that we should have been able for one campaign to have fought Great Britain single handed.... I think it will be a long time before we are disturbed again by any of the powers of Europe." Indeed it was to prove a long time—a full century in fact.[8]

Chapter Notes

Chapter 1

1. Alan Taylor, *The Civil War of 1812*, p. 205.
2. *Ibid.*, p. 103.
3. Ronald D. Utt, *Ships of Oak, Guns of Iron*, p. 2.
4. Taylor, p. 232.

Chapter 2

1. Walter Lord, *The Dawn's Early Light*, p. 33.
2. *Ibid.*, p. 35.
3. *Ibid.*, p. 36.
4. *Ibid.*, p. 48.
5. *Ibid.*, p. 53.
6. Whitehorne, *The Battle for Baltimore*, p. 117.
7. Henry Adams, *Encyclopedia Britannica*, 1911.
8. Whitehorne, p. 131.
9. Lord, p. 82.
10. *Ibid.*, p. 45.
11. *Ibid.*, p. 48.
12. *Ibid.*, p. 82.

Chapter 3

1. Lord, p. 88.
2. *Ibid.*, p. 89.
3. *Ibid.*, p. 98.
4. *Ibid.*
5. *Ibid.*, p. 107.
6. *Ibid.*, p. 124.
7. *Ibid.*, p. 125.
8. *Ibid.*, p. 138.
9. *Ibid.*, p. 147.
10. *Ibid.*, p. 151.
11. *Ibid.*, p. 168.
12. *Ibid.*, p. 200.

Chapter 4

1. Frank A. Cassell, *Merchant Congressman in the Young Republic*, p. 38.
2. John Adams to Abigail Adams, 25 October 1777, *Founders Online*, National Archives.
3. Cassell, p. 192.
4. *Ibid.*, pp. 202–203.
5. Lord, p. 250.
6. Whitehorne, *The Battle for Baltimore*, p. 44.
7. Lord, p. 233.
8. *Ibid.*, p. 228.
9. *Ibid.*
10. *Ibid.*, p. 232.
11. Whitehorne, p. 173.
12. Neil H. Swanson, *The Perilous Fight*, p. 209.
13. *Ibid.*, p. 210.
14. *Ibid.*, p. 209.
15. *Ibid.*, p. 210.
16. *Ibid.*, p. 211.

Chapter 5

1. Lord, p. 217.
2. Taylor, p. 178.
3. Swanson, p. 232.
4. *Ibid.*, p. 233.
5. *Ibid.*, p. 235.
6. *Ibid.*, p. 252.
7. *Ibid.*, p. 276.
8. *Ibid.*
9. *Ibid.*, p. 277.
10. *Ibid.*, p. 281.
11. *Ibid.*, p. 304.
12. Lord, p. 274.
13. Utt, p. 434.

Chapter 6

1. Cassell, p. 7.

2. *Ibid.*, p. 13.
3. *Ibid.*, p. 14.
4. *Ibid.*, p. 20.
5. *Ibid.*, p. 21.
6. *Ibid.*, p. 24.
7. *Ibid.*, p. 25.
8. *Ibid.*, p. 29.
9. *Ibid.*, p. 31.
10. *Ibid.*, p. 35.
11. *Ibid.*, p. 36.

Chapter 7

1. Cassell, p. 43.
2. *Ibid.*, p. 42.
3. J. Gillman and D. Paul, "Montebello, Home of General Samuel Smith," *Maryland Historical Magazine* (1947), p. 257.
4. *Ibid.*, p. 258.
5. *Ibid.*

Chapter 8

1. Cassell, p. 49.
2. *Ibid.*, p. 50.
3. *Ibid.*, p. 53.
4. *Ibid.*, p. 58.
5. *Ibid.*, p. 61.
6. *Ibid.*, p. 62.
7. *Ibid.*, p. 68.
8. *Ibid.*, p. 70.
9. *Ibid.*, p. 71.
10. *Ibid.*, p. 75.
11. *Ibid.*, p. 79.
12. *Ibid.*, p. 93.
13. *Ibid.*

Chapter 9

1. Cassell, p. 105.
2. *Ibid.*, p. 119.
3. *Ibid.*
4. *Ibid.*, p. 126
5. *Ibid.*, p. 131.
6. *Ibid.*, p. 137.
7. *Ibid.*, p. 140.

Chapter 10

1. Cassell, p. 165.
2. Lord, p. 223.
3. *Ibid.*
4. Lord, p. 224.

5. *Ibid.*, p. 225.
6. *Ibid.*

Chapter 11

1. Lord, p. 251.
2. *Ibid.*
3. John Pancake, *Samuel Smith and the Politics of Business*, p. 115.
4. *Ibid.*, p. 117.
5. *Ibid.*, p. 116.
6. Lord, p. 249.
7. *Ibid.*, p. 251.
8. *Ibid.*, p. 253.
9. *Ibid.*, p. 254.
10. *Ibid.*, p. 261.
11. *Ibid.*, p. 262.
12. *Ibid.*, p. 263.
13. Marc De Simone and Robert Dudley, *Sam Smith, Star-Spangled Hero*, p. 151.
14. Lord, p. 268.
15. *Ibid.*, p. 278.
16. *Ibid.*, p. 271.

Chapter 12

1. Marc Leepson, *What So Proudly We Hailed: Francis Scott Key, A Life*, p. 52.
2. *Ibid.*, p. 56.
3. *Ibid.*, p. 57.
4. *Ibid.*
5. *Ibid.*
6. Lord, p. 273.
7. *Ibid.*
8. *Ibid.*, p. 278.
9. *Ibid.*, p. 281.
10. *Ibid.*, p. 286.

Chapter 13

1. Lord, p. 290.
2. *Ibid.*
3. *Ibid.*
4. Leepson, p. 57.
5. Lord, p. 294.
6. *Ibid.*, p. 295.
7. *Ibid.*, p. 294.
8. *Ibid.*, p. 295.
9. *Ibid*, p. 299.
10. *Ibid.*
11. *Ibid.*
12. Lord, p. 303.
13. Lord, p. 307.

14. *Ibid.*
15. *Ibid.*, p. 309.
16. *Ibid.*, p. 321.

Chapter 14

1. Lord, p. 328.
2. *Ibid.*, p. 329.
3. *Ibid.*, p. 330.
4. *Ibid.*, p. 331.
5. *Ibid.*, p. 334.
6. *Ibid.*
7. *Ibid.*, p. 335.
8. *Ibid.*
9. *Ibid.*, p. 336.
10. *Ibid.*
11. *Ibid.*, p. 338.
12. *Ibid.*, p. 339.
13. *Ibid.*
14. *Ibid.*
15. Special Collections Exhibitions, Kings College, London.

Chapter 15

1. Cassell, p. 211.
2. *Ibid.*, p. 213.
3. *Ibid.*
4. *Ibid.*, p. 223.
5. *Ibid.*, p. 226.
6. *Ibid.*, p. 234.
7. *Ibid.*, p. 256.
8. *Ibid.*, p. 261.
9. *Ibid.*, p. 262.
10. *Ibid.*, p. 263.

Epilogue

1. Lord, p. 342.
2. *Ibid.*
3. *Ibid.*
4. Pancake, p. 128.
5. *Ibid.*
6. *Ibid.*, p. 131.
7. Matthew Page Andrews, *Tercentenary History of Maryland.*
8. Lord, p. 342.

Bibliography

Andrews, Matthew Page. *Tercentenary History of Maryland*. S.J. Clarke, 1925.

Cassell, Frank A. *Merchant, Congressman in the Young Republic: Samuel Smith of Maryland, 1752–1839*. University of Wisconsin Press, 1971.

De Simone, Marc, and Robert Dudley. *Sam Smith: Star-Spangled Hero: The Unsung Patriot Who Saved Baltimore and Helped Win the War of 1812*. CreateSpace, 2014.

Essary, J. Frederick. *Maryland in National Politics, from Charles Carroll to Albert C. Ritchie*. John Murphy Company, 1932.

George, Christopher T. *Terror on the Chesapeake: The War of 1812 on the Bay*. White Mane, 2000.

Lord, Walter. *The Dawn's Early Light*. W.W. Norton, 1972.

Marine, William M. *The British Invasion of Maryland, 1812–1815*. Tradition Press, 1965 (originally published 1913).

Muller, Charles G. *The Darkest Day: 1814: The Washington-Baltimore Campaign*. J.B. Lippincott, 1963.

Sheads, Scott S. *The Rockets' Red Glare: The Maritime Defense of Baltimore in 1814*. Tidewater Publications, 1986.

Swanson, Neil H. *Through The Perilous Fight*. Farrar & Rinehart, 1945. (This writer is aware that there are two books by the same title listed. I have relied on the one written by Neil H. Swanson.)

Taylor, Alan. *The Civil War of 1812*. Alfred A. Knopf, 2010.

Utt, Ronald D. *Ships of Oak, Guns of Iron: The War of 1812 and the Forging of the American Navy*. Regnery History, 2012.

Vogel, Steve. *Through the Perilous Fight: Six Weeks That Saved The Nation*. Random House, 2013.

Whitehorne, Joseph W.A. *The Battle for Baltimore*. Heritage Books, 1997.

Index